Other Books by Matt Leach

How Can I Believe What Can't Be Believed -
Genesis 1 – 3

Questions for a Logical Mind

Peter, the Professor, and the Blue Orb
Time Machine

A Guide to Prayer Power Set in a Science Fiction Fantasy

You've Got to Know the Territory Before You PRAY

Matt W Leach

WESTBOW PRESS®
A DIVISION OF THOMAS NELSON & ZONDERVAN

WestBow Press books may be ordered through booksellers or by contacting:

WestBow Press
A Division of Thomas Nelson & Zondervan
1663 Liberty Drive
Bloomington, IN 47403
www.westbowpress.com
1 (866) 928-1240

ISBN: 978-1-5127-4964-9 (sc)
ISBN: 978-1-5127-4965-6 (e)

Library of Congress Control Number: 2016911550

Print information available on the last page.

WestBow Press rev. date: 11/28/2016

CONTENTS

PREFACE

"Write!" said God, some thirty years ago. So I wrote. The writing flowed, filling a two-inch-thick three ring binder. I had learned much, and there was much to share. Then the flow, the inspiration, stopped. Why, I wondered. What was I supposed to do now? The answer that came I did not like. It is one thing to write glowingly from the security of an "Ivory Tower," away from real life. It is another thing to step into the real world where people live. God said, "Before you can tell it, you must first prove it."

The testing came. We went through times of desperation that forced me to my knees begging, pleading with God. It was hard to keep my mind focused on God as our source, and not people, especially when bill collectors kept calling. It has been said that to live by faith is to live in the midst of a miracle on the brink of disaster. In the time of testing God was always faithful. Our needs were always met. We stepped out on his promises and they held.

We also learned that prayer is family talk! We are God's kids. He is our father. Jesus is our elder brother. We are family. "Now," God said, "you are ready to write the book. Not the book you started to write. But the book my children, your brothers and sisters, need. They need to know the real me, the father who loves them dearly, and longs desperately to fellowship with them. Help them know that prayer is family talk."

That is why I wrote this book.

June 14, 2016

INTRODUCTION

One summer I sold gooey delicious stuff like pies and cakes and cinnamon rolls and bread, door-to-door for the Dugan bakery. The company told me I had to sell a minimum amount each day, and I had to keep my unsold returns at a minimum. Or else I would be fired. The only way I could meet or exceed my daily quota was by taking the time to know my customers. That meant getting to "know the territory". Let me explain. I had three groups of customers. There were the regular year-round residents; the Jewish group that spent their summers by the lake; and the other summer-only residents. Each group was different. The Jewish customers wanted their kosher bagels. Summer only people tended to indulge in sweets. The year round people were pretty much bread with an occasional dessert. Because I knew my customers' likes and dislikes, wherever I went all I had to do was holler "Dugan" and the doors were flung open to welcome me in.

When you stop to think about it, knowing-the-territory is how we live. It is a natural part of building relationships. Boyfriends and girlfriends, husbands and wives, friends and neighbors, and even bosses and employees, rely on knowing the territory of each other. You'd think that because it so much a part of how we live, we'd automatically apply it to all relationships. But in the one relationship where it is most needed it is often missing. That relationship is prayer.

"Wait!" you may protest. "Prayer isn't two people building a relationship. It's one person talking to God." But is it? Is there a possibility that prayer is much more than we think it is? Yes! It is. This book will help you get to know the territory that is prayer. We'll begin by learning what a nineteenth century door-to-door salesman had to know. Then we will apply that to prayer. In the late 1800's, travel was by horse or horse and wagon. A trip to town was an all-day event that took careful planning. Forgotten items stayed forgotten until time for the next trip. This age of the horse and buggy, without television or radio, was a golden age for the door-to-door salesman. A salesman who loaded his wagon with things people needed and wanted could make a lot of money. In 1887 J.P. Johnston, in his autobiography *Twenty Years of Hus'ling*[I.] wrote about his life as a salesman.

To be a success at selling, Johnston taught, you've got to know the territory. You've got to know some things. You must know yourself, your customers, and your products. The customer wants to know if you are honest and dependable. Do you value him as a person, or are you using him to get what you want? Will you make good on anything that's not right? Are you selling quality products at a bargain price? Will what he buys from you benefit him? In other words, you had to know the territory.

Prayer, likewise, has territory that must be known. Prayer isn't selling or trying to persuade God to do what you want. But like selling, you've got to know some things. You've got to know yourself; not the self you were before Jesus, but the new self you became in Christ, the you of infinite worth as seen through God's eyes. Next, you have to know, personally know, each member of your new family. Know your laughing, loving Father. Know your brother Jesus, the joy giver. Know the Holy Spirit, the one living in you as teacher and guide. Finally, know your Father's promises. Only then can you know true prayer, because prayer is *family talk*.

The Book of Acts, and the letters that follow, tell of amazing things wrought by prayer, and by the authority of Jesus' name. Paul urges us to "Use every kind of prayer and entreaty, and at every opportunity pray in the spirit" (Ephesians 6:18 GDS). Does that mean there is a formula that makes each kind of prayer work? Is learning formulas all we need to do? No! Prayer is not formulas. In his book, *Who We Are Is How We Pray*[2], Dr. Charles Keating writes that prayer is not the same for everyone. No two of us are alike. There is no one formula that fits all. Referring to the work of Myers-Briggs, who categorized personalities into four distinct types, Dr. Keating writes that each of us is a unique combination of these four types:

1. *Extrovert* (outgoing, gregarious, social) and *Introvert* (energized by being alone)
2. *Sensing* (dependent on their five senses) and *Intuition* (listening for the intuitions that come up from their unconscious)
3. *Thinking* and *Feeling*
4. *Judgment* and *Perception*

If prayer is family talk, that means that once I know myself I must concentrate on knowing my new family. If I don't get to know them prayer will be nothing more than a polite hello. How do I do it? How do I get to know intimately each member of my new family? We begin by learning the details of our shared history. We look at the love that binds us together. We look at each member of our new family. Then we boldly take our places in the family circle, bound together by love to brother Jesus, the Father, and the Holy Spirit in a beloved family.

Getting to know the territory means getting to know our shared history. That history began over six thousand years ago. It is a dark history. But momentous events happened about two thousand years ago that turned our shared history from darkness into light. Those events happened during one week that changed history forever. What that week meant for us, what our Brother did for us, and the gifts our adoptive Father gave us, are things we will never tire of recounting, rejoicing over, giving thanks for, and will never ever forget.

As you study the chapters that follow remember that the Bible is our authority for faith and practice. Any idea or statement in this book that cannot be supported by Scripture is not to be believed.

PART A

THE TERRITORY OF HISTORY

Through faith we understand that the worlds were framed by the word of God, so that things which are seen were not made of things which do appear. (Hebrews 11:3 KJV)

CHAPTER 1

THE BARNABAS DIARY

Like me you were probably born a Gentile. The Old Testament calls everyone a Gentile who wasn't born a Hebrew (Jew). The Old Testament is the history of the Hebrew people. While little is said about the Gentiles, something happened about 1885 BC that changed both of our histories. That event was the day God spoke to Abraham and Abraham believed him. God promised Abraham that he would be the father of many nations and that all the nations of the Earth, Jew and Gentile alike, would be blessed because of him.

This ancient promise, written indelibly on their hearts, kept the Hebrew people bound together as a nation even when scattered around the world. The promise spoke of one who was to come, a Deliverer who would set things right. What would the Deliverer be like? What would he do? Ideas differed. False Deliverers had arisen only to cause trouble. To the Gentiles, the Jewish nation was so obstinate they seemed to be nothing more than a thorn in the side. Little did anyone suspect that in one week on a Jewish holiday, about 30 AD, something would happen that would blend Jewish history with our Gentile history, and change time forever.

We have four recorded authentic eyewitness accounts describing the events of that week. Other references, such as those written by Titus Flavius Josephus, also describe the events. That week divided history into before (BC) and after (AD). You've heard the story many times, but have you really heard it? Let's listen to it again by telling it in a different way. This time think of it as reading your own family history. It is a history you've just discovered. You've been going through things in an old home that has belonged to your family for generations. Looking in the attic one day you find an old trunk that has been shoved back into a dark corner and forgotten. Inside the trunk, wrapped in old linen cloths, you find an old diary.

It is written in ancient Greek. You understand a little Greek but not enough to translate it. A professor at your local college is an expert in ancient Greek. You take the book to him and ask him to translate it for you. A few days later he calls. His voice is excited. Can you come right now? He sits you down and then says the last thing you could have imagined: "This diary was written by a Roman officer-turned-businessman. It includes an eyewitness account of the events in Jerusalem from Palm Sunday through Pentecost.

"It was written by a man named Barnabas. He was a proud descendent of a prominent Roman family. From what he writes we can conclude that he was stately looking, well built with light-brown hair streaked with gray. Barnabus carried himself like a Roman officer. The armor he wore in service still fit perfectly and he wore it proudly whenever opportunity afforded. When he retired, he settled up north in the city of Thyatira, one of the Roman territories on the northeastern end of the Mediterranean Sea.

"From this strategic location he built a very profitable business selling expensive dyes like royal blue (made from a variety of sea snails native to Thyatira). Business had been so profitable he decided to find new markets. He records a conversation he had with his fellow merchants.

"'Do you know what I'd do if I were you?' they asked him. 'The Jews have this big festival every year in Jerusalem. They call it Passover. Thousands come to it from all over the world. If I were you I'd plan on going to Jerusalem during Passover. It may be a Jewish holy day but they're ready to do business at the drop of a denarii. You should be able to pick up all the new markets you can handle without having to go anywhere else.'

"With that advice in mind Barnabas had planned his trip. He obtained a map of the region from the local map maker, who added the trade routes. Barnabas writes that if he starts at the seaport of Joppa, follows the mountain pass northeast to Samaria, he will intersect several trade routes. Then he can head south to Jericho, intersecting several more. Jerusalem was just a day's ride west from Jericho. With a minimum of travel, he could do a world of business.

"Barnabas writes that he packed two large crates with samples of his dyes, boarded a ship and sailed south to Joppa. There he bought two donkeys, one to ride and one to carry his samples, and set out for Samaria. His friends were right. Business was good. He signed contracts with several merchants in Samaria, Shechem, Alexandrium and Jericho. Meticulous in all that he did, Barnabas kept a daily journal of his conversations, observations and business contacts. He wrote whenever he got a chance."

The following is Barnabus' account, in his own words, as translated by the Professor.

It turns out I've timed my journey well. I will arrive in Jerusalem a couple days before Passover begins. I'll have time to get settled and look around. I made a couple choice deals in Jericho this morning with some merchants from Damascus. It was late morning before I got away. When I tell people I'm heading for Jerusalem they warn me, "Watch out for robbers along the way. Those hills are notorious for them, and if you go alone they might attack." I had come prepared for situations like this. I put on my Roman armor. It's not likely any robber will try to rob a fully armed Roman soldier. The sword hanging at my side will discourage them.

The road to Jerusalem was long, dry, dusty, and very hot. Thankfully my tunic keeps the metal armor from getting too hot. They were right when they said the road went through desolate places where robbers could easily hide. It's desolate alright! Several times I'm sure I saw men slip back into the shadows, as though they had been lookouts for a gang of robbers. But no one dared to approach me. They aren't about to take a chance on getting hurt themselves. They talk tough but they're cowards at heart. The fact that I am riding a donkey and not a war horse, seems to make no difference in their cowardliness.

I met a few caravans along the way. I warned them about the robbers. I'd hoped to learn from them what to expect when I get to Jerusalem, but they didn't have much news to share. The gossip at the Half-Way Inn was all about being happy to get out of Jerusalem before the crowds arrive. The innkeeper doesn't have much to offer, either. Travelers don't sit and talk as they are anxious to join passing caravans to have safety in numbers.

The heat on the last part of the trip was brutal, especially in my suit of armor. I felt like I was being roasted alive. At last I arrived at Bethany. It is a welcome sight. I stopped at an inn that looked inviting, and shed my armor for some cooler garments. I decide to wait at the inn for the hottest time of day to pass. I can catch up on my notes while I'm waiting. Bethany is just over the hill from Jerusalem. I figure that once it cools down I'll have plenty of time to make the short jaunt down the Mount of Olives and enter Jerusalem before the gates close at sundown.

Bethany looked pretty much deserted when I arrived. Everyone was seeking shelter from the midday heat. This inn where I'm stopped has plenty of shade, even for my donkeys. The innkeeper is obliging and lets me hobble them in the shade. I've settled down at a table in front of the inn with a cool glass of wine. A light breeze is blowing. I take my turban off to let the breeze cool my face. Sitting here relaxing, catching up on my journal, my mind wanders. I know many of the Jews who live in Thyatira. They are shrewd businessmen but honest and trustworthy. It was by their advice that I've come. "Arrive at Jerusalem at Passover," they said. What Passover is and what it means I know little about. The Jews in Thyatira kept their religious practices pretty much to themselves. I figured I'd have plenty of time to ask questions once I got here. I tried to talk to the innkeeper. He apologized for not joining me but was pretty busy at the moment. Maybe later, he said.

"May I join you?"

My thoughts are interrupted by a stranger, a fellow traveler judging by the dusty look of his robes. He is a good-looking young man, a little darker complexioned than me. His black curly hair sticks out from under his dessert turban. His beard is neatly trimmed. It'll be nice to have someone to talk to.

"Yes! Yes! Make yourself at home. I would enjoy having someone to talk to. Donkeys don't know how to carry on a conversation!"

"I know what you mean. I've been riding all day, too. You're not from around here, are you?"

"No. My name is Barnabas. I'm a merchant in dyes from Thyatira. I'm a

Roman citizen come to Jerusalem on business. You look like you might live around here. Do you? If so I've a lot of questions about what is happening."

"I'm pleased to meet you, Barnabas. My name is Jeremiah. I was named after one of our prophets, but I'm not a prophet. My family lives in Hebron. That's a day's journey south of here. We are merchants, too. But that's not what brings me to Bethany today."

"Jeremiah, you're just the man I'm looking for! I'm not a Jew. I need someone to explain to me what this Passover season is all about. Also, my Jewish friends in Thyatira are very shrewd businessmen and they suggested I try to pick up some advice from a fellow merchant before going into Jerusalem to sell my dyes."

Jeremiah's eyes light up. He is fairly bursting with excitement. "I'd love to answer all your questions. But first, do you have a room for tonight? It's going to get very crowded here in Bethany before the day ends. If you don't have a room, you'll be sleeping on the ground."

I hadn't planned to spend the night in Bethany. Neither did I have any idea how crowded it was going to get. But I didn't want to pass up this chance to have some good conversation and get some business pointers. Bethany seemed like a nice restful town. Jerusalem was only a short jaunt over the top of the hill. Besides, so many different people had told me I must enter Jerusalem the Golden from the east in the morning just as the sun breaks above the eastern hills. Well, why not? That settled it. I went inside and asked the Innkeeper for a room.

"My good Innkeeper, do you have a room for tonight?" I asked. To my surprise, he answered, "You're very lucky! I have just one room left. Normally all my rooms would be gone by now. By sundown, there won't even be standing room left in town. Here, let me help you stable your donkeys." With that, he led me to the stables and helped unload my donkeys and feed and water them.

"That young fellow you were talking to, Jeremiah. He's a good man, well respected and honest as gold. I'll bet he can answer all your questions and more besides. Dinner will be served right at sundown, so don't wander off too far," the Inn Keeper called out as I went back outside to talk with Jeremiah.

"Jeremiah, I owe you one! Thanks to your urging I was in time to get the last room. Now, you were about to tell me why you are bursting with excitement."

Jeremiah explained how every Jew saves and dreams of the day when he can go to Jerusalem to celebrate the great Holy Days. "On Passover Day Israel remembers how God delivered her from Egypt. My people, who had been treated as slaves, left Egypt wealthy and free. That's what we celebrate; the night the death angel passed over the Israelites and we were set free, made rich, and became a nation."

Obviously there is much more to learn. But before I can ask, Jeremiah continues.

"Three days after Passover we celebrate First Fruits. An omer worth of barley (that's one tenth of a bushel of stalks and grain bound together), the first grain of the newly planted crop, is baked into a loaf of bread, and the bread waved before God. It represents all the harvests yet to come. It reminds us that God brought us into this Promised Land flowing with milk and honey. It reminds us that Abraham had offered Isaac, the first fruit from which the nation of Israel sprang. It is a celebration of thanksgiving when we thank God for his faithfulness.

"Finally, fifty days after First Fruits comes Pentecost, the Feast of Weeks, marking the end of the grain harvest. But more importantly it celebrates the day when God gave us the Law on Mount Sinai. It is that Law that defines us as a nation."

I marvel as Jeremiah talks, his eyes glowing. Here it is, 30 AD and these events of which he speaks happened almost fifteen hundred years ago! You never hear of a nation lasting that long. Civilizations rise and fall, but today, almost fifteen hundred years later, scattered over most of the known world, they still believe themselves to be a nation waiting for a savior to come and reunite them. All over the world, in Africa and Egypt, in Mesopotamia, Judea and Cappadocia, Pontus and Asia, in Phrygia and Pamphylia, Libya and Cyrene, and Rome, wherever they are they keep the same holy days. They are divided by different cultures and different languages yet they continue to be united by this one idea; that they are first and foremost Jews, God's chosen people. Amazing!

The Innkeeper calls us to dinner. It's a good meal. He serves both traditional Jewish food and Roman style food. There is plenty and, despite my good intentions, I overeat! Since we'll be starting before day break, we retire early. From all accounts, tomorrow is going to be a busy day. Jeremiah reminds me once again, "There's only one way to enter Jerusalem! You must wait 'til morning and come in from the east from Bethany, over the top of the Mount of Olives. Come with the sun at your back, just as it breaks over the Mount of Olives. It is a wondrous sight!"

We wake early. Nobody can sleep with all the noise in the streets. It is the darkness just before sunrise. We eat a quick breakfast. The road is already over-crowded. Jeremiah tells me that thousands upon thousands of travelers have come by boat and camel and caravan. Many have traveled for weeks, across many miles, to make this once in a lifetime visit. I'm amazed at the size of the crowd filling the little town of Bethany. They have come to their fabled Golden City. The fame of Jerusalem the Golden has spread far and wide. It is even known to us up in Thyatira. It was said that King Herod had spared no expense on his building projects. The finest white marble, gold leaf overlay, silver, bronze, and rich Babylonian tapestry, had all gone into making Jerusalem's Temple a wonder to behold. Now I was about to find out if all I had heard was true.

"I told you there'd be a big crowd this morning," Jeremiah shouts above the noise. "Follow me. I know a path around this crowd." I gratefully follow Jeremiah. Leading donkeys through a crowd is tricky. Their stubbornness shows up at the most inconvenient times. Once we're free of the crowd, the donkeys trot right along. The townspeople, to avoid the crowds, had carved out their own little known path. When they had business in Jerusalem and the crowds were thick this shortcut saved a lot of time. We rejoin the crowd at the summit of the hill.

Looking around I sense that the air is charged with excitement, more excitement than I'd expected. The day is dawning bright and beautiful. The sky is a deep blue with white billowy clouds. It's a perfect day. But that doesn't account for all of the excitement in the air. I sense both anticipation and wonder. And I wonder, can the sight I am about to see be all that thrilling?

"Let's wait here," Jeremiah motions, "we can see the Temple from here. The path drops off so no one will get in front of us."

The Mount of Olives rises nearly four hundred feet above the city of

Jerusalem. It had kept the Golden City hidden from view as we climbed the path from Bethany. Before us, the Temple rests in deep shadow. We wait. Then, suddenly the sun breaks the horizon. Wow! The glory of the sight as the full sun strikes the Temple, leaves me breathless, speechless. It really is a wonder to behold! The gates to the temple area are overlaid with gold and silver, all except the Golden Gate that faces the Mount of Olives. That gate is made of Corinthian Bronze; far costlier than gold or silver. Each of its two doors are sixty feet high by twenty-two and a half feet wide. The doors are covered with massive plates of gold and silver.

Almost the whole Temple is overlaid with gold. The Temple stands one hundred and fifty feet high. There is so much gold reflecting the sun it is hard to look directly at the Temple. All that's not overlaid with gold is of pure white stone, like the snow on a mountain top. As my eyes adjust, I can make out a great arched bridge that stretches across the Kedron Valley to the Golden Gate. As spectacular as the Temple is, however, it still does not account for all the excitement I sense in the air. This puzzles me. I look around trying to see what I am missing. Suddenly I become aware of noises and shouts behind me. I turn and see a man sitting on a donkey.

It is then I realize that he is the source of the excitement and anticipation that I had sensed. It seems to be radiating out from him like a light more brilliant than the glory of the Temple. The crowd around him is wild with excitement and enthusiasm. The man starts down the Mount riding on his donkey, like a beloved king coming to visit his people. The crowd cuts palm branches and throws them in front of him. Others take off their coats and toss them on the path for him to ride over.

I am fascinated by what I see. Nothing on my journey has prepared me to see such an event. I watch in awe. "Praise to David's Son!" someone shouts. Others take up the chorus, "Praise to David's Son!" "God bless him who comes in the name of the Lord!" shouts another. "Praise be to God!" the crowd answers back. Soon the whole crowd is shouting and declaring the praises of God and blessing this man. I wonder what the Priests and Pharisees will say about this. They are the political leaders of the people, as well as the religious leaders. I soon learn that they totally disapprove and are upset. They shout out to the man, "Tell your followers to stop."

The man answers back, "If they are quiet the very stones will shout instead!"

"Who is this man?" I ask, turning to Jeremiah, who seems to be as excited as everyone else. "Why are the people shouting like he is your king?"

"He's Jesus. He's the promised Messiah! He is the king of kings and lord of lords!" Jeremiah answers with glowing eyes.

This is puzzling. I've never heard of this Jesus but his followers think he is even greater than Emperor Caesar! I decide to follow the crowd and see what I can learn. "Jeremiah," I ask, "are you going to follow Jesus to see where he goes and what happens?" "Yes," he nods. "Good," I answer. "I've many questions maybe you can answer." We follow the crowd down the hill, across the Kedron Valley Bridge, and through the Golden Gate. There's something about this Jesus, his magnetism, makes me want to know more. The authority that seems to emanate from him holds me in its grip. Obviously this is no ordinary man. I sense that he is a man of great honor and inner power. The people seem to share what I'm sensing because they hail him as a great, noble, and beloved king entering amidst the exaltation of his people.

Like the Priests and Pharisees, not everyone shares this adulation. In fact, the whole city is shaken, thrown into an uproar! Everywhere I turn, I hear people asking, "Who is he?" Evidently there are many thousands of visitors who had never heard about Jesus either, until this moment. They keep asking, "Who is he?" The stories that are told in answer to that question are incredulous! A man who had been born blind tells how Jesus healed him. Another tells how Jesus fed 5,000 men, plus the women and children: all from a little boy's lunch of five loaves and two fish. Soon the city, jammed full with hundreds of thousands of visitors, is abuzz with stories of miracles and the wondrous things Jesus had done.

These stories I'm hearing make me wonder. Could it be that the Jewish God has visited his people? I ask Jeremiah, "Has the promised Messiah I've heard the Thyatiran Jews talk about, really come? What do the priests say?"

"The priests say nothing," Jeremiah answers. "They want to get rid of him. They are afraid that you Romans will come sweeping down on them and destroy our nation. They are collaborationists and don't want to rock the boat or lose their easy money."

I watch to see what will happen. Looking around the temple area, I note that it seems to be filled with money changers and livestock dealers. That's when I hear Jesus' voice rise above the racket and call them "a den of thieves." Flipping tables over, scattering livestock, he drives them out of the Temple. "Ouch!" I exclaim. "They won't let him get away with that. He's hitting them in their money pouch. Mark my words, they'll find a way to get back at him."

I still don't know who Jesus is. Except for that brief display of power and authority when the money changers scramble to get away, he appears to be nothing more than a popular charismatic teacher whose pupils got carried away in their enthusiasm. Yet, I can't help but wonder, is there more to him than meets the eye? Something inside me tells me there is.

Well, enough speculating. I'm here on business. "Jeremiah, is there any possibility you could introduce me to some of the merchants here who might be interested in purchasing my dyes?"

"I'd be happy to," he answers. "In fact, my family might be interested in selling your dyes. I'll take some samples with me when I go home. Just follow me down this street. Here is where most of the merchants come to buy and sell." I follow him, and soon I am almost overrun with merchants interested in my dyes.

CHAPTER 2

Barnabus' Diary Continued When Time Was Split in Two

My days are packed full with meeting merchants, and working out business deals. They pass all too quickly. Fortunately, Jeremiah has good connections for a room, too or I would have been sleeping on the streets! Running into him was a really good stroke of luck. Thursday comes around much quicker than I expected. Thursday, Jeremiah tells me, is Passover eve. All business stops until after Sabbath. The streets of Jerusalem are empty. Jeremiah explains that every room that could be found is packed in readiness for Passover.

"Why don't you come with me?" he asks. "I'll be joining a group of friends for the celebration. I'm sure they will welcome you. We love to tell our story to anyone who will listen. They may talk your ears off! It thrills us to remember what God has done. It will help you understand us better."

I gladly accept his invitation. When it is time he leads me down several streets and past all the shops, now closed. Most families live above their shops in upper rooms, he explains. To get to them, you enter a door in the wall, climb the steps, and enter through a thick wooden door at the top. He finds the doorway he is looking for and we ascend to the door above. His friends are already gathered. He introduces me and I am welcomed like an old friend. Soon we gather round the table. The Passover lamb has already been slain and cooked. The herbs and spices are ready. The unleavened bread is baked. The Passover meal begins.

They recall the bitter years of slavery at the hands of the Egyptians.

They tell how Moses demanded that Pharaoh let the people go. They tell of the many signs and wonders, of the plagues that fell on the Egyptians but not on the Jews. They recall how the blood of the lamb that had been slain for their meal had been applied to the doorposts of their homes. They recall how, on that dreadful and glorious night, they ate their meal standing up with traveling clothes on. Their bread was unleavened because there was no time for it to rise.

They recall how the death angel could not cross that blood line into the homes of the Hebrews. Passing over them, it struck the firstborn of all the Egyptians and the firstborn of all their cattle. The next morning the grief that gripped Egypt and the Pharaoh was so strong that Pharaoh demanded that Israel leave.

"The Egyptians were so eager for Israel to go that they gladly gave Israel all their wealth just to get us to leave and to take our God with us. My people, who had been treated as slaves, left Egypt wealthy and free. That's what we celebrate; the night the death angel passed over the Israelites, and we were set free, made rich, and became a nation. We eat the meal following their age old customs." It is an uplifting experience. I am sorry to leave them but it is time to go back to our rooms and rest.

The next morning we're aroused by Jeremiah's friends banging on our door. They have extremely disturbing news. While we were celebrating Passover Jesus and his disciples were also celebrating Passover in an upper room near the Temple. We're told Jesus said some strange, puzzling things. He had lifted up the cup of wine and announced to his disciples that it was his blood, shed for them. He lifted up the bread, broke it, and said it was his body, broken for them. What do these strange words mean? His words will be repeated again and again in the days to come.

But it wasn't the words that had left them scared and bewildered. When the meal was ended it was late. Jesus and his disciples left the upper room and went to the Garden of Gethsemane to spend time in prayer. There, in the middle of the night while Jerusalem slept, the Temple soldiers came. They arrested Jesus. By the time we were awakened, the trial is over. It was an illegal trial. It violated Jewish law. In the rush to judgment, this man, who had ridden so majestically into Jerusalem on Sunday, was going to be nailed to a cross. Shocked and bewildered, we hear the full story of what happened from eye witnesses.

The news of Jesus' arrest and crucifixion spreads through the city like wild fire. We hurry to the Gate and join the crowd that is already gathering. What we see is shocking. Crucifixions are always shocking. But crucifixions of innocent men are even more so. We watch as the nails are driven into Jesus' hands and feet. Questions flood my mind. Was it all a hoax? Was he just another revolutionary who failed? If he was the Messiah, like Jeremiah claimed, couldn't he come down from the cross? Nothing happens. Others, who are only curious, rejoin the festive celebrations. But my friend, Jeremiah, drops to the ground, weeping unashamedly.

I stay to comfort and weep with my friend, although I don't understand why I, too, am weeping. This has nothing to do with me, does it? Only a handful remain to watch him die. Mercifully, death comes quickly. As he breathes his last, darkness sweeps over Jerusalem, and an earthquake strikes. A strange thought crosses my mind. "God, too, has wept." His body is taken down from the cross and laid in a borrowed tomb nearby. Slowly Jeremiah and I rise and walk back into the city. We rejoin the festivities of Passover.

Our hearts are not in it because our sorrow is too great. Later we learn that the only damage done by the earthquake was to split from top to bottom the four-inch-thick curtain that hung over the entrance to the Holy of Holies in the Temple. I can't help but wonder if God is saying something? These are strange thoughts for me to be thinking.

Sabbath day comes and goes. It is a day of grief and unanswered questions. The disciples hide themselves away. Their lives have been shaken to the core. We all wonder if they will be the next victims of the Sanhedrin. It is now early Sunday morning, the first day of the week. Jeremiah bids me farewell and leaves. But before he leaves, he explains that today will be the celebration of First Fruits. It is also the third day since Jesus was crucified. Even though it is still dark, I've not been able to sleep. I decide to go walking to try to relieve this sadness that hangs over me.

I walk near the gate when I become aware of a strange sense of anticipation in the air. It's almost as though all nature is holding its breath, waiting for something to happen. It is the dark before the dawn. I notice movement. As I watch, I see the form of two cloaked figures silently slipping out the city gate. Someone pointed them out to me yesterday. I know who they are and their mission. One is the one they call Mary Magdalene, and the other they call "the other Mary." They head towards the garden, and the tomb in which Jesus' body has been sealed. As they approach the tomb, I feel the ground shaken by another earthquake. Later I learn that they discovered that the great stone that had sealed the tomb, had been rolled away. On it, they said, sat a man whose appearance was like lightning, his garment white as snow. He spoke and said, "Jesus is not here for he has risen."

While they are visiting the tomb, I see a third cloaked figure slip silently out the city gate and make his way to a nearby field. I recognize his garments. He is a Temple priest. There, in the field, as the first rays of sunlight light the field, he finds it; stalks of barley with the grain just ripening. Without seeing it, I know it will be the first fruit of the year's crop that has come up. The priest will carefully gather an omer of the new grain. He will take it back to the Temple.

By now the city is waking up. Many worshippers are headed towards the Temple. I join them. They will be celebrating First Fruits, a celebration of thanksgiving for the first grain of the coming harvest. The priest I saw will finely grind the grain, mix it with oil, bake it, and then hold it up before the altar. He will wave it back and forth and then present it as a burnt offering. All will give thanks and praise God for the harvest that is coming.

My trip to Jerusalem has been all I had hoped it would be and far more than I had expected. In the excitement and festivities of the First Fruits celebration, I almost forget about the strange man who rode into Jerusalem on a donkey. Indeed, I would have forgotten, chalked it up to a strange Jewish happening that I had gotten caught up in; except for something else that happens. On this First Fruits, there is a second First Fruits; an event that turns the city, and my life, upside-down.

A wild rumor sweeps its way across Jerusalem on this First Fruits morning. One of the women I saw going to the tomb in the early darkness has come back declaring, "Jesus is alive. He has risen from the dead! The tomb is empty." These words might have been the ravings of a distraught woman except others are reporting, "Jesus is alive. He's appeared to Peter!" This is very strange, I think. I want to know more. Does this explain the strange feeling of anticipation I was feeling? If Jesus is really alive that would be extraordinary! Or did his disciples come and steal his body? If he is alive, does that mean that Jesus is the Messiah Jeremiah talked about? If he is the Messiah, what does that mean about our goddess, Diana?

I search for anyone who knows anything about Jesus. Soon I am spellbound as amazing story after story unfolds about his miracles, his teaching, his laughter, his fun, and now his resurrection. There can be no doubt about it. If he has really risen, then Jesus of Nazareth is the Messiah. The more I hear the more my heart melts within me. The more I hear the more I realize that the goddess Diana, and all the other Greek gods we honor, are nothing but lies. I am eager to learn all I can about Jesus. I do it in the only way I know how. I attach myself to the band of followers.

I learn that Jesus met up with two of the disciples who were walking to Emmaus. They ran back to Jerusalem to report it to the others. While they were still talking Jesus came and stood among them. He gave them last minute instructions and answered their last minute questions. "Don't leave Jerusalem," he said. "Wait here for what the Father promised that I told you about. You are going to be immersed into the Holy Spirit. It will give you power and ability and efficiency and might, and you will be able to tell people all about me with power and with attesting proofs." I hear their report firsthand.

The next forty days pass quickly. Each day new reports spread of Jesus being alive. He shows himself to the women, to Peter, and many times to the eleven. As he meets with the disciples, he eats with them, and teaches them many things from the scriptures. Then the disciples come and share it with the rest of us. Then I actually see him, too! One day some five hundred of us are gathered at the feet of the disciples. They are opening up scriptures to us that Jesus has just opened up to them. Peter is speaking. Suddenly, Jesus stands right beside Peter! He doesn't speak. His smile says it all. His hands are raised in blessing. Then he is gone.

On the fortieth day, we watch Jesus ascend into heaven. For the next ten days we stay in Jerusalem. We meet with the disciples in the Temple, praising and blessing God. When not in the Temple, the disciples and as many as can squeeze in, one hundred and twenty in all, meet upstairs in Mark's house.

Fifty days have passed since Passover. Today is Pentecost, the Feast of

Weeks, the last big festival of this holy season. It's almost 9:00 o'clock in the morning. Harvest has ended. In thanksgiving two loaves of bread are baked, ready to offer up at the high moment of sacrifice: at 9:00 o'clock in the morning. The crowds have gathered.

The 9:00 o'clock hour strikes. Then, all of a sudden, just as the priest lifts up the loaves of bread, a mighty wind roars down from heaven! What happens next is... well, all I can do is describe what I heard. Like the mighty roar of water at the bottom of a great waterfall, a mighty wind streamed down. It entered the room where the one hundred and twenty were praying. It broke into flames of fire and settled on their heads. One hundred and twenty people suddenly became animated with an exuberance of rejoicing, shouting, laughing, dancing, and singing and praising God!

The power of God gushed through their bodies. If filled the room, saturated it, filled them and saturated them. Joy unspeakable and full of glory bubbled up and flowed out. Life, God's life, surged through their veins. Gone were fear and timidity. Boldness, authority, and power, radiated from them. They couldn't sit still. They ran out of the room shouting praise and glory to God. They praised and glorified God in languages they never learned!

The visitors in the crowd know the languages! Around me are people from every nation under heaven. Like me, they too are awestruck, bewildered. Each one is hearing God praised and glorified in his own native tongue. Indeed, I am hearing God praised in my native Greek. "What's going on here?" they ask. "Aren't all these who are speaking uneducated Galileans? How is it that we each hear them in our own languages to which we were born?"

"They must be drunk," someone shouts. Others repeat the charge. Peter raises his voice to get the crowd's attention. A most amazing thing happens. He speaks, and power gushes out of him. This power radiating out from him is so strong that it makes the huge crowd get so quiet I could hear a pin drop. It makes my hair stand on end and shivers go up and down my spine. I have never heard anyone speak with such power before. I have fought in many a battle but never have I experienced such power in a leader.

I am not a Jew. I'm a Roman businessman on a business trip that has taken me to the Jews' sacred City. It should be easy for me to dismiss Peter's explanation of what has happened. I just got caught up in the drama, that's all. Jesus is a Jewish Messiah. He has nothing to do with me, a Roman citizen. But it's too late for that now. Jesus has won my heart. He's no longer just the Jews' savior. He's my Savior, too. Jesus instructed the disciples to go into the whole world preaching the Gospel and making disciples of all people. That means Jesus is for everyone. Besides, not only did he save me, He filled me with his Holy Spirit too. Yes, I, the dignified Roman Officer, am dancing for joy like all the others! My heart's desire now is to stay with the Church in Jerusalem.

But, business calls. I can neglect it no longer. There are orders that must be filled. So it is that reluctantly I return to Thyatira. But from this moment on, wherever I go, I will share what I have seen and heard. Remembering what Jesus promised I'll look for people who need to experience God's love as I love them. I will look for the sick and lay hands on them and they will recover. I'll invite people to my home and share the Good News with them. We can study the scriptures together with the help of a local Rabbi.

Barnabas' account ends with those words. Unlike Barnabas we live in a different land, and a different culture, and a different time. But those events move us in the same way. We return to them over and over again, sometimes weeping at what Jesus did for us. Always thankful, always wanting to reach out and grab His hand. We must never forget why He had to die for us. It is to that dark history we now turn, to see the full picture and understand why.

CHAPTER 3

From Glory to Darkness to Light

When the guns are silenced, when the senseless slaughter of young men ends, when the grass grows up where thousands died, we forget the horrors. Our grandparents may remember, but to us it is only a story in a history book. World War I was my dad's war. World War II is a fading memory from my grade school days, almost forgotten in the years of prosperity that followed. That is how it is with great wars fought long before our time. We put unpleasant memories behind us and hide the scars. Veterans hide their memories and grief and nightmares.

For many people Independence Day has become nothing but a day off from work with parades and fireworks. Little do people realize that those battles were merely skirmishes of an ongoing war that started eons ago. Storms, genocide, terrorism, starvation, disease and earthquakes are lingering damage from this war. The week that split time in two created a major turning point in this war. With one fell blow, man was redeemed and empowered to undo all the works of the enemy, Satan.

It is worthwhile for us to take a quick look back at how that war started. In the beginning, when God began his work of Creation he created companies of beings called angels numbering in the tens of thousands and thousands of thousands (Revelation 5:11). One archangel, Lucifer, who was considered to be the greatest of all created beings, began to nurse a spirit of rebellion. He decided that he would take God's place. "Am I not like God?" he asked himself. "Hasn't he given me his power?" Lucifer started declaring to all the angels under his leadership, "I will exalt my throne above the stars of god. I will sit on the mount of the congregation in the uttermost north. I will ascend above the heights of the clouds. I will make myself like the Most High." Rebellion began to consume his every thought. He spread his rebellion until fully a third of all the angels had joined him. When all was ready, Lucifer led his forces in an attack on the throne of God. (paraphrased from Isaiah 14:12-15)

When the smoke cleared, Lucifer was defeated. The planet where his throne once was lay devastated. The host of angels he had groomed to fight his war were now held in chains in thick gloom of utter darkness (Jude 6). After an unknown period of time passed the Spirit of God moved over the face of a chaotic sphere (we do not know if this was Satan's old planet, or a brand new planet). As the Spirit hovered, God spoke and waters were gathered together and dry land appeared. God spoke and a supremely beautiful garden emerged. God looked upon all he has made and said it is very good. Lastly, God created a man and a woman in his image and after his likeness. The glory that covers God, covered them.

God spoke to the man saying,

> I give you this planet earth to be its supreme rulers, to govern all the cities and countries and nations and world systems that come to be. I give you this earth with all its vast resources to develop them fully and make all that can be made from them, even vessels to sail among the stars. To seal this agreement, I give you this six-thousand-year lease. The only restriction is, do not eat of the tree of the knowledge of good and evil. (Paraphrase of Genesis 1:26-30; 2:16-17)

A gift was given to the man and woman; the gift of free will, the freedom to choose and make choices. The reason for this gift is that God wanted the man and woman and all their descendants to be able to choose to love and obey him of their own free will.

To choose God over someone else you must have a someone else. Satan, by his treason, had become the someone else. Satan, in his self-delusion, unaware of God's plans, believed if he could get the man to rebel against God, God would be finished. For, by law, the instant Adam rebelled, Adam's race would become Satan's slaves (Romans 6:16), and Adam's possessions (the earth) would default to Satan's ownership. That was the law.

Satan believed the end result would be that God's plans would be rendered null and void, and that he, Satan, would have finally seized God's throne. The problem was how to trick the man. Satan knew the man and woman wouldn't deliberately rebel against God. But, if he could trick them into trusting in their own wisdom instead of God's, he could get them to rebel without thinking it was rebellion. Eve was his target. Eve did not rebel. Rather, he helped her talk herself into believing it a wise thing to eat the forbidden fruit. After all, wisdom to rule wisely was what she needed. Surely God would want that.

Adam is the one who rebelled. He knowingly, deliberately, disobeyed God. When the deed was done, Satan instantly got Adam's lease to the planet Earth. In that one act of disobedience, Adam instantly lost everything including the glory that clothed him. Instantly Satan got possession of the earth. But he did not get Adam's glory covering. He soon discovered that the lease was only good for a period of 6,000 years.

The instant Adam and Eve realize the horribleness of what they have done, they experience fear for the first time. Fear of God's wrath overcomes them. They hide. They try to cover themselves so that God cannot see them. But the force of God's voice forces them to reveal themselves. Adam and Eve wait, expecting God's fury to come down upon them. The fury does not come. Instead they find a deep sadness as though God is weeping, and a great love as from one whose heart is breaking for them. As they listen, they learn that God has a secret plan, a plan unknown to Satan. A plan called Kinsman-Redeemer. A plan that was fulfilled in the week that split time in two.

CHAPTER 4

GUESS WHEN GOD THROWS A PARTY

The paradise Adam had known was lost. The future into which he looked was bleak. To an outside observer it must have seemed that God's plans and hopes were shattered. At least that was what Satan believed as he gloated over his victory, believing he had beat God. But unknown to Satan and Adam God had a plan. God had laid down a secret plan before he began the work of creation (Ephesians 1:4).

Jesus hinted at this plan in a story he told. The story is about a loving father and a rebellious son. All of us go through a rebellious stage at least once when we are growing up. When I was very young I even tied some clothes in a bundle ready to run away. My mother only smiled and told me when supper would be ready. My rebellion never made it past mealtime or bedtime.

Jesus wasn't talking about that kind of rebellion. The son in his story had reasons to rebel, or so he thought. He hated working on the farm. He resented his older brother always bossing him around. They were always arguing and fighting. Although I didn't have an older brother like this young son, I believe I understand a little of what he was thinking. For example, we both thought country life was backwards. Modern comforts had not reached us yet. In my case we had no electricity. Our bathroom was an outhouse. We used horses instead of tractors. But we did have newspapers and cars to use to go to town.

City life excited our young minds. Stories about things to see and do grabbed our attention. The city was where the action was! In the city they were doing amazing things, inventing things, and it sounded glamourous. The city cried out "come" to those of us who didn't want to be farmers. We dreamed of the day we would be old enough to work and live in the city.

That call of the city haunted the young son in Jesus' story. But there was another driving force that had to do with his older brother. Having an older brother changed everything. The oldest son would inherit two thirds of the father's wealth. If the young son stayed on the farm he would have to work for his brother. This younger brother might have expressed it this way:

"Do you know what it's like having an older brother? Nobody lets you be yourself. You're always under his shadow. It starts with the hand-me-down clothes. No matter what you do somebody says, 'Now when your brother was your age....' If your brother was good at something, they expect you to be just as good. They expect you to be just as smart. But what if you aren't like your brother? What if all your brother cares about is the family business; plodding on day by day in the same old rut? Who wants to be tied down to a boring life on a farm working for a bossy brother? The sooner I get out of here, the better."

When he could stand it no longer, he begged his father to give him his part of the estate; now! He wanted to leave and begin to live his own life without an older brother breathing down his neck. The father gave him his share of the inheritance. "Free at last!" shouted the son as he began his journey to the distant city. He was excited and full of confidence. Yes, he would make it on his own. He would prove to his father, to his older brother, to everyone, that he could succeed on his own. He was free. He had money.

He rented a room in a nice section of town. He began to study and develop his skills. But the glaring lights and his new friends were a distraction he could not resist. He was invited to parties and wasted his money on foolish things. He loved his popularity. He began to experiment with life and taste all its pleasures. He became known for his extravagance and frittering away his money on sensual pleasures and sexual lusts. "This is the life!" he declared as he let his work slip. What he thought was real freedom became an endless quest to satisfy passing whims and greedy desires that were fed but never satisfied.

And then it happened: his money was gone. Gone too were his so-called friends. His friends on whom he had squandered his wealth tossed him aside like a useless worn out shoe. He was evicted from his room. No one would take him in. No one would lend him a penny. He found that once the world has used you it doesn't want you anymore. The world treats you as a stink in its nose.

He searched but could find no work. No one would hire him, especially when they knew his reputation. He'd grown up on a farm. Perhaps, he hoped, a farmer would hire him. Farmers weren't hiring. There was a famine in the land and farmers were hard pressed. Finally, he forced himself on one of the farmers. "Go feed the pigs," said the farmer. "If they leave anything you can have it." But that could not satisfy his hunger. Nobody gave him anything better. His hunger grew.

The younger brother, who wanted to be free, who was so sure of himself when he first left home, was wretched, starving, in rags, without hope, and he stank of pigs. Day after day he fed the pigs. Day after day he longed to stuff himself with the carob pods the pigs were eating, and found no relief from the gnawing hunger pangs in his stomach. Day after day he wallowed in self-pity. Until one day, into that brain that had been so steeped in alcohol, so totally consumed with lust, pleasure seeking, and drugs, came the first sensible thought he had had since leaving home. At long last he came to himself. It was as though he had awakened from a horrible nightmare only to discover the nightmare was true.

"What am I doing here?" he exclaimed. "Why, my father's got dozens of hired servants. Every one of them has more food than they can eat, while I'm dying of hunger! I know what I'll do. I'll go home! But how can I go home after all the things I've done? How can I face my father? I don't deserve to be called his son. He has every right to disown me. I can't go home. But I want to go home. I'll go home and face my father. I'll say, 'Father, I'm so ashamed. I've dragged your name through the filth. I've done everything you're against. I've broken God's laws. I don't deserve to be called your son. Please, let me be a hired servant.'" The son turned his back on the pigs and the carob pods and began the long journey home. His only possessions were the rags on his body that smelt of pigs.

A man stood looking toward the horizon. His hand shaded his eyes.

He was searching for something, as he had been doing every day, week after week, month after month. When working in the fields he would stop and look up. When home he would rise from his chair, go to the door and look out, scanning the horizon. Lovers of bad news repeated the latest gossip they had heard about his son. He did not listen. He prayed without ceasing for his son. He prayed for the day his son would come to his senses and come home. He ceased not to watch for him.

Finally, a morning came when suddenly, in the distance, he saw the beloved form of his son. He dropped everything and ran as fast as he could down the road to meet his him. He did not greet his son with arms folded, demanding, "And just what do you think you are doing here? I've heard all about your debauchery. You've sinned against God and brought disgrace to my name. You'll find no welcome here. Get out of my sight!" No! The father uttered no such words. Instead, from him flowed unconditional love and unconditional forgiveness. Arms extended, the father embraced his son and held him close.

Then, standing back, as we often do when we want to get a good look at someone we've not seen for a while, the father beheld his son. He saw his gaunt body, his filthy clothes, and caught the smell of pigs on his unwashed body. From deep within the father's heart a great transforming love came gushing out. The son tried to say, "Father, I've sinned against you and against heaven, and I'm no longer worthy to be called your son…." He got no further for his father interrupted him saying, "This will never do for a son of mine! Servants, bring forth my best robe and put it on him."

That robe covered all the son's filth, rags, dirt, and his emaciated body. It removed his shame. Everyone would know that all was forgiven and that he was received by his father. All his unrighteousness was covered by his father's robe of righteousness (John 3:16). Next, the father had shoes brought and put on his son's feet. Those shoes marked him as a son. Everywhere he went, everyone would know that he was the son of a nobleman.

Lastly, the father had a ring put on his son's finger. This was no ordinary ring. This was a ring of power. It had carved in it the family crest. Whenever this ring was pressed in sealing wax it was exactly the same as a signature upon a letter or legal document. It was equivalent to signing a check. It was the legal signature of the family to which it belonged.

But that was not all. The father's joy was overflowing. It was as the joy of the man who, upon finding his lost sheep, calls his friends and neighbors to rejoice with him. It was like the woman who, upon finding the silver coin she had lost, called her friends and neighbors to rejoice with her. This father, upon finding his lost son, throws a party to celebrate his son's return, and invites his friends and neighbors to come rejoice with him. His son, who had been lost, was found. He had been dead and now was alive.

Jesus kept repeating that there is great rejoicing when one sinner repents. When you repented, God got excited and threw a party! The Hebrew prophet Zephaniah knew the depths of the love and delight the Father has for us. Using Hebrew words that express joy he described God's joy over a sinner who repents and comes home:

> The Lord your God is in the midst of you. He is a mighty one, a Savior - Who saves! He will brighten up over you with great joy. He will rest in silent satisfaction and in his love he will not mention or even recall past sins; his joy over you is so great that he spins around, dancing, with singing! (Zephaniah 3:17 author's translation[1])

You need to get this truth settled in your mind. The father didn't rejoice and throw a party because the younger brother was totally transformed. He threw the party because he came home and admitted he was wrong. The son repented. To repent means to change one's mind. When we repent we admit that Jesus is who he says he is, we admit our sinfulness, and ask him to take control of our lives. That causes God to throw a party for us and to give us gifts. His first gift is to do for us what we cannot do for ourselves; clothe us in righteousness. He transforms us. He makes us new. He does it for us when we allow him to do it.

CHAPTER 5

THE FACE IN THE PAINTING

God does not owe us anything. We deserve nothing. There is not one single thing we can do to earn anything from God. The fact is that we are born sinners. We can protest and say we don't believe it. But it is a fact. The evil done by men, and by ourselves, is proof. Try as we may, we can't escape the fact that we were born sinners, even gifted that way!

> Wherefore, as by one-man sin entered into the world, and death by sin; and so death passed upon all men (Romans 5:12 KJV).
>
> For all have sinned, and come short of the glory of God (Romans 3:23 KJV). As it is written, There is none righteous, no, not one (Romans 3:10 KJV).

Like the lost son, you too came to a moment of truth when you finally heard the father calling, "Come home." You heard and came home. It didn't matter what you had done, or how dirty your clothes, or how badly you smelled. Your father, because he loves you so much, instantly covered all of that up as though it had never happened. Then he threw a party and gave you gifts! You did nothing to earn them or deserve them. All you did was come home. You may have tried to say that you weren't worthy to be called his child. But he would not listen to you. Paul described God's plan, the plan he had put in place before he began the work of creation.

> He foreordained us (destined us, planned in love for us) to be adopted (revealed) as His own children through Jesus Christ, in accordance with the purpose of His will, because it pleased Him and was His kind intent. (Ephesians 1:5 AMP)

With the gift of salvation, he also gave us gifts of power and authority concerning which we've barely scratched the surface. Jesus has given us the power of attorney to use his name, saying that greater things than he did we will do. He has given us authority over demons and told us that if we resist Satan he will flee from us. He said that now we can have the things we desire when we pray in faith, and the things we say when said in faith, shall come to pass. Whatever we ask in Jesus' name, he will do. We've been given authority to do the works Jesus did, and even greater works.

This being true also means we aren't who we used to think we were. My mother spent many years tracing her genealogical roots. Other than curiosity to find out to whom one is related in the past, people seem to base their identity on finding people of nobility and distinction in their genealogy. Because God has adopted you as his child, you now have a brand new genealogy of the highest order.

There was a fascinating thing about the Roman laws of adoption which mirror God's laws of adoption. You could be the worst villain that ever lived; thief, murderer, drunkard, guilty of the most heinous crimes. But if a nobleman adopted you, the instant the adoption was final all your past and all your old wicked crimes were wiped away as though they had never happened! You could not be put on trial or sent to prison for any of your past crimes and deeds. Why? Because you are no longer who you were. That person died when the adoption papers were signed. You were forever the nobleman's child. Likewise, you are now and forever God's child.

> He planned, in his love, that we should be adopted as his own children through Jesus Christ -- this was his will and pleasure (Ephesians 1:5 PHS).

> You have been adopted into the very family circle of God and you can say with a full heart, 'Father, my Father' (Romans 8:15 PHS). For if a man is in Christ he becomes a new person altogether — the past is finished and gone, everything has become fresh and new (2 Corinthians 5:17 PHS).

Imagine it after this fashion. There is a king who has no heir, no one to succeed him on the throne. To solve this problem, he journeys around his kingdom looking for a suitable heir to adopt. He searches in every nook and cranny. That's where he finds you. You are loathsome, slovenly, disruptive and an all-round bad character. The king picks you, the most unlikely and unsuitable person, to be his heir.

You think the king must be a little looney to pick you. Your drinking buddies and fellow ne'er-do-wells agree as you laugh it up and make jokes. But, living in a castle with servants waiting on you beats spending more time in jail on bread and water. So, when the summons comes, you pack your few belongings into an old pillowcase and head for the palace.

You are stopped at the gate. You'd always figured you would be, once the king's advisors found out what a stupid choice he'd made. So you shrug your shoulders, fling your sack back over your shoulder, and turn to go.

"Halt!" the guard says. "Sit down. Wait here!"

You've heard that kind of voice of authority before! It always meant bad things were about to happen. You stop and plop down on a bench, your sack beside you, and wait with much anxiety and fear. After a few minutes you notice a man approaching from the castle. He must be pretty important from the way he's dressed. The guard brings out a table and puts it in front of you. The important looking man places a large book down on the table and sits in a chair the guard provides. He opens the book. From the look on his face you know it can't be good. One look from the man and all belligerence drains out of you.

"Stand," the man orders. You stand.

"Raise your right hand and place your left hand on this book." You do. "I am going to ask you a question. You are to answer either Yes or No, nothing else. Do you understand?"

"Yes" you mumble, like he thinks you're an idiot. You must admit, in spite of your fears, your curiosity is aroused, wondering what this is all about. He's not acting like any other judge you've stood before.

"This is the question," the man continues. "Do you freely give up all rights to your name, your lineage, your past, your present, your future, and everything that has made you who you are today? Before you answer, read the pages of this book."

You look down at the book on which your hand rests. You are shocked to find that it is your biography. Rap sheet is more like it. Strangely, it begins with Adam and lists your ancestors one by one, and what they did. It isn't until you reach the name of your great grandfather that you recognize any of the names. It is an impressive list. A few of the bad ones were most impressive. You are not so outstanding. Not much to brag about. Even your worst deeds were not anything to write home about. You weren't even good at being bad!

"I'm ready for your answer," the man speaks, interrupting your thoughts. "Do you freely give up all rights to your name, your lineage, your past, your present, your future, and everything that has made you who you are today?"

You're not one to feel guilt or repentance or remorse you tell yourself. You're feeling none of that now. But you must admit that there is nothing you saw worth being proud of or hanging on to. So it is easy to answer "Yes."

"Sign here," the man tells you.

You sign, rather curious to know what that was all about. Again the man interrupts your thoughts. Pointing to the book, he says "Look at the pages." You look and are amazed to see all the words of your biography fade and disappear. It's like you never existed. The man closes the book, turns, and says,

"Leave your sack and follow me."

No sooner do you start down the path to the castle when the king comes running towards you. He grasps you in his arms, hugs you, and says,

"Welcome home my child." He looks at you and cries out, "This will never do. Here put on my robe. Now, that is more like it. Come my child. I've much to show you."

He leads you into the great hall of the castle, where you stand gazing at the walls. His arm is around your shoulders, hugging you affectionately as though you had just come home from a long journey. On the walls are pictures of all the kings and queens going back to the very first. He names them one by one. Suddenly you catch your breath. The portrait last in line is your own portrait! The king turns and looks at you. He speaks,

"My child, this is who you now are. These kings and queens who have gone before are your lineage now. All the old is gone, erased as though it never existed. The moment I adopted you what you once were ceased to exist. You are now my own beloved child. I've called you out of darkness into my marvelous light (I Peter 2:9). The blood that now flows through your veins is the royal blood of kings. That is the law."

"In time you will learn all about your new family. But enough talk. We have a banquet to attend, a banquet in your honor. Before we go I have two gifts for you. First, I give you the clothes of a son. From this time forward, everyone will know that you are my beloved son. Second, I give you the power of attorney to use my name. I give you the authority to draw on all my resources. Where you go it will be as though I went. What you do will be as though I did it."

Our little imaginary story comes to an end but the lesson it teaches does not. God has given you a new lineage, a new heritage. He has adopted you into his family. Jesus says that God loves you just as much as he loves Jesus (John 17:23). He has adopted you as his child, a co-heir with Jesus (Romans 8:29). This means that God is now your birth daddy. That is how you must see yourself. God is not just your creator. God is your father. You are God's child. This is not to say that we ignore or diminish who he is or forget that he is God Almighty, creator of the heavens and the earth, a God whose wrath consumes his enemies. Your daddy sets your enemies at naught, too. To cement this fact in your mind is a major step in knowing the territory of who you are.

We are new creatures in Christ Jesus (2 Corinthians 5:17); we have the very nature of God in us (I John 5:10-13). We have been delivered out of Satan's power and translated into the Kingdom of his dear son (Colossians

1:12-14). It is because of who we now are that we can pray without ceasing, because prayer without ceasing is family talk, basic to who we now are.

As grandiose as the above sounds, "Isn't it time for a reality check?" you might ask. Remember the conversation Moses had with I Am? I Am had told him all the things he was to say to his fellow Israelites, and to Pharaoh. To which Moses answered, "In case you haven't noticed I stutter! I stuttered when you started talking to me, and I still stutter. No one is going to take me seriously when it takes me so long to say anything. Be real!" (Exodus 4:10) In answer God almost "bit off Moses' head," saying "Just who do you think I am? I made you and I made your mouth. As your maker I can equip you to do anything I ask you to do."

God can and does equip us. We give him permission and he changes us. We need to get that fact settled in our minds. God does the transforming. He does for us what we could never do for ourselves. His method is by transformation of our inner man.

> Be transformed (changed) by the <entire> renewal of your mind <by its new ideals and its new attitude>, so that you may prove <for yourselves> what is the good and acceptable and perfect will of God, even the thing which is good and acceptable and perfect <in His sight for you>. (Romans 12:2 AMP)

God doesn't turn us into robots. We have our part to play in the transformation process. Our part is to use words, as God once spoke words when he began the work of creation. We are to confess who we are in Christ, because what we confess is what we possess (I Timothy 6:12, Hebrews 2:1; 4:14, and 10:23). The Greek word for confession, *homologia,* means that it is by confessing who we are in Christ, and confessing what we possess in Christ, that who we are and what we possess can become realities in our lives. Do not confess the "facts" of how bad things are, but confess what faith is calling them to become.

Our confessions reinforce what God is already doing. God changed Abram's name to Abraham and Sari's name to Sarah. Their new names were Father of Many Nations and Queen of Nations. Every time they spoke their names, or the servants or anyone else spoke their names, they were calling those things that be not as though they were (Romans 4:17). They did it because they were "fully persuaded that what he [God] had promised, he was able also to perform" (Romans 4:21). They kept it up year after year, even when Sarah's womb had dried up.

You and I must become fully persuaded. Watch your words, put a guard over your mouth, so that you never speak words of doubt or unbelief, denying what God has promised. Call forth those things that be not until they are. Paul explained why our words are so important:

> Faith cometh by hearing, and hearing by the word of God. (Romans 10:17 KJV).

Remember that Jesus said over and over again, "according to your faith, expressed by your words, you have what you asked" (Matthew 9:22; 15:28; 17:20; Mark 2:5; 5:34; 11:22; Luke 5:20; 7:9; 7:50; 8:5; 8:48; 17:19; 18:42). Our ears pick up and our minds digest what our mouths say. If we want our faith to grow, if we want to live in the fullness of who we now are, we must speak out what the Bible says about us. Likewise, we must never, ever, under any circumstances, speak out anything the Bible doesn't say about us. Negative confessions cancel out positive confessions.

CHAPTER 6

Homework: Becoming Who You Are

Whoever ... does not doubt ... but believes that what he says will take place, it will be done for him," (Mark 11:23 AMP). Jesus reminds us how powerful our words are. Not only do they reveal what is in our heart (Matthew 12:34), they also have the power to create (2 Peter 2:5). Even the centurion knew that if Jesus spoke the word, the word would heal his servant (Matthew 8:8). Much has been written about the power of words to shape and mold us. While we cannot control other people's words, we can control our own words and learn to listen to what we say about ourselves, and not what others say about us or to us. When you speak the confessions that follow, you will be confessing who you are and what you possess as a child of God. Confess out loud the **bold type.** Then read the Scripture(s) on which the confession is based. Do it as often as you can.

What I am in Christ Jesus

I am a new creation in Christ Jesus. My spirit is created in the image and likeness of God. Therefore, if anyone is in Christ, he is a new creation. The old has passed away; behold, the new has come (2 Corinthians 5:17 ESV).

I am complete in Christ Jesus. For in Him the whole fullness of Deity (the Godhead) continues to dwell in bodily form <giving complete

expression of the divine nature>. And you are in Him, made full and having come to fullness of life <in Christ you too are filled with the Godhead—Father, Son and Holy Spirit—and reach full spiritual stature>. And He is the Head of all rule and authority <of every angelic principality and power>. (Colossians 2:9-10 AMP).

I am Righteous in Christ Jesus. I have right-standing with God just like I'd never done anything wrong. God made him who had no sin to be sin for us, so that in him we might become the righteousness of God. (2 Corinthians 5:21 NIV).

I am redeemed from the curse of the law (Poverty, Sickness & Spiritual Death) Christ redeemed us from the curse of the law by becoming a curse for us—for it is written, "Cursed is everyone who is hanged on a tree" (Galatians 3:13 ESV. See also Deut. 28.)

I am God's child and a joint-heir with Christ. The Spirit himself testifies with our spirit that we are God's children. Now if we are children, then we are heirs—heirs of God and co-heirs with Christ, if indeed we share in his sufferings in order that we may also share in his glory. (Romans 8:16-17 NIV).

<u>Where I Am In Christ</u>

I have been taken from Satan's kingdom and I am now in God's kingdom. For he has rescued us from the dominion of darkness and brought us into the kingdom of the Son he loves, in whom we have redemption, the forgiveness of sins. (Colossians 1:13-14 NIV).

I am part of the Body of Christ and Satan has no power over me. But I have power over him. Now the body is not made up of one part but of many.... God has arranged the parts in the body, every one of them, just as he wanted them to be.... Now you are the body of Christ, and each one of you is a part of it (I Corinthians 12:14-27 KJV). Then he called his twelve disciples together, and gave them power and authority over all devils, and to cure diseases.... Behold, I give unto you power to tread on serpents and scorpions, and over all the power of the enemy: and nothing shall by any means hurt you. (Luke 9:1, 10:19 KJV)

I am seated with Christ in heavenly places. But because of his great love for us, God, who is rich in mercy, made us alive with Christ even when we were dead in transgressions—it is by grace you have been saved. And God raised us up with Christ and seated us with him in the heavenly realms in Christ Jesus. (Ephesians 2:4-6 NIV.)

I am seated in the heavenly places far above all power of darkness and ALL things are under my feet. He raised him (Christ) from the dead and seated him at his right hand in the heavenly places, far above all rule and authority and power and dominion, and above every name that is named, not only in this age but also in the one to come. And he put all things under his feet and gave him as head over all things to the church, which is his body, the fullness of him who fills all in all. (Ephesians 1:20-23 ESV.)

What I Possess In Christ

ALL spiritual blessings in heavenly places are mine in Christ Jesus. Praise be to the God and Father of our Lord Jesus Christ, who has blessed us in the heavenly realms with every spiritual blessing in Christ. (Ephesians 1:3 NIV.)

ALL THINGS PRESENT are mine. So then, no more boasting about men! All things are yours, whether Paul or Apollos or Cephas or the world or life or death or the present or the future—all are yours, and you are of Christ, and Christ is of God. (I Corinthians 3:21-23 NIV.)

ALL my needs are supplied by my heavenly father according to his riches in glory by Christ Jesus. And my God will liberally supply (fill to the full) your every need according to His riches in glory in Christ Jesus. (Philippians 4:19 AMP.)

I don't have to worry about anything, for God has commanded me to cast ALL of my cares on him. Casting the whole of your care <all your anxieties, all your worries, all your concerns, once and for all> on Him, for He cares for you affectionately and cares about you watchfully. (I Peter 5:7 AMP.)

What I Can Do In Christ

In the power of the Holy Ghost I am a witness for Jesus. But you shall receive power (ability, efficiency, and might) when the Holy Spirit has come upon you, and you shall be My witnesses in Jerusalem and all Judea and Samaria and to the ends (the very bounds) of the earth. (Acts 1:8 AMP.)

I can and do tell others about Jesus Christ. Jesus approached and, breaking the silence, said to them, All authority (all power of rule) in heaven and on earth has been given to Me. Go then and make disciples of all the nations, baptizing them into the name of the Father and of the Son and of the Holy Spirit, teaching them to observe everything that I have commanded you, and behold, I am with you all the days (perpetually, uniformly, and on every occasion), to the <very> close and consummation of the age. Amen (so let it be). (Matthew 28:18-20 AMP.)

As a believer and in the name of Jesus Christ I cast out devils, I speak with new tongues, and when I lay my hands on the sick they do recover. And these attesting signs will accompany those who believe: in My name they will drive out demons; they will speak in new languages; They will pick up serpents; and <even> if they drink anything deadly, it will not hurt them; they will lay their hands on the sick, and they will get well. (Mark 16:17-18 AMP.)

I can do all things through Christ who strengthens me. I have strength for all things in Christ who empowers me <I am ready for anything and equal to anything through him who infuses inner strength into me; I am self-sufficient in Christ's sufficiency>. (Philippians 4:13 AMP.)

For Comfort and Strength

The joy of the Lord is my strength. ... And be not grieved and depressed, for the joy of the Lord is your strength and stronghold. (Nehemiah 8:10 AMP.)

The Lord is the strength of my life. The LORD is my light and my salvation—whom shall I fear? The LORD is the stronghold of my life—of whom shall I be afraid? (Psalms 27:1 NIV.)

Greater is he that is in me than he that is in the world. Little children, you are of God <you belong to Him> and have <already> defeated and overcome them <the agents of the antichrist>, because He Who lives in you is greater (mightier) than he who is in the world. (I John 4:4 AMP.)

I will not let the Word depart from before mine eyes, for it is life

and health. Let them not depart from your sight; keep them in the center of your heart. For they are life to those who find them, healing and health to all their flesh. (Proverbs 4:21-22 AMP.)

I let no corrupt word come out of my mouth but that which is good to edifying. Let no foul or polluting language, nor evil word nor unwholesome or worthless talk <ever> come out of your mouth, but only such <speech> as is good and beneficial to the spiritual progress of others, as is fitting to the need and the occasion, that it may be a blessing and give grace (God's favor) to those who hear it. (Ephesians 4:29 AMP.)

I refuse to give place to the devil. Leave no <such> room or foothold for the devil <give no opportunity to him>. (Ephesians 4:27 AMP.)

I speak the truth in love and grow up into him in all things. Rather, let our lives lovingly express truth <in all things, speaking truly, dealing truly, living truly>. Enfolded in love, let us grow up in every way and in all things into Him Who is the Head, <even> Christ (the Messiah, the Anointed One). (Ephesians 4:15 AMP.)

No man shall take me out of his hand. For I have eternal life. And I give them eternal life, and they shall never lose it or perish throughout the ages. <To all eternity they shall never by any means be destroyed.> And no one is able to snatch them out of My hand. (John 10:28 AMP.)

I let the peace of God rule in my heart. I refuse to worry about anything. Let the peace of Christ rule in your hearts, since as members of one body you were called to peace. And be thankful. (Colossians 3:15 NIV.) ... Casting the whole of your care <all your anxieties, all your worries, all your concerns, once and for all> on Him, for He cares for you affectionately and cares about you watchfully. (I Peter 5:7 AMP.)

That which I refuse to allow here God also refuses to allow and that which I do allow God also allows to come to pass here on earth. I will give you the keys of the kingdom of heaven; whatever you bind on earth will be bound in heaven, and whatever you loose on earth will be loosed in heaven." (Matthew 16:19 NIV.)

I am a believer and these signs do follow me. I speak with new tongues, I take authority over the devil, I lay hands on the sick and they recover. And these signs will accompany those who believe: in my name they will cast out demons; they will speak in new tongues; they will pick up serpents with their hands; and if they drink any deadly poison, it will not hurt them; they will lay their hands on the sick, and they will recover. (Mark 16:17-18 ESV.)

I am complete in him who is the head of all principality and power. And you are in Him, made full and having come to fullness of life <in Christ you too are filled with the Godhead—Father, Son and Holy Spirit—and reach full spiritual stature>. And He is the Head of all rule and authority <of every angelic principality and power>. (Colossians 2:10 AMP.)

For Financial and Material Needs

Christ has redeemed me from the curse of the law (poverty, sickness and death). Christ redeemed us from the curse of the law by becoming a curse for us, for it is written: "Cursed is everyone who is hung on a tree." (Galatians 3:13 NIV & Deut. 28.)

For poverty he has given me wealth, for sickness he has given me health. For you know the grace of our Lord Jesus Christ, that though he was rich, yet for your sake he became poor, so that you by his poverty might become rich. (2 Corinthians 8:9 ESV.)

I delight myself in the Lord and he gives me the desires of my heart. Delight yourself also in the Lord, and He will give you the desires and secret petitions of your heart. (Psalms 37:4 AMP.)

I have given and it is being given unto me good measure, pressed down, shaken together and running over. Give, and <gifts> will be given to you; good measure, pressed down, shaken together, and running over, will they pour into <the pouch formed by> the bosom <of your robe and used as a bag>. For with the measure you deal out <with the measure you use when you confer benefits on others>, it will be measured back to you. (Luke 6:38 AMP.)

I have paid my tithes and God has opened the windows of heaven and is pouring such blessings upon me that I hardly have enough room to receive them. Bring all the tithes (the whole tenth of your income) into the storehouse, that there may be food in My house, and prove Me now by it, says the Lord of hosts, if I will not open the windows of heaven for you and pour you out a blessing, that there shall not be room enough to receive it. (Malachi 3:10 AMP.)

I have all sufficiency of all things and abound to all good works, for my God has made all grace abound toward me. And God is able to make all grace (every favor and earthly blessing) come to you in abundance, so that you may always and under all circumstances and whatever the need be self-sufficient <possessing enough to require no aid or support and furnished in abundance for every good work and charitable donation>. (2 Corinthians 9:8 AMP.)

There is no lack for my God supplies all my needs according to his riches in Glory by Christ Jesus. And my God will liberally supply (fill to the full) your every need according to His riches in glory in Christ Jesus. (Philippians 4:19 AMP.)

The Lord is my shepherd I DO NOT WANT. THE LORD is my Shepherd <to feed, guide, and shield me>, I shall not lack. (Psalms 23:1 AMP.)

For Guidance and Wisdom

The Spirit of truth abideth in me and teaches me all things. He guides me into all truth. I have perfect knowledge of every circumstance I come up against. But the Counselor, the Holy Spirit, whom the Father will send in my name, will teach you all things and will remind you of everything I have said to you. (John 14:26 NIV.) But when he, the Spirit of truth, comes, he will guide you into all truth. He will not speak on his own; he will speak only what he hears, and he will tell you what is yet to come. (John 16:13 NIV.)

I trust in the Lord with all my heart and lean not to my own understanding. Lean on, trust in, and be confident in the Lord with all your heart and mind and do not rely on your own insight or understanding. (Proverbs 3:5 AMP.)

In all my ways I acknowledge him and he directs my path. In all your ways know, recognize, and acknowledge Him, and He will direct and make straight and plain your paths. (Proverbs 3:6 AMP.)

Thy Word is a lamp unto my feet and a light unto my path. Your word is a lamp to my feet and a light to my path. (Psalms 119:105 AMP.)

He will perfect that which concerns me. The LORD will perfect that which concerneth me: thy mercy, O LORD, endureth forever: forsake not the works of thine own hands. (Psalms 138:8 KJV.)

I let the word of Christ dwell in me richly in all wisdom. Let the word <spoken by> Christ (the Messiah) have its home <in your hearts and minds> and dwell in you in <all its> richness, as you teach and admonish and train one another in all insight and intelligence and wisdom <in spiritual things, and as you sing> psalms and hymns and spiritual songs, making melody to God with <His> grace in your hearts. (Colossians 3:16 AMP.)

I do follow the good shepherd for I know his voice, a stranger I will not follow. The watchman opens the door for [the shepherd], and the sheep listen to his voice and heed it; and he calls his own sheep by name and brings (leads) them out. When he has brought his own sheep outside, he walks on before them, and the sheep follow him because they know his voice. (John 10:3-4 AMP.)

I am not conformed to this world but I am transformed by renewing my mind by the Word of God. Do not conform any longer to the pattern of this world, but be transformed by the renewing of your mind. Then you will be able to test and approve what God's will is—his good, pleasing and perfect will. (Romans12:2 NIV.)

<u>If You Have Fears and Worry</u>

I am the body of Christ and Satan has no power over me. For as the body is one, and hath many members, and all the members of that one body, being many, are one body: so also is Christ. For by one Spirit are we all baptized into one body, whether we be Jews or Gentiles, whether we be bond or free; and have been all made to drink into one Spirit. (I Cor. 12:12-13 KJV.)

Greater is he that is in me than he that is in the world. Little children, you are of God <you belong to Him> and have <already> defeated and overcome them <the agents of the antichrist>, because He Who lives in you is greater (mightier) than he who is in the world. (I John 4:4 AMP.)

I will fear no evil for you are with me Lord, your word and your Spirit comfort me. Yea, though I walk through the valley of the shadow of death,

I will fear no evil: for thou art with me; thy rod and thy staff they comfort me. (Psalm 23:4 KJV.)

I am far from oppression and fear does not come near me. In righteousness you will be established: Tyranny will be far from you; you will have nothing to fear. Terror will be far removed; it will not come near you. (Isaiah 54:14 NIV.)

No weapon formed against me shall prosper for my righteousness is of the Lord. No weapon that is formed against thee shall prosper; and every tongue that shall rise against thee in judgment thou shalt condemn. This is the heritage of the servants of the LORD, and their righteousness is of me, saith the LORD. (Isaiah 54:17 KJV.)

Whatsoever I do shall prosper for I am like a tree by rivers of water. And he shall be like a tree planted by the rivers of water, that bringeth forth his fruit in his season; his leaf also shall not wither; and whatsoever he doeth shall prosper. (Psalms 1:3 KJV.)

Lord, you have delivered me from the evils of this world for it is God's will. Who gave (yielded) Himself up <to atone> for our sins <and to save and sanctify us>, in order to rescue and deliver us from this present wicked age and world order, in accordance with the will and purpose and plan of our God and Father (Galatians 1:4 AMP.)

No evil will befall me neither shall any plague come near my dwelling. There shall no evil befall thee, neither shall any plague come nigh thy dwelling. (Psalms 91:10 KJV.)

For you have given your angels charge over me and they keep me in all my ways. For he will command his angels concerning you to guard you in all your ways. (Psalms 91:11 ESV.)

In my pathway is life and there is no death. In the way of righteousness is life; and in the pathway thereof there is no death. (Proverbs 12:28 KJV.)

I am a doer of the word of God and am blessed in my deeds. But the one who looks into the perfect law, the law of liberty, and perseveres, being no hearer who forgets but a doer who acts, he will be blessed in his doing. (James 1:25 ESV.)

I take the shield of faith and stop everything the enemy brings against me. In all circumstances take up the shield of faith, with which you can extinguish all the flaming darts of the evil one. (Ephesians 6:16 ESV.)

Christ has redeemed me from the curse of the law. I forbid any sickness to come on me. Christ redeemed us from the curse of the law by becoming a curse for us, for it is written: "Cursed is everyone who is hung on a tree." (Gal. 3:13 NIV & Deut. 28.)

I overcome by the blood of Christ and the word of my testimony. They overcame him by the blood of the Lamb and by the word of their testimony; they did not love their lives so much as to shrink from death. (Rev. 12:11 NIV.)

The devil flees from me because I resist him in Jesus' name. So be subject to God. Resist the devil <stand firm against him>, and he will flee from you. (James 4:7 AMP.)

The word of God is forever settled in heaven. Forever, O LORD, your word is firmly fixed in the heavens. (Psalms 119:89 ESV.)

Great is the peace of my children for they are taught of the Lord. All your children shall be taught by the LORD, and great shall be the peace of your children. (Isaiah 54:13 ESV.)

PART B

THE TERRITORY OF FAMILY

SEE WHAT <an incredible> quality of love the Father has given (shown, bestowed on) us, that we should <be permitted to> be named and called and counted the children of God! And so we are! (1 John 3:1 AMP)

CHAPTER 7

THE ASTOUNDING GIFT

Our new lives as Christians begins with a gift, a breath-taking and astounding gift God places in our hands. It comes as an absolutely free gift! We can't earn it. We can't buy it. We can't deserve it. All we can do is open our hands and receive it! (Romans 5:15-19). However, there is something we must do once we've received it. We must use it. God's gift, the gift no one could ever earn, deserve, or buy, is the gift of redemption and adoption. It is the total and absolute forgiveness of all our sins; past, present, and future, and adoption as God's own beloved children.

It is a gift that must be possessed. It does no good if we refuse to receive it. The gift of redemption and adoption is not fully ours until we make it ours by using it. It's sort of like what we do when we are given a new toy. One Christmas I was given a wind up train with a track and tunnel. Stare as hard as I could at the box, the train did not run, the track was still in pieces, the tunnel was still two formed pieces of tin. My gift didn't work! Then something happened that made all the difference in the world. Grandpa took me by the hand and we carried the box down the road to the cold old house where my family lived in the summer. Grandpa started the fire and then we kneeled down on the carpet and took the train out of its box. We assembled the track, set up the tunnel, wound up the engine, and my train worked! I played with it joyfully all afternoon.

If we leave our salvation in the box, it's just a pretty gift that doesn't work. If you have just been given a thousand acres of land, the first thing you do is go check it out. You can't enjoy its benefits until you know what you've got, and then use it. You've just inherited a new family, power and authority. It's time to check them out to see what you got. That means getting to know the territory: the territory of God our father, who is also our daddy. It means getting to know Jesus, our bother, Redeemer, and Lord. It means getting to know the Holy Spirit who is comforter, guide, and teacher. Lastly, it means getting to know yourself, for you are now more amazing than you could have ever dreamed.

The Father, the Son, the Holy Spirit, and you together make a "fantastic four". Guard against letting any hindering aspects of your unique nature get in the way. For example, I am, by nature, a solitary, private person. Socializing is easy. I enjoy being with and working with people, but I do not develop close relationships. When the socializing is done I am happy to be alone once again. This is both my nature and my problem. To have the close intimate friendship I want with Jesus goes against the grain of my solitary nature. And yet, my solitary nature is one of my strengths. Embrace your uniqueness. You are unique for a reason. But don't let it get between you and your new family.

CHAPTER 8

At Last I See

It's weird, even scary, to think that our ideas about God are already laid down by the time we're ten years of age! But they are. During the first ten years of our life, all the experiences we've had with our natural parents form themselves into colored glasses through which we see God from then on. They are colored by both good things and by bad things called bitter root judgments. We are not consciously aware of these colored glasses. They are buried deep in our subconscious minds where they go about their work unnoticed. (See *The Transformation of the Inner Man* by John and Paula Sandford[1])

Two small boys were arguing. One said, "There is a devil." The other said, "No there ain't. It's just like Santa Claus. It's your old man!" Our childish minds see things in childish ways. We see God according to how we experienced our parents. That is, by how we perceived our parents by the time we were ten years of age. Whether our perceptions were true, exaggerated, or totally false makes no difference. They have imprinted themselves indelibly upon our minds.

Years later, when we are full grown, when we have supposedly put away childish things, our childish perceptions still rule. With our minds we learn that God is loving, kind, gentle, and cares about us carefully. But the heart says, "Oh yeah. He's just like my dad. He'll leave me, too." Or, "He will let me down, just like my father did. He's always promising to do things and never does them." Or, "He'll never be there when I really need Him." Or, "He makes a lot of promises, but he can't deliver what he has promised."

Or, "All He does is holler and punish. Not once did he tell me he loved me." The fact that the heart is already formed by the time we're ten years old, is as true for children coming from good homes as it is for children coming from broken homes and abusive parents. If the child's real or perceived experience of the father is bad, the child makes bitter root judgments against the father.

I first became aware of how these bitter root judgments influence us at a Camp Farthest Out[2]. The speaker had just ended his message. A young woman, pretty, and with a happy face, asked a question. "Why isn't God real to me?" Instead of answering her question he asked a question. He asked if she had had a good relationship with her father. "No," she said, and began to cry. Then the speaker said something that startled us. He said, "I thought so. If our relationship with our earthly father has not been good, we will not be able to experience God, our Heavenly Father, as real." He went on to explain that the only guide a person has for envisioning God as a father is the example of one's own father. This young woman's vision of a father, formed before she was ten years old, was that a father is mean, cannot be trusted, cannot be depended upon, and does bad things to you.

These judgments we make as children are called *bitter root judgments* against our parents. No one is exempt. Regardless of how good one's parents were, or how happy the home, every person makes bitter root judgments. It happens when our parents discipline us. It happens every time they thwart our wills, tell us "No," or disappoint us. Did you ever say to your parents: "Thank you for spanking me. Thank you for helping me grow up to be a good Christian. I appreciate your spanking me so very much. Please feel free to spank me every time you think it will help me."

Is that what you said? Absolutely not! You were mad at them. You might even have said something that got you spanked again! I've done that! Thanking them was the last thing you would have done. That translates into a bitter root judgment that God will never let you do what you want to do.

When your mother said, "Do the dishes again! You didn't get them clean," how did you act? What did you do? Did you say, "Thank you mother for making me do the dishes again?" No! You said, "Why do you always pick on me? You never make Sally do them over again. It just isn't fair!" That translates into a bitter root judgment that God will not be fair either.

There are other kinds of bitter root judgments. Was your father always out of town or did he have to work when you had some important event or when an emergency arose? Did it seem to you as a child that your father was never there when you needed him? That translates into a bitter root judgment that God will never be there when you need him.

Before we can know what God is really like we have to get rid of our bitter root judgments. The Jewish people were almost blinded by bitter root judgments. It started when the barrier went up between Adam and God, symbolized by covering themselves. They had not needed clothes before because they were clothed in God's Glory. The barrier grew with murder (Genesis 4:16). It grew again after the time of Moses. Religious leaders lost fellowship with God. God became holy and terrible and unapproachable in their eyes.

God tried to call them back to fellowship, but they would not come. God gave his name to Moses. "Tell the people my name is YHWH (Yahweh), which means I am for you what you need me to be." Soon the religious leaders, the priests and scribes and Pharisees, believing themselves wise, began to say that God's name was too holy to be spoken. By their own devising no longer would they know their God as the one who was for them what they needed him to be.

When Jesus was born, few were left who had seen beyond the barriers religion had erected. One was Simeon to whom the Holy Spirit had said he would not see death until he had seen the Savior. Another was Anna, a mighty prayer warrior, to whom God revealed that the baby Jesus was his son. Another was Elizabeth, John the Baptist's mother. Mary and Joseph are the only others mentioned. The average person did not know God intimately. They knew him as Israel's warrior God who had done marvelous things.

In Jesus, God tore down the wall of separation between "God and man," and "man and man" (Ephesians 2:11-22). In Jesus, God was saying, "I must give my children something that will tell them what I am really like. I must give them a picture to look at, examples of how I act and talk and think. When they know me, they will trust me. When they trust me, they will love me." How intimate do we dare to get? Jesus is our example.

There is an Aramaic word little children used when they talked to their fathers. The word was *Abba*, and it means daddy. In the Garden of

Gethsemane, when the weight of his burden was so great it caused Jesus to sweat drops of blood, when it seemed almost more than he could bear, Jesus cried out, "Daddy, you can do anything. Take this burden away" (Mark 14:36).

God wants us to be daddy intimate. The Holy Spirit makes this clear when, under his inspiration, we cry out in prayer "Daddy, my daddy" (Romans 8:15). This same Holy Spirit witnesses with our spirit that we are children of God. If we are children, we are heirs of God and joint heirs with Jesus (Romans 8:16-17). It is our daddy who has rescued us. It is our brother who died our death. This intimacy requires that we abandon our bitter root judgments. While often hard to do, the effort pays big dividends. It opens us up to be used by God to bless others.

Tommy Tyson was a popular Methodist evangelist and speaker. He had been invited to be a speaking leader at the Iowa CFO Camp. In one of his first talks he told a story that went something like this. His plane had arrived at the O'Hare Airport in Chicago. With a large complex of concourses and waiting areas it takes several minutes to walk from one airline terminal to another. Tommy had just arrived from the East on one airline and was heading towards another. As he hurried along, he noticed a couple standing at a ticket gate, getting ready to board a plane. They were a nice looking couple and he was drawn to them. As he looked at them and started to go by, he heard Jesus tell him "Go and tell that lady she's been healed. Everything's alright. She doesn't have to worry anymore."

Tommy looked at her and thought, "Lord, don't play tricks with me. That lady looks well! She doesn't look sick. But Jesus, if that is your thought, if that's what you're telling me, I want to obey. Is that really you, Lord?" Jesus didn't answer. Tommy had practiced being "Daddy intimate," listening for his voice. Now Tommy had to make a choice. Did he dare identify with a thought that seemed to come from Jesus? Or did he ignore it? When Jesus guides he doesn't grab us and shake us and say, "Now you do it or else."

Tommy continued to listen. He started walking slowly. He listened and the thought was very clear. He said, "Jesus, thank you," and turned around and went back to the ticket gate. The couple were already checked in and seated. They were seated by themselves, for which Tommy thanked the Lord! He went over to them, kneeled before the man so he wouldn't be too obvious. Even though what he had to tell the couple was good news, he had no way of knowing how they would receive it. In humility and love, he said to them, "I have not come to offend you at all. But I have come in obedience to what I believe is the word of the Lord. I heard within me as I passed this gate a minute ago, that I was to come and tell this lady, who I take to be your wife, that she need not worry. She's been healed."

The lady began to cry. Through sobs of joy, she said, "Thank you. Thank you. Thank you." and grabbed her husband's hand. The husband looked at Tommy, tears running down his cheeks, and he said, "Don't be afraid, you have not offended us. We receive this word with gratitude." Tommy said, "Thank you very much," and got up and walked away.

After sharing this story with us, Tommy led us in a short prayer: "Lord Jesus, how many times have we missed Kingdom living because we did not pay attention to the thoughts in our minds?"[4]

As illustrated by Tommy's experience, the rewards of being daddy intimate are rich. In my struggle to become daddy intimate I kept putting road blocks in my way in the form of unreachable goals! Goals are good but when your goals stop being goals and become your judge, it leads to trouble. Instead of seeking Jesus the person, I was seeking my own approval of my performance. I was defeated because I had set impossible goals for myself. I didn't understand that there is nothing we can do to impress God. He already knows us better than we know ourselves and he loves us just the way we are. He is for us. He is in our corner, our big brother backing us up.

Much of the time, we are not aware that God is there, backing us up. Often, it was in hindsight that I discovered he had been there. But once in a while, he lets us know and it feels good, as well as being humbling. The chairman of the Pastor-Parish Relations Committee came to see me one day because some people were not happy with me. Whatever it was she intended to say, she never said. As she was ascending the steps to my office, God said to her, "I sent him here." God had my back!

As we work at knowing the Father better, he helps us. One incident I enjoy telling, concerned my wife. She felt that, as a pastor, I was falling short, not living up to some of her expectations. Instead of nagging me, she talked to God about it. God answered and said, "I knew what he was like when I called him!" God put her fears to rest. It was a way of saying "Relax, I'm working on him!" If we will let God do the driving in our lives, we will discover that God rejoices in us just as we are, uses us just as we are, and sticks up for us just as we are, while molding us and remaking us. What a load that takes off our shoulders! It is as the Psalmist wrote: "in your presence there is fullness of joy;" (Psalm 16:11 ESV).

Our question is, how can we become daddy intimate with God? I don't have three easy steps to follow. But I do have some stories. Hopefully, these will ignite new ideas and insights to help you. These stories tell of other ways I have experienced God helping me to know myself and get set free from the bitter root judgments that got between me and him.

One day I was having a pity party. I wanted an ego boost. I wanted God to tell me I was special, his man. He did not oblige! I sat there, turning deep within, listening. A voice rose up from deep inside me saying, "I didn't call you because of who you are. I called you because of what you know." That startled me. I wanted an answer but I hadn't expected to actually hear an answer. It started me thinking. What did I know? I reflected back on my life. It was not remarkable, but there were some things I knew.

I started out a perfectionist. I was obsessed with the idea that I had to be perfect. Since I wasn't, I concluded I was a failure. I also concluded that, for that reason, my parents could not love me and God could not love me. I also concluded that I would never be able to earn God's love. I would fail no matter what I tried to do. But I kept trying. Then one-day God broke through my childish obsession. It happened at a Camp Farthest Out at Lake Winnipesauke, New Hampshire.

I was sitting by myself on a bench in the courtyard. An elderly lady came and sat beside me. She was known as a special lady who loved the youth. She would come and sit by and love on any youth to whom God sent her. She shared God's love silently. That day she came and sat by me! As she sat there, I suddenly realized that God loved me. He loved ME! And I hadn't done anything to earn it! He loved me just as I was. At first it was love coming from the lady. Then it was his love enveloping me. In that moment, I knew beyond the shadow of a doubt that God is real. He loved me and I felt his love. In the years that followed, when my self-esteem was low, the memory would come back to me.

Later, sitting in my office and looking back, I could see how God had worked things out so that I would desire to go to that CFO. He put me in the place where he could break through my defenses and show me that he loved me. In Hosea 4:6 (KJV) it is written, "My people are destroyed for lack of knowledge." God's answer to my pity party was to remind me that my calling was to go and tell, to spread the Good News of God's love, to tell people what I had discovered; that the God of the Bible is real. He isn't just alive; he is life itself. "Tell them I love them," was my assignment. "Tell them they are okay in his eyes, just as they are. He knows each of us personally and to the degree we will allow it, he wants to be intimately involved in our lives."

What he does not do is bring evil and tragedy to punish or teach us. The evil always comes from Satan. That is why God wants you to know that you are accepted and loved and worth everything to him. You, with all your weaknesses and strengths, achievements and failures, are his beloved. You may need to mature, even make some changes, but you don't have to do any of that alone. He is right there to help you, "both to will and to do of His good pleasure" (Philippians 2:13 KJV).

Don't make prayer a chore like I tried to do. I had been inspired by the life of John Wesley. He always rose at 4:00 a.m. to pray. I decided I would do that. At the appointed hour I got up, slipped out of the house, and went to the barnyard where I could pray out loud without being heard. I did it only once. I was just too tired to do it again. My motivation was wrong. I was trying to impress God (and myself) instead of communing with God.

I had made Jesus my ideal to emulate, and not my Lord and Saviour. I was inspired by people like Glenn Clark, Starr Daily, J. Rufus Moseley, and Frank Laubach, who had rich prayer lives. God talked to them. I wanted to be like them. Glenn Clark had a reputation of having every prayer answered. I wanted every prayer answered. Jesus had personally visited Starr Daily in a prison cell. I wanted Jesus to personally visit me. J. Rufus Moseley talked about perfect union with Jesus. Frank Laubach had personal conversations with Jesus that transformed his ministry into a dynamic literacy program that was responsible for millions of the world's illiterates learning to read. I wanted to be like them.

These men knew Jesus personally. They talked with him. When they prayed, you knew Jesus was standing right beside them. Dr. Laubach would challenge the people to pray for him as he talked. He told us that one time when he did this, the people responded with great intensity and harmony. It seemed to him that Jesus came in and took over his lips. Afterwards, six people came up to him and said, "We saw Jesus standing beside you."

"As he went out of the church a woman was sobbing was sobbing with her head on the seat. He sat down beside her and asked if he could help her. 'I don't believe in such things,' she said, 'but what can I do? I saw Christ myself!'"[5]

Dr. Laubach did not use the traditional "Thee's" and "Thou's" with which I'd been raised. He spoke simply, as he would to anyone standing next to him. His prayers conveyed the awareness that Jesus really was standing there. I decided that that was how I wanted to pray. From that time on, I would talk to Jesus just as though he was right beside me. I wouldn't use a lot of fancy words. I wouldn't try to impress him. I would be myself, trusting him.

> Just as I am, thou wilt receive,
> Wilt welcome, pardon, cleanse, relieve;
> Because thy promise I believe,
> Oh Lamb of God, I come, I come.
>
> (Charlotte Elliott, 1835)

What is the proper way to speak to Jesus? Because he is both creator and savior, shouldn't our speech be formal? We'll find the answer when we listen to how the disciples spoke to him before and after his resurrection. They always spoke in the familiar, intimate speech of family and friends. In fact, Jesus calls us his friends. Paul tells us that Jesus is the firstborn of many brethren (Romans 8:29), which means he is our brother. Familiar speech is not disrespectful. Its family talk. It's relating to Jesus as a brother.

On the theological level, he is creator (Colossians 1:16). He gave the Law (Exodus 20:3-17). He is the one whose coming is foretold. He is the one who died for our sins, rose, and is alive forevermore. He is the one who works with us, confirming his word by signs following (Mark

16:20). He is the one who is with us always, even to the end of the world (Matthew 28:20). He is the one that is coming again (John 14:3). That is the theological Jesus (Hebrews 4:13).

But he is also the same Jesus with whom we fellowship in the intimacy of friend and family. How do we talk to God? He is our father in the very formal sense of creator. But he is also our daddy. Jesus called God daddy (Mark 14:35). Jesus told Philip, "Have I been with all of you for so long a time, and do you not recognize and know me yet, Philip? Anyone who has seen me has seen the Father" (John 14:9 AMP). Jesus made it clear that it is a family relationship. God is our father. Paul further highlights this family relationship when he tells us that because we have been adopted into God's family, we can say with a full heart "daddy, father" (Romans 8:15).

As the Jesus of the Gospels became more and more real to me, it became easier to talk with him. Because Jesus said that he and the father are one, it also became easier to pray to the father. I began to talk to God as a son who both loves and has respect for his father. I was simply myself, his kid. There was no sense in trying to hide anything, because nothing is hidden from his eyes (Psalm 69:5). I didn't try to make excuses. I was just me and nothing else. What really helped was getting a simple fact through my head. I finally figured it out that my salvation was God's idea. He did it for his sake, not mine (Isaiah 43:25-26). He deliberately chose to wash us with the blood of the Lamb. "Your assignment," God told me, "is to go and tell people all about this."

He has covered us with the blood of Christ. He has declared us clean (Jeremiah 31:34; Hebrews 8:12; 10:17). He has adopted us as his very own children. Why should we act like we're unclean and unworthy when he has washed us clean and made us worthy? Isn't that the same as saying his words are untrue, that he is a liar? It is he who washes us clean, not ourselves (I John 1:9). God sees us through the blood of Jesus and it is just-as-if-I'd never sinned (Romans 5:9; Titus 3:7). Read Ephesians 1:3-12. Too often we do not see clearly because we see through dirty lenses. We must let the washing of the word (Ephesians 5:25) cleanse our vision so that we can see clearly ourselves, the Father, the Holy Spirit and Jesus. Washing in the word is the best way I've found to clean my vision.

CHAPTER 9

LEARN TO TRUST

Learning to trust can be very difficult. If one has felt betrayed by a parent, teacher, pastor, friend, or anyone he trusted, the emotional pain cuts deeply. It can prevent us from trusting anyone. If we cannot trust those we have seen, how can we trust Jesus, who we haven't seen? A baby begins to learn trust from the moment it is born. Except for the traditional slap on his bottom to help him start to breathe, babies experience warmth, the mother's love as she holds him close, and the satisfying flow of milk when he is hungry. Helplessness is rewarded by help.

Trust is learned. Just as a baby learns trust by experience, trust can be rebuilt by experience. The first step in building trust in Jesus comes as you study the scriptures. What do the stories tell you Jesus was like? What do the stories tell you he wasn't like? You need to examine them carefully to avoid any misunderstanding. By so doing, you will not be disappointed from wrong and misguided expectations. Let's look at what the scriptures tell us.

There was a group who trusted Jesus, but didn't understand what he came to do, even though he explained it many times. This group got to know him, eat with him, walk and talk with him. It seemed to them that events were all coming to a glorious head when the whole world would know who Jesus is. They thought that day had come when Jesus rode into Jerusalem on a donkey. It was a most glorious day, that Palm Sunday. Thousands of people lined the short road from Bethany to Jerusalem. Perhaps Jesus radiated the brilliance of the temple. Whatever it was, the moment they saw Jesus, the crowd received him as king.

Four days later, everything changed. Joy was turned to stark terror. Stark terror turned to utter disbelief. Utter disbelief to unfathomable sorrow. The disciples were with Jesus in a garden where he had gone to pray. It was late. They were tired and could not stay awake. Suddenly they were startled wide awake. A multitude of soldiers had come, led by Judas, their treasurer. The soldiers grabbed Jesus. For an instant, maybe they thought Jesus would call down fire from heaven. Then they saw their danger. Soldiers' swords flashed in the light of torches.

Terrified, the disciples fled and hid. The soldiers led Jesus away. Peter and another disciple followed the soldiers to see what would happen. Peter feared he would be recognized, but he just had to follow. When someone did accuse him of being with Jesus, he denied ever knowing him, so great was his fear. It was a nightmare. The trial was illegal. The witnesses false. The death undeserved. Before evening had come it was over. Jesus was dead, and his body was laid in a borrowed tomb. The disciples were numb with shock and horror.

Disillusioned, torn with grief, unable to believe, unable to understand, the disciples and the women met together secretly, for fear of the Jews. Would the next knock on the door be a friend or would it be soldiers come to kill them, too? The Sabbath passed. At early dawn, as the first rays of the sun began to penetrate the darkness, two of the women slipped out into the empty streets. Cautiously they stole quietly among the shadows. Slipping out through a small door in the city gate, they walked quickly to the tomb. Everything had happened so fast. There had just been time, before the Sabbath began, to take Jesus' body down from the cross and lay it in a borrowed tomb. There had been no time to prepare it properly.

The women came bringing aromatic spices and ointments to anoint Jesus' body. They hoped the guards would roll the stone away, and let them in. But when they arrived at the tomb the guards were gone. The stone had already been rolled away. They went inside. To their dismay that which they feared had happened. The body of Jesus was gone. Suddenly two men in shining garments appeared. Terrified, the women bent their faces to the ground. "Why are you looking for the living one among the dead ones," the men asked? "He isn't here. He is risen. Don't you remember? Back in Galilee he told you he would be crucified and on the third day he would rise again."

The women rushed back and told this news to the eleven and the others. They said they had seen a vision of angels who said Jesus was alive. This report struck the apostles as an idle tale told by distraught women. Peter and John got up and ran to the tomb. Peter stooped down and saw the linen clothes lying there all by themselves and he went home wondering what had happened. Was this just another cruel indignity heaped upon tragedy?

That is how it was the morning of that first day of the week, when Cleopas and another man began to walk to a village called Emmaus. They were in deep conversation about everything that had happened. As they talked a stranger drew near and walked along with them. He listened a little, and then asked, "What is all this discussion that you are having while you walk?"

"You must be the only visitor to Jerusalem," Cleopas said, "who hasn't heard all the things that have happened there recently!"

"What things?" the stranger asked.

"About Jesus, from Nazareth. There was a man - a prophet strong in what he did and what he said.... We were hoping he was the one who was to come and set Israel free.... And now," said Cleopas, in a voice of great and deep grief, "it is all over. The authorities crucified him." And so they began to tell the story of their hopes and dreams, now shattered. They told about Peter and the miraculous catch of fish. They told of traveling with Jesus about all Galilee. They told of the camaraderie, the laughter and the joy. He taught with authority. He was their friend and companion. The traveler listened intently as they spoke. He urged them to go on. They told of the signs and wonders that attested to what Jesus taught. He healed every disease and disability. He commanded unclean spirits to leave and they did. Deaf and dumb both heard and spoke. Blind eyes opened. The lame leapt and danced with joy. The dead were raised to life. Withered limbs grew out to normal size. They told how amazed the crowds were, saying "Nothing like this has ever been seen is Israel." It was sheer joy to be known as one of his close associates, to have people point at you and say, he's one of them.

"He sent ordinary people out with power to overcome all the enemy's power. When they reported back, Jesus danced for joy and shouted praises to God! Anyone to whom he gave it, had the power and authority to heal the sick, raise the dead, cast out devils, and even walk on the water like Peter did. He told a paralyzed man his sins were forgiven and to rise up from his bed and walk."

These were some of the stories and feelings and great grief Cleopas and his friend shared with the stranger who walked with them. When Cleopas finished, the stranger began to speak. What they heard was the last thing they expected to hear!

"O foolish men and slow of heart to believe all that the prophets have spoken! Was it not necessary that the Christ should suffer these things and enter into his glory?" Then, beginning with Moses and all the prophets, he explained to them everything in the scriptures that referred to himself. When they reached Emmaus they asked the stranger to eat with them. While he was sitting at table he took the loaf, gave thanks, broke it and passed it to them. Their eyes opened wide and they knew him! It was Jesus! But he vanished from their sight. (Luke 10:17-19; 24:17-24 PHS; see also John 15:14-15)

> Later when all the Disciples were present Jesus said "Here and now are fulfilled the words that I told you when I was with you: that everything written about me in the Law of Moses and in the prophets and psalms must come true." Then he opened their minds so that they could understand the scriptures. (Luke 24:25, 26, 32-45 PHS)

Consider all Jesus did and all he taught. Reflect on the power and authority he had given first to the twelve, and then to the seventy. See the deaf ears unstopped, blind eyes opened, and the slaves of sin set free. Know this: The resurrection of Jesus was God's stamp of approval on all Jesus said and did. The Resurrection was God's "Yes" and "Amen." The wonder and the glory had not ended but had only just begun! They now knew "joy unspeakable and full of glory" (I Peter 1:8 KJV).

While with them, Jesus had told them that they would do greater works than he had done. It was true! Their power to heal was stronger than ever before. Their power over evil spirits was greater than ever before. Their power grew so strong that they would speak, and thousands would believe and be baptized. Those thousands received the same power and authority to heal the sick, cast out devils, and raise the dead.

Look back on the camaraderie and the joy and laughter of their fellowship together. The disciples had known Jesus as a person, as well as teacher and healer and miracle worker. They had known him as one with whom they laughed and cried, sang and danced, feasted and worked. He was confidant and friend. They talked and joked with him as friends do. Jesus was all of these. He was also much more and now they knew that, too. They knew he was a prophet of God (Luke 24:19), that he alone had the words of eternal life and was the Holy One of God (John 6:68). Yes, they now knew Jesus in his fullness, as Lord and Christ. But they knew him first, as teacher and friend. And that made all the difference in the world. In return they trusted him with their lives and were willing to suffer and die for him.

The only begotten Son of God was their brother and kinsman, their teacher and friend (Matthew 28:10). They always regarded him as such. In J.R.R. Tolkien's *Lord of the Rings,*[1] we first meet Aragorn when he is one of many "wanderers" who secretly fought to keep places safe, like the Shire, homeland of the Hobbits. When the Hobbits meet him, he becomes their friend, guide, and protector on the long journey to the elven city of Rivendell. At the end of the story, Aragorn assumes his rightful role as King. The Hobbits knew him as a very dear friend, as a protector, and now as King. But he was the same Aragorn. Although he was their King, they continued to fellowship with him in the comradery of friendship.

Before he ascended, Jesus gave his disciples the power of attorney to use his name (Matthew 28:18-19a; Mark 16:17-18; Luke 24:47; John 20:21). As they went out and preached, Jesus worked with them, confirming the word with signs and wonders (Matthew 28:20; Mark 16:20). It was they who were to do the works now, using the power and authority of Jesus' name. He was there with them all the time just as he said he would be, talking with them, teaching them, guiding them, telling them what to do (John 16:13). Their teacher, their friend, was now with them in a far more powerful way (John 14:18) as the only unfailing trustworthy teacher and friend.

Jesus wants us to relate to him like the disciples did; as friend, teacher and kinsman. It is in that kind of intimacy; of brother to brother, of friend to friend, of teacher to student, of Lord to friend, that Jesus can commune and communicate with us. He is our big brother, the first born of many brothers and sisters (Romans 8:29). In the quiet, I can talk to my friend. In the stillness, I listen. I expect him to talk back to me. Even when I am talking, I stay alert. It may be a thought, an idea. But I know he will answer. Sometimes when I am making excuses, and I do a lot, I stop, for I almost see his face, and I know the look he is giving me. That is communion and communication.

Following are some of the occasions and events that shaped the relationship shared by Jesus and his disciples. Those were exciting days, days of classroom instruction (Mark 4:34), days of miracle filled open air meetings (Mark 6:56, 8:1-10), days of practicing what they had been taught (Mark 6:7, 30). They laughed and played together with the one who said "I have told you these things that my joy and delight may be in you and that your joy and gladness may be of full measure and complete and overflowing" (John 15:11 AMP).

> FISHERS OF MEN: Jesus, walking by the Sea of Galilee, saw two brethren, Simon, called Peter, and Andrew his brother, casting a net into the sea: for they were fishers. And he saith unto them, follow me, and I will make you fishers of men (Matthew 4:18-19 KJV).

> KINGDOM LIVING: Jesus went about all Galilee, teaching in their synagogues and preaching the gospel of the kingdom and healing all manner of disease among the people. And his fame went throughout all Syria: and they brought unto him all sick people that were taken with divers diseases and torments, and those which were lunatic, and those that had the palsy; and he healed them. And there followed him great multitudes of people from Galilee, and from Decapolis, and from Jerusalem, and from Judea, and from beyond Jordan (Mathew 4:23-25 KJV).

A TEACHER WITH AUTHORITY: The people were astonished at his doctrine: for he taught them as one having authority, and not as the scribes (Matthew 7:28-29 KJV).

LEPER HEALED: There came a leper and worshiped him, saying, Lord, if thou wilt, thou canst make me clean. And Jesus put forth his hand, and touched him, saying, I will; be thou clean. And immediately his leprosy was cleansed (Matthew 8:1-3 KJV).

SINS FORGIVEN: They brought to him a man sick of the palsy, lying on a bed; and Jesus seeing their faith said unto the sick of the palsy; Son, be of good cheer; thy sins be forgiven thee.... But that ye may know that the Son of man hath power on earth to forgive sins, (then saith he to the sick of the palsy,) Arise, take up thy bed, and go unto thine house. And he arose, and departed to his house. But when the multitudes saw it, they marveled, and glorified God, which had given such power unto men (Matthew 9:2, 6-8 KJV).

THE DEAD RAISED: There came a certain ruler, and worshiped him, saying, My daughter is even now dead: but come and lay thy hand upon her, and she shall live.... he went in, and took her by the hand, and the maid arose (Matthew 9:18, 23-25 KJV).

THE DEAF HEAR, THE DUMB SPEAK: As they went out, behold, they brought to him a dumb man possessed with a devil. And when the devil was cast out, the dumb spake: and the multitude marveled, saying, It was never so seen in Israel.... And Jesus went about all the cities and villages, teaching in their synagogues, and preaching the gospel of the kingdom, and healing every sickness and every disease among the people (Matthew 9:32-35 KJV).

DEMONIC FORCES OBEY: There was in their synagogue a man with an unclean spirit; and he cried out, saying, Let us alone; what have we to do with thee, thou Jesus of Nazareth? art thou come to destroy us? I know thee who thou art, the Holy One of God. And Jesus rebuked him, saying, Hold thy peace, and come out of him. And when the unclean spirit had torn him, and cried with a loud voice, he came out of him. And they were all amazed, insomuch that they questioned among themselves, saying, What thing is this? what new doctrine is this? for with authority commandeth he even the unclean spirits, and they do obey him (Mark 1:23-28 KJV).

JESUS EMPOWERS THE 12: And when he had called unto him his twelve disciples, he gave them power against unclean spirits, to cast them out, and to heal all manner of sickness and all manner of disease.... Behold, I give unto you power to tread on serpents and scorpions, and over all the power of the enemy: and nothing shall by any means hurt you (Matthew 10:1; Luke 10:19 KJV).

JESUS FEEDS THE MULTITUDE: He commanded the multitude to sit down on the grass, and took the five loaves, and the two fishes, and looking up to heaven, he blessed, and brake, and gave the loaves to his disciples, and the disciples to the multitude. And they took up of the fragments that remained twelve baskets full. And they that had eaten were about five thousand men, beside women and children (Matthew 14:15-21 KJV).

JESUS AND PETER WALK ON THE WATER: Peter answered him and said, "Lord, if it be thou, bid me come unto thee on the water." And he said, "Come." And when Peter was come down out of the ship, he walked on the water, to go to Jesus (Matthew 14:22-33 KJV).

GLORY ON THE MOUNTAIN: After six days Jesus taketh Peter, James and John his brother, and bringeth them up into a high mountain apart, and was transfigured before them: and his face did shine as the sun, and his raiment was white as the light. And, behold, there appeared unto them Moses and Elijah talking with him.... A bright cloud overshadowed them: and behold a voice out of the cloud, which said, "This is my beloved Son, in whom I am well pleased; hear ye him" (Matthew 17:1-5 KJV).

AUTHORITY GIVEN TO FORGIVE SIN: "Verily I say unto you, Whatsoever ye shall bind on earth shall be bound in heaven: and whatsoever ye shall loose on earth shall be loosed in heaven. Again I say unto you, That if two of you shall agree on earth as touching any thing that they shall ask, it shall be done for them of my Father which is in heaven. For where two or three are gathered together in my name, there am I in the midst of them" (Matthew 18:18-20 KJV).

YOUR WORDS HAVE POWER: "For verily I say unto you, That whosoever shall say unto this mountain, Be thou removed, and be thou cast into the sea; and shall not doubt in his heart, but shall believe that those things which he saith shall come to pass; he shall have whatsoever he saith. Therefore I say unto you, What things so ever ye desire, when ye pray, believe that ye receive them, and ye shall have them" (Mark 11:23-24 KJV).

JOY AND LAUGHTER: "These things have I spoken to you that my joy might remain in you, and that your joy might be full" (John 15:11 KJV).

LAUGH AT THE RIDICULOUS: The man who acts humble before God but struts before men (Matthew

> 23:5-12). Blind guides that strain at gnats but swallow camels, who meticulously clean the outside of the cup but leave the inside full of creepy crawlers, who look beautiful on the outside like a sepulcher but are full of dead bones (Matthew 23:24, 25, 27). The dismal looking Pharisees who succeed at looking dismal (Matthew 6:16 KJV).

How many times have you discovered that someone you thought you knew, you didn't know at all? It is that way with knowing Jesus. He wants us to know him in all his ways because he wants us to include him in all our ways. If you will trust Jesus, and follow his teachings, you will never be disappointed. Need more proof that you can trust him? Then take a closer look through the eyes of his mother, his disciples, and three women whose lives he touched.

CHAPTER 10

MOTHERS KNOW BEST

The dirt road, packed solid from the many feet and caravans that had passed along it, wound its way northward, down the hill from Nazareth. It led around the western edge of the Great Reed Marsh and up the hill to the village of Cana. The breeze was fresh and warm, full of the fragrance of flowers. At times it rippled among the reeds, wave upon wave, transforming the reed grass into an ocean of gently rolling waves. The blue sky, dotted with billowy white clouds, made a perfect background for the feast of colors below.

Among the reeds, the flowers were a rainbow of colors of purple and yellow and red and blue. On the hillside, there was hardly room for the green grass amid the blanket of flowers. Children had great fun lying on their backs in the grass along the edge of the marsh; smelling the sweet smells of the flowers and herbs; bathing in the warm sun; watching the billowy clouds and imagining all sorts of animals in the cloud shapes; listening to the melodies of the birds and trying to find their nests.

A perfect day. A perfect day in June. A perfect day for a wedding. The kind of day for which every bride hopes. To attend a wedding, a special wedding, was why Jesus and his disciples were walking along the road to Cana enjoying the peace and beauty. A beautiful day. A glorious occasion. Jesus, who loved to laugh and have a good time, was looking forward to the celebration of his beloved cousin's wedding. John was as nervous as a bridegroom could be. He was glad his cousin would be there. Already Aunt Mary was working on the provisions, seeing that everything was just right.

It took a lot of planning and a lot of food and wine for a Jewish wedding feast. A Jewish wedding was a luxurious event.

The father, who was head of the household, on behalf of his son, usually began the plans for marriage. He selected the bride his son desired and arranged payment of a bride price. The bride price, a suitable gift agreed upon by the bride's father, was given by the groom to the bride's father. The bride price was not a purchase price. Marriage is a covenant relationship between two families. The giving of gifts (the bride and the bride price) sealed the covenant between the two families. There were no hasty weddings. Family approval was essential. The wedding itself was a purely extravagant occasion. Special colorful wedding clothing was worn. The bride and bridegroom were adorned with all manner of festive adornments: jewelry, garlands, and a veil for the bride.

The festivities began with festive processions of gaily dressed attendants and musicians dancing and singing. The bride and bridegroom, each coming from a different starting point, met at the house were the feast was held. It was a sensuous feast of colors and sights and sounds and tastes. Delicacies of food excited the taste buds as never before! In a life that was often harsh, when people worked long and hard hours with few, if any, luxuries, a wedding feast was the social event of the year. The feasting and drinking lasted many hours. Wine was one of the special sensuous enjoyments. Without wine there is no joy, the Rabbis had said. Ben Sirach said wine was one of the good things especially created for good people (Ecclesiasticus 39:25-26).

What a feast this was! This wedding was the social event of the year. The evening was as fine as the day had been. The gentle breeze was warm, but comfortable. The moon was full. The food was most excellent. Everything seemed perfect. That is, almost perfect. That kind of night and such a joyous occasion caused people to drink much more heartily of the wine than had been planned for. It wasn't that they became drunk. Drunkenness was an evil thing, not allowed by respectable people. As a matter of fact, the wine was mixed with water, two parts wine to three parts water.

But this night, so perfect in every way, had called for drinking much more wine than had been anticipated. The most horrible disgrace that could come upon a Jewish family, was to run out of food and drink at a wedding feast. That would be a terrible source of shame for the family and mar the rest of the celebration. During the next week, the bride and groom, dressed in their wedding robes, wearing crowns, would keep open house. They were to be treated as king and queen. Their word was law. Failed provisions would be a terrible humiliation for the bride and groom to face that week. So Mary told Jesus about it.

"My dear Lady," Jesus said. "Never mind; don't be worried. I must wait for the right opportunity." Once in a while mothers see things a little bit more clearly than we! It's hard to admit, but sometimes they do. And mothers don't take "No!" for an answer. Mary knew her son. She knew from experience that Jesus would do the right thing. Knowing this, Mary immediately ordered the servants, "Do whatever he tells you to do." What did Jesus do? Did he panic? Did he rush off to see if he could buy some wine somewhere? Did he go on a three day fast? No. He did what he always did. He did what was as natural to him as breathing. He talked to his Father. "Father, John is going to be terribly embarrassed if we don't do something. Would it be alright with you if I turn water into wine? I know that is what you would do." (John 5:19).

And Father God said, "Son, you do that. But, make it the best. Make it Helbon vintage wine. And make so much of it, it can't possibly run out. I want to bless young John and his bride with this wine." Did you realize that the first miracle Jesus did was to pamper sensuous pleasure! There were six stone water pots that held about 20 gallons apiece. "Fill them to the top," Jesus said. And so the servants filled them to the brim. "Draw some out and take it to the Master of Ceremonies." This they did. Now when the Master of Ceremonies tasted the water that had been turned into wine, he was amazed. And he said to the bridegroom, "You know, most people serve the good wine first and then end up with cheap wine. But you saved the best wine until last!"

What is Jesus like? His mother knew. This incident tells it all. The very first miracle Jesus did, the very first demonstration of his glory, was at a wedding feast! It wasn't to heal some devastating illness. It wasn't to confound the authorities or prove that he was God's Son. The very first miracle happened at a fun time, a time of feasting and laughter and merry making. It involved turning water into wine, of all things! And its purpose was to save some people from public embarrassment. The first miracle Jesus did, turning water into wine, was a miracle pampering sensuous pleasures! The wine he created by that miracle was not just grape juice or cheap wine, it was the finest of wines, a wine to tickle the taste buds. In fact, it was so exquisite a wine that the Master of the Feast declared to the bridegroom, "You have kept the best wine 'till last!"

Those who drank the water-become-wine experienced sensuous pleasure as only God can provide. We are forced to believe what Mary knew: that God delights in giving his children sensuous pleasures and saving them from embarrassment. That first miracle was God shouting that he cares about you intimately and carefully. It says you are the object of God's love and care. All too often we talk ourselves out of God's help by thinking, "He's probably not going to do anything about it. God's got other things to worry about besides me and my unruly hair or stuck zipper. He's too busy with important things." By our attitude and lack of expectation, our unwillingness to trust him, we block God out and he cannot give us the help he wants to give.

Mary knew that everything that concerns us is important to God. Wine running out might seem unimportant, but Mary knew God. God wouldn't want anyone to be embarrassed. She had learned that from Jesus. That is why it was so natural, so instinctive for Mary to tell Jesus the wine was running out. That is why Mary expected God, through Jesus, to replenish the wine, and immediately told the servants to do whatever Jesus said to do. That is why Jesus turned instinctively to his father, expecting God to approve of his first miracle being done to help with a simple problem of hospitality. (See Matthew 7:9-11; 10:30.)

Whatever the need, whatever the situation, how big or how small, how monumental or insignificant, we can turn to Jesus in trust, and, if we will let him, he will do the right thing. Whenever Jesus comes into our lives, he brings a quality that is like changing water into wine. When Jesus comes into our lives, life becomes vivid, sparkling, and exciting. With Jesus life is thrilling and wonderful and exhilarating. That is what Mary teaches us.

Do you know Jesus as his mother knew him? Do you trust him as Mary trusted him?

CHAPTER 11

GOOD FISHING

The Sea of Galilee (Lake Gennesaret) is a heart shaped body of water lying in a dip in the earth's surface, some 690 feet below sea level. It is approximately thirteen miles long, eight miles across at its greatest width, and four miles at its narrowest width. Its waters vary from green to blue. It is encircled by a ring of green or yellow vegetation, depending on the season. Surrounded by mountains of considerable height, the lake is a vast bowl, around 200 feet deep. On the east, the cliffs rise steeply to the Jaulan Plateau. On the west, the mountains form an amphitheater, backed by mountains with valleys and gullies. When a wind comes from the west these valleys and gullies act like gigantic funnels. They compress the wind, so that when it comes out, it bursts forth with savage violence upon the lake. The sea, calm one moment, can be instantly whipped into a raging torrent of foam crested waves, which can swamp the strongest boat and overcome the staunchest men.

Fishing was the main industry of the nine large cities on the shores of the lake. There were over 330 fishing boats on the lake. The city of Bethsaida (House of Fish), on the northeast end, processed tons of fish that were shipped north. On the west, the city of Magdala Taricheae (Magdala of the Fish Salters), was famous for its salted fish, which it shipped as far away as Rome.

One of the biggest fishing companies was the Zebedee Wholesale Fish Company, headquartered in the city of Nahum on the north. Like many a successful and respected business, this had started as a family enterprise and had grown into a large operation employing a sizable number of people. Some estimate, considering the size of his operation, that Zebedee (who was Jesus' uncle) was a millionaire! He was sufficiently wealthy to have servants, and his wife, Salome, contributed towards Jesus' support.

The Zebedee Wholesale Fish Company specialized in deep sea fishing. The boat used in this kind of fishing was large, equipped with both sails and oars, and required several men to handle both it and the heavy nets. One of Zebedee's sons, James, had a crew of five men in addition to hired servants. Along with Zebedee's sons, James and John, their cousins Peter and Andrew were partners. Peter and Andrew also employed large crews to man the big boats and handle the heavy nets. These four men, uneducated in a formal sense, were neither poor nor ignorant. They had the practical and tested wisdom of men who are hardworking, sharp-dealing businessmen.

Jesus, a direct descendent of King David, and James and John were cousins. Andrew and Peter were cousins of James and John. From the first, James, John, Peter and Andrew admired their cousin with whom they grew up and played and laughed. He was their friend, their kinsman, and even though he was trained to be a carpenter, you can be sure that he spent many a night with them fishing on the Sea of Galilee. He was one of them. And yet, from the first they knew there was something different about Jesus. Some said that the blood of his ancestor, King David, ran true in his veins. Those who dared dream the "impossible dream," dared to dream that, perhaps, Jesus was the one who would redeem Israel. These cousins carefully watched for any telltale signs.

Jesus was full of joy, laughing and bringing joy wherever he went. Underneath the joy, however, there was also seriousness, determination, and kingly character. He was always quick to lend a helping hand and to share his money. Although they had all grown up together and played together, they really didn't know him. But one thing they knew for certain, when Jesus was there, it added a big plus to life. Jesus was deeply loved and admired.

It wasn't just Jesus' kingly bearing that made them think Jesus might be the one to redeem Israel. There were the stories, too; born of a virgin, blessed by Simeon and Anna, who both said that Jesus had come to redeem Israel, at the age of twelve discussing deep issues of faith with the learned men in the Temple. The real question in their minds, the critical point they zeroed in on, was what would Jesus do on his thirtieth birthday when he became of age?

That day had come. Now they were waiting. Peter and Andrew had been fishing all night. They hadn't caught a thing. They brought their boats in to shore and set about mending their nets. As usual these past few days, they began talking about Jesus and the mighty things that had happened. They had been there when John the Baptist had baptized Jesus in the Jordan. They had heard John tell about Jesus in glowing words. They had seen Jesus go into the water. They saw Jesus come out of the water, changed. As he stood in the water, a dove came and settled upon him. There was a noise like thunder. John the Baptist said that it wasn't thunder. He said that God spoke and said, "This is my beloved son, in whom I am well pleased."

Then Jesus had gone off alone, into the wilderness, to pray. Meanwhile, John and James and Peter and Andrew had returned to their fishing. Jesus had been gone about forty days. Ever since he'd come back, amazing stories about him began flooding the countryside. He was traveling from town to town teaching the scriptures. He was a fantastically good teacher. People would sit and listen to him hour after hour. But even greater than that, he had the power to heal all kinds of diseases. There wasn't a sick person left in the city of Nahum by the time he left there.

But, boy did he stir up a hornets' nest in Nazareth! They tried to kill him. The story was that he was standing on the edge of a hill, the town's people ready to throw him off the cliff, when suddenly no one could see him anymore. Jesus returned to the city of Nahum. Everyone was amazed when even unclean spirits obeyed him. He had even stood over Peter's mother-in-law, as she lay sick on her bed, and commanded the fever to leave her, and it did, right then. She felt so good she got up immediately and cooked dinner.

That evening, they brought every sick person they could find and he touched them and they were all healed, everyone. He cast devils out of a lot of people and as they left, the devils called him the Christ, the Son of God. It didn't seem like the people would ever leave. But, finally they did. The next morning Jesus left, saying he "must preach the kingdom of God to other cities also: for therefore am I sent" (Luke 4:43 KJV).

These were the things Peter and the others were talking about as they worked on their nets. They would have liked to have gone with Jesus, but there was work to do, a business to run, a living to be made. As they continued to talk, they heard noises in the distance. It sounded like some sort of celebration, or a big parade. As the crowd drew closer they heard shouts of "Jesus," and "Blessed is he who comes in the name of the Lord." Just then, they caught sight of Jesus' robe and saw that it was Jesus coming, followed by a large crowd.

The crowd kept pushing, trying to get ever closer to Jesus. They were about to crowd him right into the lake. "Peter, give me a hand. Help me into your boat." Peter scrambled into his boat and then, reaching over the side, he took Jesus' hand and helped Jesus into the boat. "Thank you, Peter," said Jesus as he hugged his friend. "Now, if you'll push back from the shore a little, I will speak to these people. They are like sheep without a shepherd."

Peter pushed off a little from shore, mumbling under his breath, "They're more like a crowd of beggars!" Jesus sat down on the cushioned seat at the stern of the ship near the helm. From there he taught the people, his voice loud and clear above the lapping of the waves. When Jesus had finished speaking to the crowd, he turned to Peter. "Peter," he said, "row out into the deep water and let out your nets for a catch." Peter answered, "Teacher, you know this isn't the time of day to catch fish. Besides we worked all night and didn't catch a thing. Nevertheless, because you said to do it, I will go out and let down the nets."

Peter knew the sea and he knew fish. All his experience told him there would not be any fish out there. In the daylight, under the hot sun, the fish go down to deeper, darker waters. That was why he fished at night, the time when the fish come to the top. But Jesus said to do it, and if Jesus said to do it, he'd do it. Gathering up his crew and his nets, Peter put out into the deep water. They looked. There was not a sign of fish. But Jesus said, "Let down your nets." And when they had done this Peter was utterly amazed to discover that his nets had enclosed a great multitude of fish! The nets began to break. They motioned to the other boat to come and help them. They came.

It happened so quickly. First, not a fish could be seen as they looked down into the water. But when they let down the nets as Jesus said to do, suddenly there were more fish than Peter had ever seen in one catch. As the nets started to break every man worked hard to harvest the fish and save the nets. Still the fish came. They eased the other boat up and carefully transferred the net to it. Still the fish came. Peter looked. Goosebumps stood out all over his body. Chills ran up and down his spine. The very air was charged with electricity as though lightning was crackling all around.

There was no way to explain what had happened except to say that God had worked a miracle through this man who was teacher and relative and friend. Just as Isaiah, when he saw the Lord, cried, "Woe is me! For I am a man of unclean lips" (Isaiah 6:5), Peter fell at Jesus' knees and cried, "Depart from me; for I am a sinful man, O Lord." Looking at Peter, Jesus said, "Peter, don't be afraid. From now on all of you will be catching men" (Luke 5:8-9 KJV). As soon as they got the two boats to land, they left everything and followed Jesus.

In the eyes of the fishermen, Jesus was a man totally worthy of trust. Regardless of how impossible or foolish it sounded when they did what Jesus said to do, they always came up with their nets ready to burst. Peter also sensed, on occasions like this, that when he was in the presence of Jesus, he was in the presence of God, Israel's redeemer, David's descendant. Do you know Jesus like Peter did? He wants you to know him as kinsman, as friend, and as God's son.

CHAPTER 12

The Lifter Up of the Fallen

The Scribes and Pharisees had little respect for women. There are few things worse, they said, than being born a woman! That was what the learned men believed. Men are blame shifters. They're always blaming someone else. It started back in the Garden of Eden. God created Adam and gave him dominion to rule, to develop, to create. The woman, Eve, was created from the man's side to be a help to him and be cherished by him (Genesis 2:18). The man was to be the head of the wife as Christ is the Head of the church. The man was to love his wife with the same love as Christ had for the church and gave himself up for her (Ephesians 5:23-25).

In the Garden of Eden, it was Adam's responsibility to keep his wife from doing the thing God had forbidden. He didn't. Instead, he was with her and did nothing as he watched her eat the forbidden fruit. In fact, he even took a bite himself. When confronted by God, the man abruptly denied any responsibility. First, he tried to blame God, then shifted the blame to the woman. The truth is, Eve did not deliberately sin (I Timothy 2:14). She was deceived by the serpent. It was the man who deliberately sinned. But the man denied his guilt and still does. Shifting the blame onto the woman, blaming her for his own sin, he began treating the woman as inferior to men and under the authority of men.

This attitude about women was so bad that St. Thomas Aquinas wrote, "As regards the individual nature, woman is defective and misbegotten, for the active power of the male seed tends to the production of a perfect likeness in the masculine sex; while the production of a woman comes from defect in the active power."[1] The woman was considered to be little better than a slave. "Sin began with a woman and thanks to her we all must die" (Ecclesiasticus, 25:18, 19 & 33 KJV).

That is what the Sadducees and Pharisees believed about women on this fateful day. They brought a prostitute to Jesus. Have you ever been caught "red handed," caught in the act of committing a crime? All of us at one time or another have been caught "with our hand in the cookie jar." It was embarrassing to be caught, if not painful! You were yelled at, maybe even spanked. You were not killed or you wouldn't be reading this! There were crimes believed to be so bad that the penalty was death. Adultery was one of those crimes.

The religious authorities knew the Law and knew it had to be obeyed. The Law laid it down that

> The man that committeth adultery with another man's wife, even he that committeth adultery with his neighbor's wife, the adulterer and the adulteress shall surely be put to death (Leviticus 20:10 KJV).

Death was by stoning. In the years since Moses gave the Law, they managed to forget about stoning the man. It was always the woman's fault.

The authorities wanted to discredit Jesus. They had not been able to trap him with legal questions. They wanted to ruin Jesus' reputation, cause his followers to become disillusioned. In the wee hours of the night, they hatched a scheme they were sure would work. There was a certain woman, a prostitute, "a worthless piece of trash" they called her. She made her living by selling her body. They would pay a man to go into her. Once he had her in bed the Pharisees would come bursting in and grab her. This they did. Then, dragging her half naked and cringing in fear, they threw her in front of Jesus. With looks of smugness, they waited to see what Jesus would say.

There was no way Jesus could worm his way out of this one. If Jesus said she should be stoned, as the Law said, he would lose his reputation. Never again would he be called the friend of sinners. He'd be discredited. He'd lose his followers. That would be the end of him. On the other hand, if Jesus recommended pardon, they could accuse him of teaching men to break the Law of Moses. They could label him a heretic and rebel and therefore a threat to Rome.

The Scribes and Pharisees were sure they had Jesus in their trap. There was no way he could get out of this! You could almost see them gloating, rubbing their hands together in self-satisfaction. Ah, yes! They'd trapped Jesus this time. They had him cornered.

"Well, Master," they said in derision. "What is your sentence?"

Jesus wouldn't look at them. Instead, he stooped down and began writing in the sand. We aren't told what he wrote. We only know what happened when he gave them his answer.

"All right," said Jesus. "Stone her! Only let the man who is without sin be the first to cast a stone. You are right about what the Law says. She deserves to be stoned. But you may stone her only if you never wanted to do the same thing yourselves."

There was silence. Then slowly the accusers drifted away. Did they see their secret sins exposed in the sand? We don't know. It could have been the fear that if they picked up a stone, Jesus would openly confront them with their sins. Jesus and the woman were left alone. A great misery standing face to face with a great compassion.

"Woman, where are your accusers? Has no one condemned you?" Jesus asked.

"No man, sir," she replied.

"Neither do I condemn you," said Jesus. "That does not mean that what you did was right. It does not mean that you can go back to your sinful ways. It means that I set you free to go and sin no more. I set you free to go and start a new life. You've made a mess of things; but life is not finished. I send you forth to go and begin again."

Suddenly this woman discovered she was a somebody after all. How did she experience Jesus? She experienced him as one in whom was great compassion. She experienced him as one who looked upon her and saw, in her, infinite worth. In the words Jesus spoke to the woman, we hear an echo of the words God spoke through Isaiah: "I, even I, am He Who blots out and cancels your transgressions, for My own sake, and I will not remember your sins." (Isaiah 43:25 AMP).

In Jesus, God has done a new thing. New worlds of possibility have opened up to us. God gives us victory over everything that would drag us down, everything that would destroy us, everything that would leave our lives in misery. God has given us victory in Jesus.

In Jesus' day, the land of Palestine was about one hundred and twenty miles long. In the extreme south was the southern kingdom of Judea. In the extreme north was the northern kingdom of Galilee. In between lay a land, bordering on the Sea of Galilee, called Samaria. For centuries, a feud raged between the Jews and the Samaritans. It began when most of the Jews from Samaria were taken to Babylon as prisoners, where they remained. The Assyrians brought in other people to replace the Jews who had left. A lot of inter-marrying went on so that the Samaritan Jews were no longer pure blood Jews. Consequently, they were looked down upon and despised by the "pure" Judean and Galilean Jews. To make matters worse they built their own Temple on Mount Gerizim. This was an abomination to the Judean and Galilean Jews. As a result, there was constant feuding between the Jews and the Samaritans.

Travel time between Judea and Galilee could be shortened a full three days by going through Samaria. Even though the pure blood Jews of Judea and Galilee wanted nothing to do with the mixed blood Samaritan Jews, they would tolerate them for the sake of saving three days' travel time. So it was that Jesus, wanting to escape discussions about baptism, decided to go to Galilee by way of Samaria. It was a long walk, and tiring. They came to a town called Sychar. About a half mile outside of town was an ancient well. Jacob had dug this well several hundred years before. Jesus was tired and sat down to rest. The disciples went on ahead to the village to buy food.

About midday, while Jesus sat there, a woman of Samaria came to the well. Why she came to draw water at that hour is not explained. There was water in the city. Perhaps she shared the same contempt as her fellow adulteress in Jerusalem and the village women drove her away. A Jew, especially an orthodox Jew, wouldn't be caught dead talking to a Samaritan. Jesus startles the woman when he does the unheard of thing. He speaks to her, not just a Samaritan, but a woman who is an adulteress. He asks for a drink. She can't believe her ears. Astonished she blurts out: "How come you, a Jew, are asking me, a Samaritan woman, for a drink?"

She is even more astonished and puzzled at the answer Jesus gives her. "If you knew the generosity of God and who I am, you would be asking me for a drink, and I would give you fresh, living water." She looks at Jesus. He appears to be normal. Unlike someone who is mocking her, his eyes radiate compassion and generosity. But his words are confusing. Taking a deep breath, she answers him.

"Sir, you don't even have a bucket to draw with, and this well is deep. So how are you going to get this 'living water'? Are you a better man than our ancestor Jacob, who dug this well and drank from it, he and his sons and livestock, and passed it down to us?" She is really asking Jesus; What kind of man are you? I have been mocked and ridiculed too many times not to know when it's happening. You aren't mocking me, or ridiculing me. Everything about you, the glow in your eyes, your gentle manner, your tone of voice, all say that you are serious, that you are speaking to me, a woman of Samaria, as an equal. As these thoughts rush through her head, Jesus answers.

"Everyone who drinks this water will get thirsty again and again. Anyone who drinks the water I give will never thirst—not ever. The water I give will be an artesian spring within, gushing fountains of endless life."

Not only is the woman amazed that Jesus would talk to her, she is even more amazed that he would offer her such a precious gift. This gift would be wonderful. To never be thirsty again, to never have to come to this well again; what a blessing he holds out to her. Her response is immediate. "Sir, give me this water so I won't ever get thirsty, won't ever have to come back to this well again!"

"Go call your husband and then come back," Jesus answers.

"I have no husband," the woman protests.

"That's nicely put: 'I have no husband.' You've had five husbands, and the man you're living with now isn't even your husband. You spoke the truth there, sure enough."

The woman is taken by surprise. This man knows everything about her! He knows all about her shameful lifestyle, even though he has not condemned her. This is intensely embarrassing and uncomfortable because only a prophet of God could know those things. That means God himself knows them. She feels undone. Quickly, she switches his attention away from herself and poses a theological question. "Oh, so you're a prophet! Well, tell me this: Our ancestors worshiped God at this mountain, but you Jews insist that Jerusalem is the only place for worship, right?"

Once again she is not prepared for the answer she gets, nor for the revelation that comes at the end of Jesus' answer. "Believe me, woman, the time is coming when you Samaritans will worship the Father neither here at this mountain nor there in Jerusalem. You worship guessing in the dark, we Jews worship in the clear light of day. God's way of salvation is made available through the Jews. But the time is coming—it has, in fact, come—when what you're called will not matter and where you go to worship will not matter.

"It's who you are and the way you live that count before God. Your worship must engage your spirit in the pursuit of truth. That's the kind of people the Father is out looking for: those who are simply and honestly themselves before him in their worship. God is sheer being itself—Spirit. Those who worship him must do it out of their very being, their spirits, their true selves, in adoration."

This was getting at thoughts the woman had never thought. But she was not totally without hopes for the future. "I don't know about that. I do know that the Messiah is coming. When he arrives, we'll get the whole story." Then it came. The revelation that set her spirit free, filled her with excitement, and sent her rushing off, running to tell it to the whole city. Jesus said, "I am he. You don't have to wait any longer or look any further."

Just then the disciples came back and the woman ran off, leaving her water pot in her excitement. She rushed into town saying, "Come see a man who knew all about the things I did, who knows me inside and out. Do you think this could be the Messiah?" This aroused the people's curiosity so much that they went out to Jacob's well to see for themselves.

Meanwhile the disciples laid out the food, but Jesus didn't eat. "Rabbi, eat. Aren't you going to eat?" To which Jesus answered, "I have food to eat you know nothing about. The food that keeps me going is that I do the will of the One who sent me, finishing the work he started. As you look around right now, wouldn't you say that in about four months it will be time to harvest? Well, I'm telling you to open your eyes and take a good look at what's right in front of you.

"These Samaritan fields are ripe. It's harvest time! The Harvester isn't waiting. He's taking his pay, gathering in this grain that's ripe for eternal life. Now the Sower is arm in arm with the Harvester, triumphant. That's the truth of the saying, 'This one sows, that one harvests.' I sent you to harvest a field you never worked. Without lifting a finger, you have walked in on a field worked long and hard by others."

With those words, something no one had ever suspected could happen, did happen. God reached down on the despised Samaritans and harvested them into the Kingdom. The Samaritans were so eager to hear him, and so eager to accept him, that they invited him to stay. And he stayed with them two days. As he left, the townspeople said to the woman, "We're no longer taking this on your say-so. We've heard it for ourselves and know it for sure. He's the Savior of the world!" (All quotes are from John 4:3-43 MSG).

How did the Samaritan woman experience Jesus? God is a God who does the unexpected, using the unlikely. The woman of Samaria came humbly as who she was. Then she let God use who she was to bring salvation to a despised nation.

If being a Samaritan woman was a bad thing, being a Syrophenician woman was even worse. Like the woman taken in adultery, and the woman at the well, this third woman, a Syrophenician woman, was about to open the door of redemption to the Gentile world.

Jesus and the disciples crossed the Sea of Galilee, tying up their boat at Gennesaret. Gennesaret was on the northwest shore. From there they journeyed northwest into the Gentile region of Tyre and Sidon, probably to get away from the Jews for a little rest. At least Jesus said that he did not want anyone to know that he was there. But peace was not to be found. (The words quoted are from Mark 7:24-30 PHS.)

"For no sooner had he got there, then a woman who had heard about him, and who had a daughter possessed by an evil spirit, arrived and prostrated herself before him." The woman had a great need and she knew Jesus had the answer. But it wasn't that simple. She was Greek, a Syrophenician by birth, a despised Gentile. She knew that Jews did not have anything to do with Gentiles. She knew that because she a Syrophenician woman she would probably be pushed away by those guarding Jesus. But need drove her. Her little girl, her most precious possession, lay at home tormented by an evil spirit. Falling at Jesus' feet she begged,

"Please, drive the evil spirit out of my daughter."

Jesus answered her with words that seem to us to be totally out of character for Jesus. How could the one who preached love and never condemned anyone, say what he said to her? Dogs were not well-loved pets. A dog was a symbol of dishonor. To call a man a dog was about the worst insult you could give him. And yet, "Jesus said to her, 'You must let the children have all they want first. It is not right, you know, to take the children's food and throw it to the dogs.'"

It didn't matter that the word he used for dog actually meant a little house dog, as compared to the wild dogs. He still called her a dog. The woman had two choices. She could walk away offended. A lot of people are like that. They "wear their feelings on their sleeves," as the saying goes, taking offense at anything and everything. This woman wasn't like that. She chose the other path. She chose not to be offended. She looked at Jesus, saw the love in his eyes, although the expression on his face was stern. Standing her ground, she spoke up with all the courage she could gather up.

"Yes, Lord, I know, but even the dogs under the table eat the scraps the children leave."

Jesus looked at her with admiration. This woman had passed the test. She had the faith to believe. "If you can answer like that," Jesus said to her, "you can go home! The evil spirit has left your daughter." And she returned home and found the child lying quietly on her bed, the evil spirit gone.

How did the Syrophenician woman experience Jesus? She came to him as an outsider and found him to be the answer to her deepest need. She would be the first, the forerunner. People would look at her and know they were getting a glimpse of God's purpose, kept secret since the world began, that through Jesus all the Gentiles would turn to God in the obedience of faith.

CHAPTER 13

TOUGH BUT OH SO GENTLE

God has an enemy. We know him as Satan, although he has many other aliases. One of his primary tactics is to "lie through the skin of his teeth." He does this by doing what many of us have learned to do with finesse; lie like crazy to shift the blame from ourselves to others. After Satan became the God of this world (2 Corinthians 4:4; Ephesians 2:2; Luke 4:5-7), things went from bad to worse. He planted doubts and unbelief every chance he got. Even though he is the father of all the evil present in this world, his goal is to lie his way out of the blame and get everyone to blame God for their problems, their sickness, their failures, their tragedies.

Satan wants us to join his side by becoming God haters. When Satan stole Adam's lease and became the prince of this world, he thought he had defeated God's plans and shut God out. But God had written an open door clause into Adam's lease. If we ask him, and if we meet the requirement of faith, God can intervene to help us. Unfortunately, by the time some drunk has rammed your car, killing your loved ones, it is too late to ask God to intervene. The evil has already been done.

Satan seizes on our grief, because grief is a strong emotion that makes us vulnerable to his attacks. While we grieve, Satan plants his seeds of anger against God who allowed this to happen. That's how Satan works. First, he causes bad things to happen to us and then he tries to get us to blame God. If we turn against God or start blaming God for the bad things, we block God from being able to help us. Satan is counting on that. If we don't want to fall into Satan's hate trap, we must know some things about God. It is vitally important for us to know what God's nature is really like.

Some speak of God's wrath falling on us, like a parent spanking his child. The truth is God's wrath is reserved for his enemies and not for us, his children (I Thessalonians 2:16; 5:9). Every time God warned Israel what would happen to them if they went whoring after other gods, he always added that if they would remember him and come back to him, he would bless their socks off! Not because they deserved it. Not because they've done penance. But simply because he loves them! So, read with pleasure the verses given below that tell you what God is like.

I. God IS Love.

Paul describes love in I Corinthians 13. God deliberately chose Israel and set his love upon her. Having set his love upon her, he does not let go. He does not change his mind. He asks that she be careful to do the commandments and the statutes and rules that he commands. In return he will bless her with riches. At the same time, he warns them that he knows she won't be faithful. He warns her of the troubles she will reap when she goes whoring after other gods. But when she remembers him, he adds, and repents and seeks his face, he will restore her and pour out blessings upon her once again (Deuteronomy 7:6-13; 30:1-9; 2 Chronicles 7:14). He will blot out her transgressions and remember them no more for his own sake (Isaiah 43:25).

John tells us we need to love like God loves. We can do it, he writes, because God loved us first, and proved it by sending Jesus so that we might live through him. He's set us free to love. John explains that if we love one another, God dwells in us, and his love is perfected in us. John explains that if we don't love, it means we never did know God (I John 4:7-19).

2. The Nature of God Is Perfect.

Perfection means to be complete, lacking nothing. You might say perfect about the turkey or sirloin steak that has just been set before you with its mouthwatering aroma tickling your nose. What you mean is that it lacks nothing because the animal was the right age and fed just right, was cooked just right, has the right moistness, the right amount of spices, and looks just right on the platter.

When we apply this to God we are saying that everything about God is just right, lacking nothing. How he loves us is just right, is just what we need. It lacks nothing and is far greater than we could have imagined. Jesus tells us to be perfect, in the same way that God is perfect. The Message Bible renders it like this:

> In a word, what I'm saying is, Grow up. You're kingdom subjects. Now live like it. Live out your God-created identity. Live generously and graciously toward others, the way God lives toward you." (Matthew 5:48).

That is possible because God is working in you, "for His good pleasure and satisfaction and delight." (Philippians 2:13 AMP)

3. The Nature of God Is Joy.

Our God is a joyful God. The prophets tell us that joy is our heritage.

> For you shall go out in joy and be led forth in peace; the mountains and the hills before you shall break forth into singing, and all the trees of the field shall clap their hands." (Isaiah 55:12 ESV)

> The joy of the Lord is your strength and stronghold." (Nehemiah 8:10b AMP)

> The Lord your God is in the midst of you is the mightiest of the mighty; he will save! He will exuberantly rejoice over you with mirth and gladness and joy and pleasure; He will be silent and not remember past sins, or even recall them, so great is His love; He will spin around, dancing over you with loud singing. (Zephaniah 3:17 author's translation)

> In your presence there is fullness of joy; at your right hand are pleasures that never end. (Psalm 16:11 ESV)
>
> Though you have not seen him, you love him. Though you do not now see him, you believe in him and rejoice with joy that is inexpressible and filled with glory. (I Peter 1:8 ESV)
>
> When the morning stars sang together, and all the sons of God shouted for joy. (Job 38:7 KJV)
>
> I have told you these things, that My joy and delight may be in you, and that your joy and gladness may be of full measure and complete and overflowing. (John 15:11 AMP)

4. The Nature of God Is Abundant Life.

> The thief <Satan> comes only in order to steal and kill and destroy. I came that they may have and enjoy life, and have it in abundance (to the full, till it overflows). (John 10:10 AMP)

The absolute fullness of life which belongs to God is the life Jesus is talking about. Abundant is over and above, more than is necessary, exceeding abundant, supremely abundant. The life is life intensive, a principle of power and mobility in holiness and righteousness. This Life is possessed of vitality, absolute fullness of life, alive as God is alive; who is the fountain of life. "For with You is the fountain of life; in Your light do we see light" (Psalm 36:9 AMP).

5. The Nature of God Is Light.

> God is Light, and there is no darkness in Him at all <no, not in any way>. Spotless, holy, majestic, free from every imperfection. God dwells in light. (I John 1:5 AMP)

> "In him was life; and the life was the light of men." (John 1:4 KJV)

> "... his light so bright no one can get close. He's never been seen by human eyes—human eyes can't take him in! Honor to him, and eternal rule! Oh, yes...." (1 Timothy 6:16 MSG)

6. The Nature of God Is Unparalleled Beauty.

> And he that sat on the throne was like in appearance to a jasper (a green translucent agate) and a sardis stone (a clear, deep-red stone), and there was a rainbow round the throne like to an emerald in appearance (a transparent stone light green in color) ... and before the throne there was a glassy sea, like to crystal (clear and colorless in itself) ..." (based on Revelation 4:2-3, 6)

> "And the building of the wall (New Jerusalem) was of jasper (a translucent stone of various colors) ... the city was pure gold, like unto clear glass. And the foundations of the wall of the city were garnished with all manner of precious stones." (based on Revelation 21:10-21)

The first foundation was jasper (transparent green); the second, sapphire (transparent azure blue with gold); the third, a chalcedony (translucent red); the fourth, an emerald (transparent light green); the fifth, sardonyx (red and white); the sixth, sardius (transparent red); the seventh, chrysolite (golden yellow topaz); the eighth, beryl (sea-green stone); the ninth, a topaz (transparent yellow); the tenth, a chrysoprasus (apple green); the eleventh, a jacinth (dark blue as sapphire); the twelfth, an amethyst (transparent purple).

7. The Nature of God Is Goodness.

> And God saw everything that He had made, and, behold, it was very good. (Genesis 1:31 KJV)

Everything that he had made was a perfect reflection of his thought. Jesus put it this way:

> If you then, evil as you are, know how to give good things to your children, how much more will your Father Who is in heaven give good things to those who ask Him! (Matthew 7:11 KJV)

> There is only One who is good (Matthew 19:17 ESV).

Good (agathos) describes that which, being good in its character, is beneficial in its effect. God is essentially, absolutely and consummately good. God is good (Mark 10:18; Luke 18:19). He who is born again, who becomes a Christian, becomes good because he is recreated in God's image (Romans 15:14; Galatians 5:22; Ephesians 5:9; 2 Thessalonians 1:11).

8. The Nature of God Is Jesus.

> Anyone who has seen me has seen the Father....I am in the Father, and...the Father is in me." (John 14:9, 10 NIV)

> God was reconciling the world to himself in Christ. (2 Corinthians 5:19 NIV)

> He is the image of the invisible God, the firstborn over all creation. (Colossians 1:15 NIV)

> The Son is the radiance of God's glory and the exact representation of His being, sustaining all things by his powerful word. (Hebrews 1:3 NIV)

> For by him all things were created: things in heaven and on earth, visible and invisible, whether thrones or powers or rulers or authorities; all things were created by him and for him. (Colossians 1:16 NIV)

> He is before all things, and in him all things hold together. (Colossians 1:16 NIV)

> In the beginning was the Word, and the Word was with God, and the Word was God. He was with God in the beginning. Through him all things were made; without him nothing was made that has been made.... The Word became flesh and lived for a while among us. We have seen his glory, the glory of the one and only Son, who came from the Father, full of grace and truth. (John 1:1-3, 14 NIV)

9. The Nature of God Is Embedded in The Nature of His Image.

> So God created man in his own image. (Genesis 1:27 KJV)

Man was created to be like God. God is characterized by universal benevolence, unconquerable goodwill, and constant seeking of the highest good of every man. The great characteristic of God is his love for saint and sinner alike. No matter what men do to him, God seeks nothing but their highest good.

> A man...is the image and glory of God. (I Corinthians 11:7 KJV)

Image means a being corresponding to the original. The condition of man as a fallen creature has not entirely effaced the image; he is still suitable to bear responsibility, he still has Godlike qualities, such as love of goodness and beauty; none of which are found in a mere animal.

10. The Nature of God Is to Be Restored in The Image.

> As we bore the image of the earthly man, we shall bear also the image of the heavenly man. (I Corinthians 15:49 KJV)

> You have...put on the new man being renewed in full knowledge according to the image of him that created him. (Colossians 3:10 KJV)
>
> Because whom he foreknew, he also foreordained to be conformed to the image of his son, that he should be the first born among many brothers. (Romans 8:29 KJV)

We are to be like God in love and goodness. We are to show forth his character. This isn't going to be something we do by force of will. It is something we are to allow to spring forth like a well of water bubbling up out of us (John 7:38). The Spirit dwells within us, and these are the Spirit's fruits that we allow to spring up within us. (Romans 8:11; Galatians 5:22)

CHAPTER 14

Homework: Plant a Tree

Many years ago, more than I like to remember, I planted 1,000 evergreen trees. To a small lad, which I was, 1,000 was a huge number. The trees were seedlings, more like twigs in size. I had to be careful not to trample on them. Today, some seventy plus years later, they are giant trees. What had once seemed a fragile little seedling has become strong and unmovable by storm or wind. Writing hundreds of years ago, the Psalmist said that a blessed man is like a tree.

> Blessed is the man
>
> who walks not in the counsel of the wicked,
>
> nor stands in the way of sinners,
>
> nor sits in the seat of scoffers;
>
> but his delight is in the law of the LORD,
>
> and on his law he meditates day and night.
>
> He is like a tree
>
> planted by streams of water

that yields its fruit in its season,

and its leaf does not wither.

In all that he does, he prospers.

(Psalm 1:1-3 ESV)

Your assignment is to draw a *Dream Tree.* On a blank sheet of paper draw the outline of a tree. There will be three equal parts: The top with three branches, the trunk, and three large roots at the bottom. Write your name on the trunk. On the left branch write, Persons. On the center branch write, Places. On the right branch write, Things. The roots of the tree will list your Biblical authority, or promises from which your tree will draw nourishment. On the left root write Old Testament. On the middle write Gospels. On the right write New Testament.

Now you can begin to fill in your tree. Each of your people, places, and things will be smaller branches branching off the main branch. Your Biblical authority will be little roots branching off the large roots. A tree is a growing thing. So your tree will grow, adding more branches and perhaps losing a few branches. The root system just keeps growing, supporting and supplying nourishment for the branches.

PART C

The Territory of Myself

For if a man is in Christ he becomes a new person altogether — the past is finished and gone, everything has become fresh and new. (2 Corinthians 5:17 PHS)

CHAPTER 15

FORGET AND FORGIVE YOURSELF

We looked at Jesus through the eyes of those who knew him. We found him to be altogether loving and worthy of our trust. We looked at the Father and found he is just like Jesus. It is good to know that in our minds. But knowing it in our minds is not the same as knowing it in our hearts where trust and confidence and faith reside. To know it there we must know it in our experience. Paul tells us how to do it.

> Do not be conformed to this world, but be transformed by the renewal of your mind, that by testing you may discern what is the will of God, what is good and acceptable and perfect. (Romans 12:2 ESV)

Imagine that you were born into poverty. Your clothes have been patched so many times the patches have patches. You think poor. You have no hope. Your dreams for the future go no farther than finding enough food for your next meal. Suddenly, with the speed of a bolt of lightning you are instantly rich. You are also the President seated in the White House. But you are still wearing your patched clothes. Your world, once a few acres, has grown to include the whole world. Waiting for you in the next room are the greatest and smartest men and women of the world. They are waiting for you to counsel them with your wisdom. To say that you suddenly feel very awkward and extremely out of place is putting it mildly.

Something similar happens to us when Jesus redeems us. We feel awkward, undone in his presence (Isaiah 6:5) as though we are still wearing dirty patched clothes of sin. We feel even more awkward in God's presence. The trouble is that we are remembering what he has forgotten (Isaiah 43:25; Jeremiah 31:34). We remember because we haven't forgiven ourselves. This interferes with prayer. If prayer is family talk, and if I want to take my place as a blood-bought part of that family enjoying and soaking up the love and joy of my family, then I need to be transformed.

Think of yourself as a very unique ball of clay, a self-evolving ball of clay. A ball of clay that has within it a perfect plan for what that clay is to become, just as a tree is in the heart of the seed. As the clay starts to evolve, emerging as a tiny baby growing in stature, outside forces begin to poke at the clay. Some try to distort it. Some try to force it into a different shape.

When the clay has reached its maturity it has been buffeted and poked so much it is hard to tell what it was designed to be, much like a tree that has been buffeted by storms, insect infestation and disease. It hardens into its misshapen form. One day, someone comes along and sees your misshapen form and asks, "How did you get to be that way? Tell me what happened to you." That's a question you've never asked yourself. Could it be that the real you is not what you see? Is there a real you hidden inside? Is it possible for a hardened lump of clay to be softened and reshaped into its original design?

I discovered that the answer is Yes! I used to jokingly admit I had a fault or two. But I didn't believe any of my problems were caused by any of my faults. I laid the blame on my high school, on the "backwoods" rural environment in which I grew up, and on my parents. The problems that engulfed me when I started college were not my fault. Or so I believed. Then one day my bubble got burst. My college psychology professor made a statement I did not like. He said, "Your parents provided the environment; what you did with it was your own contribution." The only way I could enjoy a good pity party when things were going wrong was if I could play the part of the powerless victim and blame everybody else. Then my professor made that statement ruining my pity party!

At the same time, it was also one of the most liberating statements I had ever heard! He was telling us quite simply that we had the power to change things. We were not victims. We were discoverers. We were discoverers of what works and what doesn't, of which decisions were good, and which were bad. Because we were the ones who made the decisions, we also had the power to change those decisions. That is a key concept. You have the power to change things, to make new decisions. Use the stories that follow as stimuli to help you think about your own story. Identify the things that need to change. Change the ones you can change. Ask God to change the things you can't change.

CHAPTER 16

NOT SO OKAY

We moved from town to the country when I was five. My mom, a nurse, needed to care for her parents who lived on the family farm. I was alone, out in the country. There were no neighborhood kids to play with like I had had in town. No cellars to explore, no homemade root beer to drink with friends on a hot summer day. That left me with only two things to do. The first was to annoy and tease my older sister, which I did with relish. The other was to create my own little world. I nailed some boards across two tree limbs for a platform. I could climb up and pull the ladder up after me. Up there I was in my own kingdom. It could be whatever I wanted it to be. No one could get to me. There I could read, eat my lunch, and dream of adventures.

In those days before cell phones, iPads, and television, and with no neighbors to play with not much exciting or interesting happened. The trains still ran. There was one across the valley that went by a couple times a day. My dad rode the train to the big city where he worked. But soon the trains stopped coming. The tracks were torn up. In the country we had no exciting places to explore, no people to watch, no stores with all kinds of magical things in the windows at which to gaze in wonder. The only place to go was church. For the youth there was no social life apart from the church. Our youth group met at the church or in each other's homes. We played games like musical chairs and spin the bottle. Sometimes we had youth rallies when we got together with youth from other churches.

At first we used kerosene lamps. Electricity had not yet come to the country. Our toilet was a little outhouse outside the back door, with three holes. We did use toilet paper although my great uncle, who lived way out in the country, still used pages from the Sears catalog. Our bathtub was a laundry tub. In the winter it sat by the stove. In the summer it sat on the back porch. Our water came from a hand pump. We heated water on the big wood burning kitchen stove. In that old stove mom could bake a cake or a pie and roast a turkey without an oven thermometer or timer. Our refrigerator was a bucket we lowered into the cool water of the well. Life in the country seemed to have stood still, frozen in time.

In the eyes of a child growing up in the country all the exciting things happened in the city. It wasn't until electricity came to the country that things began to change. To those of us growing up in our rustic rural settings even small towns enchanted us like a temptress. They called out to us with messages of culture, of excitement and opportunity in science and industry. They also tempted us with lights and flashing signs, promising thrills and excitement. There were the latest in movies, stage shows, symphony orchestras and beautiful show girls. There were exotic foods and drinks from strange lands to excite your tongue. For culture, there were gigantic museums and parks and zoos displaying the wonders of the world.

I was not a prodigal son. The dark side of cities held no attraction for me. I was looking for opportunities for growth and development and a career. The only way to fulfill my dreams was to begin with college. That is where the painful process began of learning unpleasant things about myself. With great confidence, I wrote my first Freshman English composition. I was sure I would get an "A" because it was one of the best compositions I had ever written. In high school I got "A+'s". The professor returned my composition filled with red ink and one big "F". In this shocking way I began to learn that my rural high school had not prepared me for college.

That was a horrible shock to my self-esteem. This country boy who thought he was pretty smart had stumbled and stumbled hard! It didn't stop there. My self-confidence shaken, I let TV with its live shows seduce me. I wasted my time in front of the TV set. My studies were neglected enabling me to have the excuse that I would have gotten an "A" if I had studied. I was afraid that if I studied hard and still got an "F," my ego couldn't handle it.

That's how I dealt with the discovery that I was not the "A" student I had thought I was.

This way of dealing with setbacks was not a good choice. One day I received a letter from the College Dean. I was invited to leave the college. Their motto was, An Adventure in Excellence. I had failed to qualify for the adventure! This forced me to make a decision. Was I going to be defeated or was I going to cast aside the country boy and grow up? Uncle Sam said, "I'll help you grow up." And so I began another journey that took me around the world, exposed me to different cultures and readied me for the next step. That next step was to learn I was not a victim and I could change things.

None of us wants to go through the pain of admitting we aren't okay and need to change. First, it is very painful to our self-esteem and second, we don't know how to change or maybe don't even want to change. It was at this point that I made a great discovery. God did something that reversed the process for becoming okay! He reversed it by making us okay as our starting point. Once we become Christians we can change, precisely because, now we are okay! True, our thoughts try to accuse us. But we can be sure we are okay because God said so. God has made us okay in Christ. Change for a Christian is good, to be desired, and doable. We don't change to become okay. We change because Christ has made us okay. Paul writes,

> This is how we … can reassure ourselves in the sight of God, even if our own conscience makes us feel guilty. For God is greater than our conscience, and he knows everything. (I John 3:19, 20 PHS).

Paul tells us how to do it. It is a process of transformation, wherein we allow the word of God to do the work.

> Be transformed (changed) by the <entire> renewal of your mind, so that you may prove <for yourselves> what is the good and acceptable and perfect will of God, even the thing which is good and acceptable and perfect <in His sight for you (Romans 12:2. AMP).

The knowledge that I had in my hands the power to change came too late to keep me in college. But it started to pay off after my military service. I reapplied to my old college. They said I could come back if I took some summer school classes and passed them. I did and was back in college that fall. This led to a rather interesting situation. My grades were so high the first semester I was back that I was put on the Dean's honor list. That meant I could take unlimited cuts in all my classes. However, my accumulative average was still so low that I was on probation and not allowed to cut any classes!

Jesus had made me okay. Because he had made me okay I went on to graduate from college and seminary *cum laude* (with honor)! The fact that Jesus has made you okay is the key you need to grab and hang on to. This is what sets you free. Jesus has made you okay. That is why you can change.

> But all of us who are Christians ... are transformed in ever-increasing splendor into his own image" (2 Corinthians 3:8 PHS).

CHAPTER 17

GHETTOS IN OUR MINDS

True, we can change. But the fact is that when we get down to the nitty-gritty some things seem impossible to change. Nevertheless, in Christ and only in Christ are all things possible. I'd been invited to attend a conference in Chicago in the early 1960's. One of the speakers was from VISTA - Volunteers in Service to America. He talked about the problems of the people living in the ghetto areas of the cities. He told about the things VISTA was doing to help bring the ghetto victims out of the ghetto. We were stirred by his talk. Someone asked, "What can we do to help?" We were expecting him to say something about raising money. The answer he gave was not what we had expected to hear. But it stirred our imaginations.

His answer had to do with an old saying that goes, "You can take the boy out of the country, but you can't take the country out of the boy." He said it was like that with the people who lived in the ghetto. You can take the people out of the ghetto, but you can't take the ghetto out of the people. He said the real need was a transformation of the inner man. The ghetto mindset held them trapped. Not until people get a new *mindset* will they change things on the outside. As a very wise man once said,

> Where there is no vision the people perish (Proverbs 29:18 KJV).

Everyone has a mindset. A mindset is an ingrained habitual mental attitude, a set of assumptions that determine what we believe and how we act. Our mindset determines how we respond to the environment in which we live, to our culture, and to our history. When the ghetto mindset is pounded into an individual's head over and over, and he repeats over and over that he is trapped, that nothing can change, he will eventually accept that as absolute truth.

People who become kings and queens aren't born with different genes. They too are subjected to a mindset, a ruler mindset. Their training and expectations from the time they are conceived in their mothers' wombs is that they were created to rule. They grow up believing they are different. They expect to be obeyed. They expect to be rich and live in grand palaces. Growing conditions and expectations shape them and make them what they are.

In the late sixties we took a bus load of youth from the Midwest to visit Washington, D.C. and New York City. We slept in church basements and cooked most of our meals. One of our stops was at an inner city church in Philadelphia. It was an old church with an attached gym. When we arrived some youth were shooting baskets in the gym. A couple of them talked with us a little and helped us unload our big yellow church bus. Then they left.

The pastor gathered us around and talked about the neighborhood, about the dangers of gang wars, and about staying inside the walls at night. He said that because we were staying at the church our church bus was safe. Otherwise, it would be stripped clean in five minutes! While he was talking we heard police cars go by with sirens wailing.

We went out for supper and when we came back we had a shock. One of the youth who had been shooting baskets when we arrived, who had helped us unload, and then walked down the block towards home was shot when he reached the end of the block. That's what the sirens had been about. Then the pastor told us that the word was out that there was going to be a gang war that night. Since neither side really wanted it both sides had passed the word to him so that he could alert the police. With that alarming news, we went to bed hoping for a peaceful night.

Next day we went on a bus tour of the area. The pastor pointed out rundown apartment buildings that were standing empty. Windows were broken. Doors were smashed down. The buildings were shabby. The pastor said that inside all the plumbing had been ripped off the walls and the water left running. The police didn't dare go in to shut the water off. It was a scene of mass destruction. We assumed that these were old slum dwellings and that the landlords had gotten what they deserved. We were shocked when he said that all those apartment buildings had been new low-rent housing for the ghetto people. As soon as the people moved into the buildings, they began to vandalize them. Until you take the ghetto out of the people every place they go will become a ghetto.

It works that way with us, too. Each of us has his own destructive mindset. It might be a ghetto mindset. It might be a self-adoring mindset like the king's. It might be a timid mindset, like the person who is afraid to do anything new. It might be an I-can't-do-anything-right mindset, like the person who knows nothing works out for them. All of us grew up with our own hindering mindset. When we became Christians, that mindset was cracked open. We were set free, made new. Once the mindset trap is broken, God has to rebuild in us the mindset he wants us to have. That process can be painful and it can take some time to complete.

Many years ago, a young man raised with a mindset of great self-importance, acted, as he thought, with kingly wisdom. He killed a man. The people he thought he was helping rejected him and he had to flee for his life. Adopted as a baby, he had been raised in the luxury of a palace. His adoptive mother showered him with all that great wealth could buy. He had the power of her name. Servants and soldiers had to obey him. He had been brought up to be arrogant, obeyed and pampered. All those traits from the palace stuck to him like a vile smell. Now, he was cringing with fear.

His natural parents were members of a race of slaves, who were oppressed by his adoptive family. When he tried to break up a fight between two of them, they asked him, "Are you going to kill us too, like you did the foreman? Who made you our leader?" He had been seen and was rejected. Soon Pharaoh would know. In great fear he fled to another country where he was alone, without money or power or a job, and without a people to lead. In a moment of anger, he had gone from wealth and power and dreams of being a great leader, to the life of a penniless, powerless, wanted fugitive. He was reduced to poverty without reputation and powerless.

He found a man who was willing to take him in. He married one of the man's daughters. For the next forty years, he cared for his father-in-law's live stock. He was a man of shattered dreams, a man who had nothing to offer. Little did he realize, and none of us would have realized, that living in the desert away from wealth and power was the place he needed to be. It was the place of the right growing conditions. This place would grow him into the leader he had once dreamed of being. Too often, like Moses, we rely on our own wisdom for achieving our goals and end up in the desert.

Moses gave up all his dreams. He did the only thing he could do; he became the shepherd of his father-in-law's sheep. His mind was no longer scheming and planning as it had been for many years, relying on his own wisdom. God could now develop Moses into the man he needed. So it happened that one day in the distance Moses saw a bush on fire. As he looked the bush burned but was not consumed! Hmm, he thought. That's curious. What's going on? I'm going to have a closer look.

He approached the bush, when suddenly, "Moses, Moses!" spoke a voice from out of the bush. Startled, he jumped back, the hair on his neck sticking up, his adrenalin rushing through his veins. "Do not come near." the powerful voice commanded. "Put your shoes off your feet, for the place on which you stand is holy ground. I am the God of your father, the God of Abraham, the God of Isaac, and the God of Jacob."

There is that about the presence of God when he speaks to you after this manner, that ignites an awesome fear in your heart. Moses knew, felt all through his body, that he was in the presence of tremendous Power. He knew the voice. He knew it from the gentle voice in his quiet times of prayer. Never like this. He was afraid to look and hid his face.

God continued,

> I have surely seen the affliction of my people who are in Egypt, and have heard their cry because of their taskmasters and oppressors; for I know their sorrows and sufferings and trials. And I have come down to deliver them out of the hand and power of the Egyptians, and to bring them up out of that land to a land good and large, a land flowing with milk and honey, a land of plenty. Come now therefore,

> and I will send you to Pharaoh, that you may bring forth My people, the Israelites, out of Egypt.

"You can't be serious!" exclaimed Moses in alarm. "I'm wanted for murder. The people don't want me for a leader. I tried once. Nobody would listen to me then. Nobody will listen to me now. The Israelites won't. I know Pharaoh won't. Who am I that I should go to Pharaoh and bring the Israelites out of Egypt?"

Don't misjudge Moses. He had once been the "I'm your man" kind of guy. Since then he had learned to face the truth about himself. He wondered if God understood the truth. It would be utter disaster to return to Egypt. God knew what he was about. "I will surely be with you," he said.

"All right," Moses conceded, "suppose I do go. When I come to the Israelites and say to them, the God of your fathers has sent me to you, and they say to me, what is his name? What shall I say to them?"

"Say to them," ordered God in a commanding voice that sent the flames shooting high into the sky,

> I AM WHO I AM and WHAT I AM, and I WILL BE WHAT I WILL BE; you shall say this to the Israelites, I AM has sent me to you! God, the Creator, the One who made heaven and earth, and then formed Adam and Eve from the earth. He is the One Who sent me to you.

Moses was thinking God must be crazy if he thinks that will work. "Look, God. Let's be realistic," Moses argued. "They won't believe me. They'll say, 'You've finally cracked! That's what happens when you kill someone and then go off living like a hermit. You crack, you go off the deep end. Now you're trying to tell us God really appeared to you? Go on old man, before we throw stones at you.'"

"What is that in your hand?" the Lord God asked.

"A rod," Moses answered.

"Cast it to the ground," commanded God.

Moses did. It became a serpent, and Moses ran away from it. (The serpent was the symbol of royal and divine power worn on the crown of the Pharaohs.)

"Put forth your hand and take it by the tail," demanded God, his voice ringing with impatience.

Moses hesitated. This was not a serpent one wanted to be friendly with and Moses was not a snake handler. Taking a deep breath, watching his chance, Moses stretched out his hand and caught it and instantly it became a rod in his hand. For a moment, anxiety gripped him. What would happen if he let loose of his stick? Would it turn into a snake again? Those questions were answered when God told him when and where to do the miracle.

"Do this," said God, "so that the elders will believe that the Lord, the God of their fathers, has appeared to you, indeed. If this won't persuade them put your hand in your bosom."

Moses did, and when he pulled it out it was leprous. When he did it again it was restored.

"If they won't believe those two signs, pour water from the Nile on the dry land."

Moses did, and it became blood.

God's signs were quite impressive, but Moses still tried to get out of going.

"Okay," he protested. "Let's suppose the elders believe you appeared to me. Suppose I do all the things you tell me to do. It won't work for a very simple reason. You're forgetting that I am not a good speaker. I'm not good with words. I never have been and, in case you haven't noticed, I haven't gotten any better since talking to you. Besides that, I stutter. Nobody is going to take a stutterer seriously."

In those forty years in the desert he had finally gotten honest about himself. He had no false illusions about marching off and accomplishing what God was asking him to do. It had to be God doing it all the way or it wouldn't happen. God had to be the speaker of every word spoken. God had to do the miracles. God had to instruct Moses every inch of the way. In the next words God speaks he tells Moses he need have no fear. God will be in his mouth.

"Who has made man's mouth?" questioned the Lord. "Or who makes the dumb, or deaf, or the seeing, or the blind? Is it not I, the Lord? Now GO! And I will be with your mouth, and will teach you what you shall say."

In one last desperate plea Moses begged,

"Please, Lord. Send someone else."

In a voice that must have startled Moses, God answered.

"NO! Is there not Aaron your brother, the Levite? I know he can speak well. Also, he is coming out to meet you and when he sees you, he will be overjoyed. You must speak to him and put the words in his mouth; and I will be with your mouth and with his mouth, and will teach you what you shall do." (The preceding story is from Exodus 3:5-17 AMP)

So it was that Moses, the real Moses now, freed from all the false wisdom of his youth, set out to do the thing he had once dreamed of doing. But this time, it was God doing it, and doing it in a way that far surpassed any plan Moses may have had. The growing conditions he needed to prepare him to perform the task God set before him, had done their job.

The first step in preparing Moses to fulfill the plan God had for him was to break the bondage of his ruler mindset. When you became a Christian God broke the mindset that was holding you in bondage. God's plan for Moses far exceeded in greatness anything Moses could have dreamed. God's plan for you far exceeds anything you can plan for yourself. Being set free from the bondage of your mindset, sets you free to take your seat at Jesus' right hand at the throne of God (Ephesians 2:6). When your inner image and self-expectation are right, it's your right to reign as a king in life (Romans 5:17).

> Jesus said, "I came that they may have life as God has it, and that they may have it in superfluity, exceeding, beyond measure, abundance," (John 10:10 author's translation from the Nestle Greek Text).

CHAPTER 18

GET A NEW MIND

Dr. H. got our attention in a hurry! The information sheet said that he was a professor of theology in a Methodist Seminary. Theologians can be rather boring speakers. They tend to use big words and answer questions nobody is asking. We were prepared for the worst. Imagine our shock when Dr. H's opening words were,

"I've just been converted!"

Dr. H. explained that he got converted while trying to grow an avocado tree! He prepared the ground. He went to the nursery and bought a healthy avocado tree. He brought it home and planted it. It died! Every avocado tree he planted died. He was ready to give up on the idea, but decided to give it one last try.

As he was getting ready to plant the tree, Dr. H. happened to read the label and it said, "Given the right conditions this tree will grow." He suddenly realized that he didn't know what the right conditions were. He went to the nursery and got a book. It told him what to do. He did it and now he has a healthy avocado tree.

Dr. H. reminded us that the Greek word "conversion" means to "have a new mind." He got a "new mind" about how to grow an avocado tree and the tree flourished.

"Everyone," Dr. H declared, "has a green thumb in the sense of having the power to control the growing conditions. Given the right conditions anything can grow."

Listen to that again. "Everyone has the power to control the growing conditions. Given the right conditions anything can grow." What is true for avocado trees is true for our damaged self-image. Our innermost being can be likened to an avocado tree. In the heart of the avocado is a divine plan for a tree that is perfect. You might call it, its self-image. The ground in which it struggles to grow is filled with things that want to distort, cripple, and even destroy it.

Like the avocado tree each of us has a Divine Plan[1], a perfect self-image deep in the heart. But poisons in the soil, weeds, bugs, and worms disfigure and distort our self-image. Bitter root judgments and a destructive mindset are two of the poisons. This disfigured self-image controls how we live. It controls what we expect of ourselves and others. If the damage is too severe we are unable to function, unable to love even ourselves. The idea of being conformed to the image of Christ (Romans 8:29) may seem impossible.

Dr. H. said change is possible because we can change the growing conditions. Everyone has the power to control the growing conditions for his self-image. Evangelism in the New Testament was an announcement of a joyful message of Good News. It was the message of forgiveness, mercy, new beginnings. That is the message we must bring to our self-image. A gardener does not harangue at a drooping flower. He fertilizes, weeds, and nurtures it. Or, more precisely, he loves it. Just as true evangelism is loving the sinner into the kingdom of God, we must love ourselves into our God given self-image. (see Romans 8:29)

Sometimes we do things on purpose or unconsciously that keep us in misery; a sort of self-imposed self-punishment or self-hate, because we don't live up to our expectations. Or we convince ourselves that healing, prosperity, and success are for others but not for us. This is a form of false pride, pride that it's not for us. We call down fire on ourselves; perhaps in the form of losing jobs, or driving our loved ones away, claiming that this confirms what we already knew about ourselves. If God spanked, that kind of talk would earn a good a spanking!

The task God sets before us is to see ourselves as he sees us. We are to fertilize, weed, love and nurture ourselves. We are to supply the right growing conditions to our self-image. Step one is to get a clear picture of the self-image we are seeking to grow. Because we are created in the image of God we need to know what that image is. Step two is to learn what growing conditions are required for the image of God to grow. Step three is to develop and act on a systematic plan to provide the correct growing conditions. Before Moses could rise to the stature he had once dreamed of having, he had to come to the point where he was totally dependent upon God to accomplish it.

Look at your prayer tree. In the midst of the people, places and things you will begin to see your real self as God sees you. Over time, the unique expression of the image of God that is you, will emerge. It may not be what you expected. It may be an image you, like Moses, never dreamed possible. What is making it possible is nothing you did or will do. It is possible because of a marvelous thing God did for you when you received Jesus as your Lord and Savior. God gave you the gift of righteousness. Paul writes, "For he hath made him to be sin for us, who knew no sin; that we might be made the righteousness of God in him" (2 Corinthians 5:21 KJV).

A gift is not a reward. A gift cannot be earned. A reward is earned. A gift is not deserved. A gift is something the giver gives because he wants to give it. Once a gift is given it cannot be taken back. A gift comes to you unasked for, unearned, and undeserved. When you receive a gift it is your absolute possession. God gave you the gift of righteousness, the gift of right-standing with him, as his very own child. It is your lawful possession. You are in right-standing with God regardless of how many times you fall into sin, do bad things, fail in spiritual disciplines or do the worst things you can imagine. Because righteousness is your legal possession, all you have to do to keep it working is do what John tells us: "If we confess our sins, he is faithful and just to forgive us our sins, and to cleanse us from all unrighteousness" (I John 1:9 KJV).

This amazing good news sometimes seems too good to be true. Lest you think this, or think it only wishful thinking, look back at what Balaam saw when he was asked by Balak to curse Israel. The Israelites were a stubborn nation that God had threatened to destroy many times. That is not what Balaam saw. Balaam saw the people as God saw them:

> (God) hath not beheld iniquity in Jacob, neither hath he seen perverseness in Israel: the LORD his God is with

> him, and the shout of a king is among them." (Numbers 23:21 KJV)

There was a time when I did not know God had made me righteous. My head and my heart did not agree. My heart knew the truth and so my heart condemned me. Many suffer from self-condemnation of the heart. In my case, I was trapped by perfectionism. I set this trap for myself. I'm not sure when or why. Use my story to help you uncover some things you may have unknowingly done to yourself.

In 1938 we moved to the old family farm, to be near Grandma and Grandpa. World War II broke out, and dad took a job in a defense plant 90 miles away. Somehow I got a very strange idea that had nothing to do with facts. My little child mind got the idea that I had to earn my father's love. I started to believed my father wouldn't love me if I was bad. I had to earn his love by being perfect when he came home on weekends. If I wasn't perfect, my dad wouldn't love me. The worst thing I could imagine was for my dad not to love me. I looked forward to the weekends. I wanted everything to be just right, because I loved my dad and almost worshiped him.

One-night dad and I were having a lot of fun. He was sitting in a chair next to a wall. A mirror hung on the wall above him. I stood in front of him and we bounced a ball back and forth. I was having so much fun and everything seemed so wonderful. My dad loved me. My dad was laughing with me. My dad was playing with me. Then it happened. I threw the ball too hard. It bounced high. Dad missed it. It hit the mirror. The mirror shattered. As that mirror shattered, I shattered. I had committed the unpardonable sin. In that one foolish moment I had lost my father's love.

That is how I felt in my little child's mind and heart. Mom and dad tried to console me. They could not understand why I cried so hard. It didn't matter what they said. They could tell me over and over again that it was all right. But I knew the truth. I knew I'd lost my father's love. I had tried to be perfect and I'd failed. Because I had failed, because I had cost myself the love of my father that I desired so much, I could not forgive myself and I could not love myself.

That belief carried over into how I related to my heavenly Father. Because, in my heart, I knew what I was like I knew that God could not love me. We pick up strange ideas as children. We think we outgrow them. But those strange ideas remain with us, often buried in our deep minds, haunting us and making us miserable. They block our efforts to build a healthy relationship with God as well as with others. The only guide a person has for envisioning God as a father is the example of one's own father. My bitter root judgment robbed me of intimacy with my earthly father and now my heavenly Father.

Another source for bitter root judgments is other people. A child who is put down by parents, friends, teachers and other people; who is told he is bad, lazy, and will never amount to anything, may lose all hope and live under the curse of condemnation, living out everything he believes he was cursed with.

The remedy that transforms these poisons into vital nutrients, regardless of how much condemnation we feel, is the fact that God has declared that we are the righteousness of God in Christ Jesus: and that not of ourselves

> It is the gift of God: Not of works, lest any man should boast, For we are HIS workmanship, created in Christ Jesus unto good works, which God hath before ordained that we should walk in them" (Ephesians 2:8-10 KJV).

This is a fact that cannot be changed. It may be hard to believe. The idea of being declared righteous without doing anything to earn it sounds too good to be true. Not wanting to be taken in we deliberately keep trying to prove it is wrong. This is a poison that needs to be transformed.

Another poison that Christians imbibe unknowingly, is the habit of putting the cart before the horse. Some even think it is spiritual to do so! We think that if we are obedient enough maybe God will bless us. If the thing for which we pray doesn't come to pass we slip into self-condemnation. We ask, what did I do wrong? Maybe I didn't pray or fast enough. Maybe I didn't have enough faith. Maybe I need to work my faith up again. Maybe I've committed some sin I don't remember and I need to repent of it.

On and on we go trying to figure out "where I went wrong, where I missed it." That is the wrong question. God does not bless us or answer our prayers as a reward for obedience. His blessings are gifts, not rewards.

Righteousness is a gift, not a reward. We put the cart before the horse when we fail to understand how faith works. Jesus said that if we would seek first the kingdom of God and his righteousness, "all these things [blessings] would be added unto us" (Matthew 6:33 KJV).

Jesus is talking about relationship, not works. He does not want our deeds. He wants our hearts. It is what is in our hearts that he cares about.

> A good person produces good things from the treasury of a good heart, and an evil person produces evil things from the treasury of an evil heart. What you say flows from what is in your heart" (Luke 6:45 NLT).

In practical terms, to be Christ's is to be a descendant of Abraham (Galatians 3:29), which automatically makes us an heir of all the blessings promised to Abraham and his descendants. Because of Christ, we have an advantage those people never had. We have righteousness placed on us as a free gift. In Jesus we are righteous. Because Jesus has done it all there is nothing more we can do to qualify for God's blessings. As Paul says, "There is therefore now no condemnation to them which are in Christ Jesus, who walk not after the flesh, but after the Spirit" (Romans 8:1 KJV).

Our task is simply to take it. If we have questions, we search the Scriptures for the answers. Our relationship with God is based on his gift and not on how good we've been. God said we are righteous and that settles it. Paul explains, "He that spared not his own Son, but delivered Him up for us all, how shall He not with Him also freely give us all things?" (Romans 8:32 KJV). Don't try to argue about it, God says: "This is the way it is" says God. "I do it for my sake, and not yours. Now deal with it!" (author's paraphrase of Isaiah 43:25-26)

Through his blessings, we gain confidence in God and the desire of our hearts is to be like Jesus. The more we are like Jesus the more we are obedient. Obedience is our love response to God's blessings. We love God because he loved us first and blessed us (I John 4:19). We can forget about trying to put ourselves down, John writes, "For God is greater than our hearts, and he knows everything." (I John 3:20 NIV).

As we begin to reach out and receive his blessings, faith grows in our hearts until that bondage to self-condemnation is broken. It is as Balaam asked, "How can I curse whom God has blessed?" (Numbers 23:21 KJV).

He blesses us first, breaking our bondage, so that we can be obedient as a love response.

> He breaks the power of cancelled sin,
> He sets the prisoner free;
> His blood can make the foulest clean,
> His blood availed for me.
>
> (Charles Wesley)

CHAPTER 19

BREAKING THE UNBREAKABLE

There are a variety of conditions, situations, experiences and environments that add their damage to a destructive mindset; if we let ourselves accept them. The real life examples that follow illustrate this variety, and give examples of how God broke these people free. Do not yield to the temptation to blame others. We cannot blame others for our own responses in any given situation. Our responses are our own contribution. The simplest explanation is to say that we are all born into a sin environment with a sin nature. God is always present waiting for us to turn to him. Because Satan is the god of this world (2 Cor. 4:4) God can do nothing until we ask him. These stories will help you identify some things that need breaking up.

Jim was young, happy, and talkative. He got along well with his parents and with others. He had not had any serious childhood tragedies. There were none of the usual telltale emotional signs. His sociological adjustment was good. He did not appear to be the kind of person who would be in trouble with the Law. Yet he was in prison serving five to ten years for stealing.

As part of our seminary training, a few of us spent one day a week counseling prisoners at a men's reformatory. We observed, talked with the staff, talked with the inmates, ate with them, and led discussion groups. Their participation looked good on their records when it came time for parole. The inmates, for their own amusement, tried to con us into believing wild stories, about themselves. If they couldn't con us we were okay. To help us sift through their stories the Chaplain let us study the records of the men. The records included reports from social workers as well as details of the crime.

As I studied Jim's records, I discovered something unusual. Jim had been raised in a family and among friends for whom stealing was a way of life. Jim stole because he had been brought up to steal. He believed there was nothing wrong with stealing. The social worker concluded that Jim was actually a well-adjusted person. He was just well-adjusted to the wrong culture. Jim's situation is a good illustration of the Law of the Generations of Exodus 20:5. Jim was in bondage to the sins and beliefs of his fathers. Only the transformation of the inner man could change him (Romans 12:2).

The sins of the fathers is one of the Biblical subjects we have a tendency to gloss over without fully understanding it. The Bible speaks of the sins of the fathers in Numbers 14:18:

> The LORD is longsuffering, and of great mercy, forgiving iniquity and transgression, and by no means clearing the guilty, visiting the iniquity of the fathers upon the children unto the third and fourth generation." (KJV)

To visit the iniquity of the fathers means to bring the punishment, or curse, or repetition of the fathers' crimes and depraved actions to rest upon the children. We see this whenever we see a child do what his or her parents always did. We see the bad habits, the unproductive ways of acting, and the peculiar mannerisms of the parents being repeated by the children. In other words, it gets passed from generation to generation. People often say it's in the genes, or it's bad blood, or the apple doesn't fall far from the tree. Sin itself is a very infectious disease. It infected the whole human race (Romans 3:23; 5:12). It infected creation (Romans 8:22) and reached to the very temple of heaven (Hebrews 9:23). The earthly father literally does pass down the curse through the genes in his seed.

Abused children tend to become abusing adults. Many psychological problems pass from parent to child. There is evidence that emotional and spiritual problems can often be traced back to a parent, grandparent, or another ancestor who practiced the occult. Less dramatic are the negative emotional chains forged between husbands and wives, between parents and child, between brothers and sisters. This bondage is expressed in arguing, bickering, etc. Chains are also forged when we become angry and unforgiving towards someone or they become angry and unforgiving towards us. Jeremiah writes, "Our fathers have sinned and are no more, and we have borne their iniquities" (Lamentations 5:7 KJV). He quotes an old saying of the people, "The fathers have eaten a sour grape, and the children's teeth are set on edge." (Jeremiah 31:29 KJV).

Since Jesus came this law of the generations can be broken. Catherine Marshall tells about her experience.[1] She had some personal problems she could not get rid of. The possibility that it might be generational was raised. When she studied, she found that her grandparents had practiced witchcraft. She then had her son pray using the words from Hebrews 4:12, saying that he took the sword of the spirit, which is the word of God, and using it he severed the cords they had been talking about that were binding his mom to her grandparents. She was set free.

Larry Huch[2] tells about his own bondage to the spirit of anger and family curses that had been passed down to him through his family. He tells of his bondage to drugs and the violence of the street and gangs. These were bondages he could not break. They held him prisoner. But they were broken through the power of Jesus' name using the sword of the spirit which is the word of God.

Our growing conditions provided the circumstances that helped shape and mold us into who we are. The good news is that what we did with those growing conditions was our own contribution. That is good news because it means that if our response was unproductive, or even destructive, we can change our response. We can do whatever is necessary to promote growth and health. We do not have to remain the victims of the past, because we can change how we respond to the past.

God has provided the means of grace by which we can be set free from both bad growing conditions and the bad fruits of bad growing conditions. These means of grace work regardless of how we feel or whether we believe they work or not. They work because God's word works, because working is built into the very nature of his words:

> For as the rain cometh down, and the snow from heaven, and returneth not thither, but watereth the earth, and maketh it bring forth and bud, that it may give seed to the sower, and bread to the eater: so shall my word be that goeth forth out of my mouth: it shall not return unto me void, but it shall accomplish that which I please, and it shall prosper in the thing whereto I sent it. (Isaiah 55:10-11 KJV)

Our parents raise us in the best way they know how. Unfortunately, some parents only know how to belittle us just as their parents belittled them. In their own frustrations they may say they wish we'd never been born. They might say they hate us and curse us. A child raised in that environment may give in to it and allow it to form a destructive mindset of bitterness and worthlessness. That is what happened to Dick. I first met Dick at a Camp Farthest Out where we became friends. Dick was a seminary student at the university I attended. After two years of army food I was ready for home cooked meals. Dick and Carolyn agreed to let me eat my meals with them. We both benefited. They got extra spending money. I got to witness a miracle. Through Dick God taught me that in his eyes we are of infinite worth.

The events and circumstances of his childhood had left Dick emotionally crippled. He was unable to receive love or give love. He had suicidal tendencies. He was without hope. That all changed the day Dick received Christ as his Savior. Hope awoke as a light suddenly turned on in a dark room. He knew that in Jesus there was a way out of his darkness into God's marvelous light. His search led him to the Camp Farthest Out where I met him. It had already led him to attend the Seminary at the university where I was in college.

That Fall, back at seminary, Dick read a book that dramatically changed his life. Agnes Sanford, author of *The Healing Light*[3], was a daughter of missionaries and the wife of an Episcopal Priest. She suffered from deep depression. A pastor visited her one day when her baby was sick. He laid his hands on her sick baby and it was instantly healed. Later, in the midst of her depression, the Holy Spirit sent her to that same pastor. With a simple prayer the depression lifted. Agnes was set free. The anointing for healing came upon her and she began a healing ministry that touched countless thousands.

Agnes described a prayer for the healing of the subconscious mind (a part of man's soul). When Dick read about that prayer he immediately wrote to Agnes and asked for an appointment. Agnes wrote back and said that she and her husband conducted a School of Pastoral Care. She invited Dick to come and attend one of the week long schools. Dick went. We waited for his return not knowing that an amazing story awaited us.

When Dick returned, he didn't tell us anything about the school. But, a most fascinating thing happened. His children, Carl and Martha, climbed up onto his lap, and refused to get down. They clung to Dick tenaciously. Dick looked at Martha and asked, "Martha, what do you see in my eyes?" "Love," Martha answered. Then I understood. Dick had never been able to really love his children. Because he hadn't known love as a child he didn't know how to give love. But now a wonderful thing had happened. Dick had been set free so that not only could he receive love he could give love freely and unhindered for the first time. Carl and Martha were hungrily soaking up that love. After Carl and Martha went to bed, Dick told us what had happened.

Agnes had arranged for the chaplain of the Good Samaritan Hospital in Los Angeles to come to Massachusetts for the School of Pastoral Care. At the last minute the chaplain called and said he just couldn't make it. At first Agnes accepted that. But the Holy Spirit worked on her until she called the chaplain back and said, "I don't know why, but you just have to come." The chaplain came. As the week progressed the chaplain kept looking and wondering who the person was for whom God had had him come. During this time, he observed Dick and he said to himself, "If that man doesn't come to me by the end of the week, I'm going to him." The last day of the School came and Dick did go to the chaplain. He told the chaplain about his early home life, the lack of love, his feelings towards his parents, and his suicidal tendencies.

Immediately the Holy Spirit told the chaplain just how to pray for Dick. He led Dick in a prayer of confession of all hate that had built up within him. Then he pronounced Dick forgiven and prayed the prayer of healing the memories. Just one thing remained. Somehow he had to show Dick God's Love. Again, the Holy Spirit told him what to do. He put his arm around Dick and the love of God poured in. In that moment Dick knew that he, too, was a beloved of God. God had brought the Chaplain all the way across the United States, forced schedules to be changed, just for Dick. God loved Dick so much he moved heaven and earth just for Dick.

Dick was special to God, just as you are special to God. God did not go to all that trouble because he had plans for Dick. God did it simply out of love because Dick needed it, and Dick was open to receive it. He remained an architect with a Master of Divinity degree, who had been an air force bomber pilot in World War II. It was the severity of his need that called for that kind of medicine. God tailors our experience of him to match our need. Dick had to see the lengths to which God would go to bring life to him, one of God's beloved children. The shackles of his childhood were blasted open. Dick was finally able to remove each one and toss it aside. It wasn't always easy, but it was now possible.

My story was not dramatic like those above. Mine was self-imposed. While I was in my mother's womb, mom had a vision. She believed God had called me for some special purpose. This belief, mom planted firmly in my mind. My child mind, acting very childishly, did two things. First, it made me believe I was someone special set apart from others. Second, my mind seized on that thought and turned it into an impossible self-expectation of perfection, of acting and being perfect. Those unrealistic expectations created a mess in my child's mind. I've already shared how it turned into a bitter root judgment, which ended up erecting a barrier in my mind between myself, my dad, and God. What troubles has your child-mind caused you?

Believing I was special I also believed I had to be perfect. But no matter how hard I tried, I failed. My self-image was a mess. As a result, I couldn't forgive myself or love myself or believe God loved me or that my father loved me. As I grew up I learned about God, but I didn't know him personally as my God, and my father. I learned about Jesus Christ, but I did not know him as Savior and Lord. Jesus was an ideal to be admired, a pattern to be followed to which I could never attain. My childish bitter root judgment was to blame.

That all started to change in 1950. Jim, a young student pastor, came to our church. He told us about Glenn Clark, author, college professor, coach, and man of prayer. In 1929, on an island farthest out off the coast of Maine, God gave Glenn Clark a dream of groups of people coming apart together for a few days to come into balance spiritually, mentally, and physically. He believed that men and women should become athletes of the spirit. These training camps, he called Camps Farthest Out. In the summer of 1950 Jim took me to a CFO Camp on the shore of Lake Winnipesauke, New Hampshire.

I saw God's love power in action. I saw it in Ruth Robison, a Methodist pastor's wife, whom God healed of a terminal cancer. I saw it in J. Rufus Moseley, a saintly man whose books have become classics on the Spirit filled life. He was equally at home with the President in the White House and the black man on death row. I saw love power in the compassion of Frank Laubach, whom God raised up to develop a simple method to teach illiterates how to read their own language. He taught them that Jesus loves them and wants them to be able to read so that they can live better.

But something was missing. These experiences fed my idealism while reinforcing my feelings of failure because there was no way I could live up to the ideal. One day I went into New York City with some friends to attend a Jack Wyrtzen's Word of Life Rally. At the end of his message, the speaker asked those who wanted to be saved to come forward. I went. It's funny. I had always assumed that I was saved. Hadn't they made me Sunday School Superintendent? But that night I was compelled to go forward. I prayed the sinner's prayer. I asked Jesus to come into my heart as my Lord and Savior.

I thought if I did what I was feeling compelled to do I would feel different. I didn't feel any different. No great load was lifted from my shoulders. No bells rang. No lights flashed. I wasn't bubbling over with new joy like everyone else. So I doubted that anything had happened. Maybe I hadn't really repented. Maybe God had rejected me. Maybe my sins weren't forgiven after all. I was mixed up and disappointed. I'd invited Jesus to come into my heart and I couldn't feel him there.

One of the girls in our group, Louise, went to the counseling room with me.

"Are you saved?" Louise asked.

"I don't know," I confessed. "I don't feel any different."

That answer did not satisfy Louise. She was not about to let me doubt God's Word just because my feelings didn't match up with it.

"What does the Bible say in Romans 10:9, and I John 1:9?" she demanded.

I read:

> If thou shalt confess with thy mouth the Lord Jesus, and shalt believe in thine heart that God hath raised him from the dead, thou shalt be saved. ... If we confess our sins, he is faithful and just to forgive us our sins, and to cleanse us from all unrighteousness. (KJV)

"Did you confess your sins? Did you confess the Lord Jesus with your mouth? Do you believe in your heart that God raised Him from the dead?"

"Yes," I answered to all three questions.

"Well, if God said it, and you believe it, that settles it," Louise said with finality. "Now, are you saved?"

"I don't know. I don't feel saved. I don't feel like Jesus came into my heart. I don't feel anything."

It's a wonder Louise didn't hit me on the head! We had just established the fact that it didn't depend on my feelings, but on God's word. God bless Louise for her persistence! It took a while, but it finally got through my thick skull. Because I had repented, confessed, believed, and received, it was done; regardless of what my feelings said. I had to learn that feelings are fickle and cannot be trusted. I had been ruled by feelings for too long. I had to learn not to trust my feelings until my feelings came into line with the Word of God. If I put my trust in my feelings instead of God's Word, then the moment I felt down or depressed I would have thought I'd lost my salvation!

Do not believe the evidence of your feelings or what your natural eyes see until your feelings and the evidence of your eyes come in line with God's Word. I've noticed that some of the people who exhibit all the feelings produce little or no fruit. I've also noticed people not caught up in feelings and chills up and down the spine produce a mighty harvest of fruit. I was at a Bible Study where the anointing of the Holy Spirit was very strong.

We left with the assignment that each of us would bring at least one new person the next week. When the next week came there were fewer people there than before. The enthusiasm and anointing of the week before had fizzled out. James said, "Faith, if it is not accompanied by corresponding action, is dead" (2:17 Author's paraphrase).

The same can be said of feelings and chills.

CHAPTER 20

THEY BROKE THROUGH

Huckleberry Finn, one of Mark Twain's characters, once said, "what's the use you learning to do right when it's troublesome to do right and ain't no trouble to do wrong, and the wages is just the same?"[1] Change is not easy. It takes much effort. Often frustrated, we ask if it is worth the struggle. Suddenly the idea of stepping out of the old life into a brand new one is not so exciting. It means giving up beliefs once tightly held; the destructive-mindset and bitter root judgments that have been our life's anchor. They are fallow ground; hard, bare, lifeless ground that must be broken up, so that new, life giving nutrients can be worked into it.

Breaking it up forces us to make a quality decision. The decision we have to make is to decide to accept, believe, and act like the Bible is one hundred percent accurate, word for word. That's what I had to do. Paul told Timothy, "Study and be eager and do your utmost to present yourself to God approved (tested by trial), a workman who has no cause to be ashamed, correctly analyzing and accurately dividing <rightly handling and skillfully teaching> the Word of Truth" (2 Timothy 2:15 AMP).

I did it and it worked!

The following two stories are about real people. The first is about Fred. The second is about Starr Daily who shared his story in two books and in numerous talks. Fred's early environment caused him to develop a mindset of rebellion against poverty at whatever the cost. He was born and raised in poverty in New York City. He wanted to be like all the rich folks and not like people in the church he attended who wore ragged clothes. Fred wanted money in his pocket, fine clothes and a nice place to live. He saw only one way to break free.

He stopped going to church and went the way of the streets. He sold booze, ran notes, hustled street women, and card games. He shined shoes for guys in organized crime. He left home at fifteen and had younger kids working for him selling newspapers. He learned all the tricks of making money the easy way. By the time he was twenty-one he was married and owned a gas station with an operational bookie joint in the back. Some days he made as high as $10,000. He was arrested twenty-three times during his criminal career. But he was always able to use money and clever lawyers to keep out of jail. When the FBI got on his trail, he moved to another state. This was his life style until one day he lost his temper one too many times.

There was a guy who was causing him a lot of trouble. This guy was badmouthing him, boasting he was going to kill him, and "ratting" on him to the police. Fred went to this man's apartment with the intention of beating him up. But when the man began running off at the mouth again, Fred killed him. It took a year for the police to build a case against Fred. The jury found him guilty of murder and the judge sentenced Fred to life in prison and an additional ten to fifteen years for running wild. More than once, while Fred was in the prison, the warden declared that after Fred died he was going to keep Fred's body in that cell for fifteen more years until his sentence was finished! The parole board told him, Come back in 2021. During his first year in prison, his wife divorced him.

Prison turned out to be the same lifestyle Fred had known in the streets, but tougher. It all came to a head when a prison uprising broke out. Fred was forced back to his cell by riot guards. There, frustrated and enraged he asked God,

"God, are You for real? I'm tired of killing and trying to be killed."

He picked up a Bible and read from Luke 4:18 where Jesus quoted from Isaiah's prophecy that one was to come who would bind up and heal the brokenhearted, proclaim liberty to the captives, the opening of the prison and the eyes of those who are blind. As Fred read these words his heart melted. He began to cry, and cried for three and a half hours. While he cried, all the anger and bitterness and hatred fell off him and he felt washed clean.

Fred's life changed drastically. He started liking people of all races, even the guards. Then he realized it was because he had started liking himself. He threw out all his pornography, stopped drinking, snorting cocaine and dropping pills of every kind. He was even delivered from his ten cigar a day habit. One day a guest preacher left the pulpit in the prison chapel and headed towards Fred in the back. He placed his hand on Fred's shoulder and said to him,

"Isaiah 61:1 and 2, Fred."

From that time on two things began to happen to Fred. First, God directed him in a program to help Christian ex-convicts make it on the outside. Second, God prepared Fred to make it on the outside himself. One day Fred's lawyer came to see him. He said something about a technicality he was taking before the court to see if he could get Fred out. That is when they overturned Fred's murder conviction. Fred then pled guilty to second-degree murder and was put on ten years' probation. He was freed on January 16, 1981. When his handcuffs were removed that day the last reminders of his imprisonment fell away. A totally free man, he began to do Isaiah 61:1-2,

> The Spirit of the Lord GOD is upon me; because the LORD hath anointed me to preach good tidings unto the meek; he hath sent me to bind up the brokenhearted, to proclaim liberty to the captives, and the opening of the prison to them that are bound; To proclaim the acceptable year of the LORD, and the day of vengeance of our God; to comfort all that mourn (KJV).

Fred had to come to the point where he no longer wanted to live the kind of life into which his antipoverty mindset had locked him. He gave God permission to break up the fallow ground. But he also knew he had to do his part. He took responsibility. He deliberately put his old lifestyle behind him by throwing away those things that been part of it; pornography and drugs. He replaced the destructive mindset with a "Child-of-the-King" mindset. The motto of his new life became; I choose to believe the Word of God. God said it. I believe it. That settles it.

There is a good reason for setting your mind on this motto. Faith demands it. God is always true to his word and we can always depend on him. In human relationships trust in another person is hard to establish and almost impossible to restore. If your parents, a boss, a friend, your mate, your child, or any other person betrays you, it is almost impossible to restore faith in that person. Once wounded, we ask, will they do it again? We don't want to be gullible like Charlie Brown who always believes Lucy when she says that this time she will not take the football away. But she does, and Charlie, once again, falls on his back.

Not so with God. We can trust God always. God does not let us down. He is not a man. What he says he will do, he always does (Numbers 23:19). He sends his word to heal (Psalm 107:20) and values his Word so highly that he magnifies it above his name (Psalm 138:2). God further declares that his Word will accomplish the purpose for which it was spoken (Isaiah 55:11).

Sometimes the negative mindset grips so strongly that a man must go to the end of human endurance before his will cracks and God can melt his frozen heart. Starr Daily spoke with a deep voice and a laugh that was contagious. Love for his audience, with a consuming desire to convey to them how much God loves them, flowed from him. He wanted us to know that love will open our prison doors and set us free, too. He has written his story in two books: *Love Can Open Prison Doors*[2] and *Release*[3].

Starr's mother died in childbirth. His step mother couldn't be bothered to come and hear him recite a four-line poem in front of his third grade classmates and their mothers. He longed to have someone there who could give him a reassuring smile. When it was his turn to recite he began confidently, and immediately forgot a line in the middle. His face turned red with embarrassment. A child giggled. Then everyone laughed, including his teacher who chose to laugh at him instead of supporting him and helping him do it right. It so traumatized him that he turned and ran from the room emotionally wounded.

That event was catastrophic. It launched him into a life of crime as he chose to hate the people who mocked him. He began drinking at age twelve. By his early teens he was a major criminal, well trained by master burglars. His goal was that the deadliest criminal would pay him respect. Prisons, jails, penal farms, chain gangs, the third degree beatings by the police world, did nothing to reform him. He had been in and out of prison so many times he was labeled a hardened criminal. Starr said he started out by hating God and wound up hating everything including his own infallible wisdom. Hating all things sacred and decent, as evidence of his rebel spirit, was the popular thing to do in the circle in which he moved. He said of himself that he was so poor a criminal he carried around with him a whole pack of defeatist's philosophy.

The price he paid for that was to spend the greater part of his time behind iron bars. It all came to a head during Starr's last imprisonment, when the warden accused him of a crime he did not commit. He was thrown into solitary, a small dungeon hole with frosted walls, filthy shirt and pants, and only a slice of bread and water to eat. Weeks later, too weak to move, too weak to will his hatred, he drifted into delirium. One day Jesus came to him and filled him with love in place of all his hate. Those who he had hated, he now loved and they began to respond with love. Then one day a miracle happened. He, who was to never get out, walked out the door free by the grace and mercy of God.

CHAPTER 21

HOMEWORK: TRIMMING THE TREE

James had something to say about the reasons why some prayers are not answered that is well worth listening to. His statement makes it clear that there are rules and laws that govern prayer. We need to follow these rules and laws if we want our prayers answered.

> You do not have, because you do not ask. <Or> you do ask <God for them> and yet fail to receive, because you ask with wrong purpose and evil, selfish motives. Your intention is <when you get what you desire> to spend it in sensual pleasures. You <are like> unfaithful wives <having illicit love affairs with the world and breaking your marriage vow to God>! Do you not know that being the world's friend is being God's enemy? So whoever chooses to be a friend of the world takes his stand as an enemy of God (James 4:2-4 AMP).

James is speaking about motivation. Look at the people, places, and things you've written on your prayer tree. In Isaiah 43:26 God urges us to plead our case before him as a lawyer prepares for and pleads his case before a judge or jury.

> "Put Me in remembrance <remind Me of your merits>; let us plead and argue together. Set forth your case, that you may be justified (proved right)" (AMP).

There is nothing wrong with wanting something just because you want it. Don't fall into the trap of trying to justify it. To want something for the pure pleasure of enjoying it is okay. To want something so that you can indulge in sin is not okay. The reason for being specific about your motivation is to help you in choosing your scriptural authority for asking for it.

When a lawyer prepares for a trial, he researches all his law books to find every law and every precedent and law that applies. Law and precedent help him win his case. Arguing your case means to find every scripture promise that can in any way be applied to your request. It also means to find examples of God's mercy and blessing that prove that he grants our requests because it pleases him to do so. He doesn't bless because we've earned it. He blesses because it is his nature and will to bless. Jesus said so (Matthew 7:11). As a way of reassuring yourself about God's willingness to grant you your desires, let's examine some of the attributes of God as seen in his many names.

His name is YHVH: I Am

God's name for himself, in Hebrew, is YHVH, and comes from the verb HVH with the idea of being or existence. HVH carries these shades of meaning: to be, to exist, to be to, to belong to, to serve for, to be about to do anything. When God told Moses his Name (Ex. 3:14), God wanted us to know that he is everything his name is. That name said some very important things. My name, said God, is YHVH, meaning,

> "I ever shall be the same that I am right now. I am what I am and who I am, and I will be what I will be. I ever shall belong to you the same that I belong to you today. I am for you what you need me to be."

Much more than eternal and unchanging existence is meant by God's name. YHVH means God is for us now and ever will be for us. YHVH means God loved us, loves us now, and ever will love us. YHVH means God will be and will do all that he must be and do to enable us to become all that he created us to be. He created us to be like him, an image of himself.

God revealed different aspects of his nature, his love, and his being for us what we need him to be, by combining his name, YHVH, with key words. These compound names of God are exciting. But more exciting than what God's names reveal about him is the fact that God's name, and all that God is, he was before the foundations of the earth were laid! God did not become YHVH after the fall of man. He has always been what he is. He has always been all that we need:

> Before the mountains were brought forth, or ever thou hadst formed the earth and the world, even from everlasting to everlasting, thou are God (Psa. 90:2 KJV).

> [God] hath chosen us in [Christ] before the foundation of the world...having predestinated us unto the adoption of children by Jesus Christ to himself, according to the good pleasure of his will (Eph. 1:4-5 KJV).

Jehovah-Tsidkenu: Jehovah-Our-Righteousness.

The disobedience of Adam was disastrous. It polluted man so completely that even his most righteous and glorious deeds were worse than rotten scum. It polluted words, words by which God had created, and by which man had named animals. Isaiah writes, "But we all are as an polluted thing, and all our righteousnesses are as a menstrous cloth" (Is. 64:6 KJV).

By his name, Jehovah-Tsidkenu, God wants us to know that he is our righteousness. He has taken upon himself the penalty for our sin. He has provided the blood of the Lamb that cleanses us of all sin. He has paid the price so that we can reign as kings and queens in this life we are now living, with the power to whip Satan up one side and down the other (Romans 5:17).

> For he hath made him to be sin for us, who knew no sin; that we might be made the righteousness of God in him (2 Corinthians 5:21 KJV).

> But of him are ye in Christ Jesus, who of God is made unto us wisdom, righteousness, and sanctification (I Corinthians 1:30 KJV).

Not only has Jehovah-Tsidkenu done that, Paul writes that he has declared us complete in Christ; "For in him dwelleth all the fullness of the Godhead bodily. And ye are complete in him, which is the head of all principality and power" (Colossians 2:9-10 KJV).

Jehovah-M'Kaddesh: Jehovah-Our-Sanctifier.

God called Moses to come up the mountain and God would give him tables of stone, and a law, and commandments with which to teach the people. There were instructions about the ark of the testimony, the table for the showbread, the golden candlestick, the tabernacle, the altar, the clothing of the priests, the consecration of Aaron, the order of sacrifices and offerings. Lastly, God commanded that the Sabbath was to be kept as a sign. It was a sign` between the people and God throughout all generations, that God is Jehovah-M'Kaddesh, Jehovah our sanctifier (Ex. 24-31).

It isn't enough to be declared righteous. That takes away the penalty for the sin but it leaves the sinner unchanged. Jehovah-our-sanctifier also changes the sinner by sanctifying him, that is, recreating his spirit, thus enabling him to separate himself from evil things and evil ways.

> "That ye may know that I am Jehovah-M'Kaddesh [The Lord that doth sanctify you]" (Exodus 31:13 KJV).

> "And the heathern shall know that I am Jehovah-M'Kaddesh [I the Lord Do Sanctify] Israel, when my sanctuary shall be in the midst of them for evermore" (Ezekiel 37:28 KJV).

> But ye are washed, but ye are sanctified, but ye are justified in the name of the Lord Jesus, and by the Spirit of our God (I Corinthians 6:9-11 KJV).

Jehovah-Shalom: Jehovah-Is-Peace.

Gideon built an altar at Ophrah as a reminder of God's word. He named it Jehovah-Shalom, The Lord-is-peace (Judges 6:24). Shalom is God's word to us. It tells us that God's will for us is wholeness, completeness, peace. Shalom is a word that reaches its fulfillment in the gift of the Holy Spirit. When the Holy Spirit is in you and you allow the Holy Spirit to bear his fruit, accomplish his work; you have within you love, joy (gladness), peace, patience (an even temper, forbearance), kindness (benevolence), faithfulness, meekness, humility, gentleness, self-control (self-restraint, continence) (Galatians 5:22-23).

> "And, having made peace through the blood of his cross, by him to reconcile all things to himself; by him, I say, whether they be things in earth, or things in heaven" (Colossians 1:20 KJV).

Jehovah-Shammah: Jehovah-Is-There.

Ezekiel concludes his description of the New Jerusalem by giving the city a new name: Jehovah-Shammah, Jehovah-is-there (Ezekiel 48:35). The knowledge that God is here is central. Ours is not a God who has withdrawn to some distant place where we have to search and shout and cry and try everything we can think of to get his attention. Paul reminds us, "Know ye not that ye are the temple of God, and that the Spirit of God dwelleth in you?" (I Corinthians 3:16 KJV).

Jehovah-Rophe: Jehovah Heals, Restores, Pardons, Comforts.

> If thou wilt diligently harken to the voice of the Lord thy God, and wilt do that which is right in his sight, and wilt give ear to his commandments, and keep all his statutes, I will put none of these diseases upon thee, which I have brought upon the Egyptians: for I am Jehovah-Rophe - the Lord that healeth Thee (Exodus 15:26 KJV).

> But he was wounded for our transgressions, he was bruised for our iniquities: the chastisement of our peace was upon him; and with his stripes we are healed (Isaiah 53:5 KJV).

> Who his own self bare our sins in his own body on the tree that we, being dead to sins, should live unto righteousness: by whose stripes ye were healed (I Peter 2:24 KJV).

> Who forgiveth all thine iniquities; who healeth all thy diseases (Psalm 103:3 KJV).

Jehovah-Jireh: Jehovah's-Provision-Shall-Be-seen.

Surprising as it may seem, Abraham approached the sacrifice of Isaac with great joy and anticipation. He was excited about what God was going to do. He knew that God would either provide (Jireh) an alternate sacrifice, or else raise Isaac from the dead (Romans 4:13-21; Hebrews 11:17-19). It was with this confidence that Abraham assured Isaac, "My son, God will provide (Jireh) himself a lamb for the burnt offering" (Genesis 22:8).

Jehovah-Nissi: Jehovah-My-Banner.

Following the momentous events of their deliverance from Egypt, the parting of the Red Sea, the giving of manna, the water miraculously supplied, Moses led the Israelites south towards Mt. Sinai, following the cloud by day and the pillar of fire by night. They came to the territory of

Amalek in Rephidim. There a great battle ensued. For reasons not given, Amalek chose to attack Israel (Exodus 17:8-16). Amalek shouldn't have done that! He made an enemy of God, and gave God the opportunity to prove to Israel that God is a strong defense:

> With whom My hand shall be established and ever abide; My arm also shall strengthen him. The enemy shall not exact from him or do him violence or outwit him, nor shall the wicked afflict and humble him. I will beat down his foes before his face and smite those who hate him (Psalm 89:21-23 AMP).

Jehovah-Rohi: Jehovah-My-Shepherd.

God would have us know that he is our shepherd. We can trust him. We can place our confidence in him without fear. No one can snatch us out of his hand. He has sent his son to bring us safely home.

> "My sheep hear my voice, and I know them, and they follow me: and I give unto them eternal life; and they shall never perish, neither shall any man pluck them out of my hand. My Father which gave them me, is greater than all; and no man is able to pluck them out of my Father's hand. I and my Father are one." (John 10:27-30 KJV)

Praying the Scriptures

There are many scripture passages that can be converted into prayers. Try using Ephesians 1:17-23 or 3:14-19, and rewrite it putting in your name. Ask God to grant you the things Paul is asking be granted to the Ephesians. Another way of praying the scriptures is to collect scriptures dealing with the topic that concerns you. For example, if you want to pray for your children you might use passages like Jeremiah 1:12; Isaiah 54:13; Isaiah 49:25; 1 Peter 5:7; 2 Timothy 1:12; Ephesians 6:1-3; Deuteronomy 30:19-20; Deuteronomy 28:13, 3, 6; Psalm 91:11, 2; Psalm 3:3; Colossians 3:21; Ephesians 6:4; Proverbs 22:6; Psalm 8:1-2; Psalm 9:2-3; Luke 2:52. To make these passages a prayer, personalize them to fit your situation. If you do not know what scriptures to use, get a book that lists scripture passages by subject.

Do not be afraid of repetition. You can only be blessed by praying the same scripture prayers over yourself hundreds, even thousands, of times. In like manner, those for whom you are praying can only be blessed as you pray the same scripture prayers over them day after day. Words are creative and you are creating good things by your words.

PART D

The Territory of Power

For the weapons of our warfare are not of the flesh but have divine power to destroy strongholds. (2 Corinthians 10:4 ESV)

CHAPTER 22

IN HIS MAJESTY'S SERVICE

Imagine you are on assignment as a new real-life James Bond. You have been given a new arsenal of weapons. What would you do first? Wouldn't you begin by learning all you can about your new weapons? You want to know what each can do. You want to know how to use each weapon. Your life and the success of your mission depend on how well you use your weapons. In true James Bond style, you go out not knowing what tactics the enemy will try to use. You need to be prepared for anything, knowing that your enemy never fights fair.

Even though you aren't James Bond, you actually are a special agent in His Majesty's service. You have been empowered to fight a war against a diabolical enemy named Satan. War is not pleasant. Fighting is not pleasant. Even though you don't want to be in a war, Satan has brought the war to you. It is a war that began ages ago. Your enemy is worse than any enemy James Bond ever faced. However, your weapons are more powerful than any weapons James Bond ever possessed. Knowing your enemy and how he works, and knowing your weapons and how to use them, guarantees your victory over him. (James 4:7)

Keep in mind that you once belonged to Satan, bound to him in servitude. When we chose Jesus, instead of Satan, we automatically became Satan's enemies, equipped by God to be victors in life. We were given the assignment to stop Satan in his tracks and send him fleeing from us. To do this, we were given two very powerful, almost godlike weapons. They are called *authority* and *power*. Paul tells us "For the weapons of our warfare

are not of the flesh but have divine power to destroy strongholds." (2 Corinthians 10:4 ESV)

Possessing these weapons does not mean we know how to use them, any more than having a bicycle means we know how to ride it. Work and learning come first. Work had to be done before we could enjoy the fresh fruits and vegetables from my dad's garden. The ground had to be prepared, seeds planted and weeds removed. Being a little boy who thought he was much bigger than he really was, I wanted to help. My dad would put a spading fork in my hands and tell me to start digging. I wasn't strong enough to push it into the ground. So I'd straddle the handle, stepping on the top of the tines, and wiggle the fork back and forth. Slowly it worked its way into the soil. Slowly the clump of dirt would come loose and I could flip it over. It was a lot of work. But it was the only way to prepare the soil. The seeds were the promise. Preparing the soil, planting, cultivating and weeding it were how we laid claim to the promise and got to enjoy the harvest. There were no short cuts. No fruits and vegetables ever tasted better than the ones I helped grow.

There are no short cuts in learning to use our power and authority. Short cuts end in disaster. Jesus told about two people who built houses. One took a short cut and built on sand. The house collapsed when the storms hit. The other built his house on solid rock and it withstood the fierce storms (Matthew 7:24-27). Our weapons of power and authority must have a good foundation in order to maximize their power. The foundation is the continual confessing of who we are and what we possess in Christ. God told Joshua that if he immersed himself in the Word he would be prosperous and have good success (Joshua 1:8).

Next comes knowledge of the enemy. Before James Bond left on assignment he learned all he could about his enemy. Enemies use our ignorance against us. Satan is our enemy. One of his favorite weapons has become one of his titles. He is called "the great deceiver".

And the great dragon was thrown down, that ancient serpent, who is called the devil and Satan, the deceiver of the whole world—he was thrown down to the earth, and his angels were thrown down with him (Revelation 12:9 ESV).

One of his favorite deceptions is the instant potatoes trap. He tries to convince us that we don't need to study the Bible. He tells us, "You don't need to do anything in order to use your power and authority. It's like instant potatoes, you just add water." If we go out to fight the enemy without adequate preparation, he'll have us running all over looking for a place to hide! Without preparation we will not have authority and power.

There is no such thing as instant faith. Just as piano skills are developed through practice and study, faith is developed through practice and study. Our goal is to always be on top of our game, to always put a guard over the words that escape our mouths. We must affirm daily who we are in Christ and what we possess in Christ. In all the cases of healing in the Gospels in which details are given, Jesus attributes the healing to the recipient's faith, or to the faith of the ones who brought the sick person to Jesus. To get that kind of faith, we must spend time in the Word. If we let our faith slip it won't be there when we need it.

A second trap Satan sets for us is the "unworthy" trap. Can you imagine James Bond, at a critical point, saying "I can't use this weapon. I'm so unworthy. It'll never work for me!" You'd turn the movie off in disgust. Everyone knows the weapons work if you use them the way they were designed to work. Whether or not our authority and power work has nothing to do with whether or not we feel worthy or unworthy. The power is in the weapons. If we have been doing our part to develop our confidence, our knowledge, that is all it takes. At the first hint that we lack faith and confidence, Satan pulls out all the stops to bluff us and get us to turn and run. We must have enough faith, enough trust, in our weapons to use them and stand firm, never wavering.

> Only it must be in faith that he asks with no wavering (no hesitating, no doubting). For the one who wavers (hesitates, doubts) is like the billowing surge out at sea that is blown hither and thither and tossed by the wind" (James I:6 AMP).

A third trap Satan sets is to trick us into neglecting to load our weapons. There is a man side and a God side to every scripture promise. The man side must be done before God can do the God side. Not only must we know what our weapons are and know how to use them, we must have faith in them. Then God acts. God has not sent us into battle alone to succeed or fail. When we go into battle God guarantees we will succeed. Fighting side-by-side with us is a helper, the Holy Spirit. He empowers us to win.

> But you shall receive power (ability, efficiency, and might) when the Holy Spirit has come upon you, and you shall be My witnesses in Jerusalem and all Judea and Samaria and to the ends (the very bounds) of the earth. (Acts 1:8 AMP)

CHAPTER 23

THE WORK OF HELPER POWER

The Holy Spirit is the means whereby God changes us and empowers us. In Joshua 1:8, God wrote the first self-help book ever written. In Acts 1:8, he wrote the second edition! They tell what happened when the Spirit came on Joshua and then on the Church. The Holy Spirit came on Joshua to accomplish the work to which God had called him. In the process, Joshua found his way prosperous and had good success. Prosperity and success were not earned or deserved. They were given as an undeserved blessing. "But thou shalt remember the LORD thy God: for it is he that giveth thee power to get wealth" (Deuteronomy 8:17-18 KJV).

We can't change who we are by our own will power. Who we are is determined by our genes, the influences of our environment, and our mindset. No amount of effort on our part can change our genes. Only with extreme effort can we overcome the grip of our environment and our mindset. Even then, we are not fully free from them. But the Holy Spirit can set us free! The Holy Spirit comes upon us as an enabler when we allow it and are willing to obey his guidance. Paul tells us to "Work out your own salvation with fear and trembling, for it is God who works in you, both to will and to work for his good pleasure." (Philippians 2:12, 13 ESV)

We see an example of this enabling power of the Holy Spirit at work in the life of an Old Testament man named Saul. No matter from what side you looked at him, Saul was not kingly material. He did not have charisma. He did not have wisdom. He was not smart enough. He did not have a following. But he was tall and well built. Still, those who knew him would never have imagined him as a king. The people had been clamoring for a king "like all the other nations have." Finally, God said, "Okay, they want a king, I'll turn Saul into a king."

The kind of transformation required to turn Saul into a king would leave no doubt in anyone's mind but that God had done a major piece of work! This worked to Saul's advantage. With a change so dramatic, no one would question the fact that he was now a powerful king. God began the process. God called his prophet Samuel, saying, "Samuel, I've got a job for you."

> "Tomorrow about this time I will send you a man from the land of Benjamin, and you shall anoint him to be leader over My people Israel; and he shall save them out of the hand of the Philistines." (I Samuel 9:16 KJV)

Meanwhile, Saul's father's donkeys had wandered off and were lost. He asked Saul to take a servant and go look for them. Saul looked in all the likely places but couldn't find them. He was ready to give up when his servant reminded him that the prophet Samuel lived nearby. Maybe Samuel would know where the donkeys were.

Samuel was not impressed when he saw Saul. He was sure God had made a mistake. Nevertheless, he related God's message to Saul. Saul responded with surprise. He knew himself well enough to know that it would take some doing if God was going to make it happen. So he asked the logical questions such an announcement would raise.

> "Am I not a Benjamite, of the smallest of the tribes of Israel? And my family the least of all the families of the tribe of Benjamin? Wherefore then speakest thou so to me?" (I Samuel 9:21 KJV)

Samuel answered by telling Saul that this was God's idea, and then explained how God would equip him to do the job.

> THEN SAMUEL took the vial of oil and poured it on Saul's head and kissed him and said, "Has not the Lord anointed you to be prince over His heritage Israel? ... The Spirit of the Lord will come upon you mightily . . . and you will be turned into another man." ... And when <Saul> had turned his back to leave Samuel, God gave him another heart, and all these signs came to pass that day. (I Samuel 9:16, 21, 10:1, 6 AMP)

Saul was transformed and empowered by the Holy Spirit. Evidence of this was seen when Saul began doing what only the prophets could do; speak in an ecstatic language. His expression changed from common to kingly. But underneath it all, he was still Saul. Samuel instructed him that if he wanted God's promises to him to be fulfilled he had to obey God. Unfortunately, Saul being Saul, chose to rely on his own wisdom rather than obey God and God's prophet. His rebellion caused the kingship to depart from his house (I Samuel 15:3-23). When God anoints and empowers us, he does not turn us into robots. He does not take away our free will. It is up to us, as it was up to Saul, to choose to obey or disobey.

King Saul was a light bulb with a poor connection. A bulb burns brightly only as long as it is connected to the power source. Remove the power source and the light goes out. Weaken the connection to the power source and the bulb burns dimly or flickers. Saul made the mistake of thinking he was a self-contained power source. Forgetting that he was nothing without that connection to God, he almost severed the connection.

Up until the day of Pentecost, the equipping power of the Holy Spirit was only poured out on a select few. That changed on the Day of Pentecost. On Pentecost it was poured out first on the one hundred and twenty who were praying in an upper room, and then on everyone who was added to the church. Its coming was dramatic. It came as a mighty wind and flames of fire settling on their heads. They began to speak in other languages as the Spirit gave them utterance. Like Saul, each of the one hundred and twenty was turned into another man, given power, ability, efficiency and might they had not possessed before. Each was the same person, and yet a new person. A formally scared Peter suddenly declared the Good News fearlessly, boldly.

Since the Day of Pentecost, the Holy Spirit has been poured out on all believers. When you are born again the first step in your transformation begins. You get a recreated human spirit and the Spirit of God dwells in you permanently. That is not the same as what was happening to the one hundred and twenty. When you are born again it is like drinking a glass of water. Whereas the one hundred and twenty jumped into an ocean! Throughout the New Testament, we find all the new Christians jumping into the water of the Holy Spirit baptism. Speaking in tongues quickly became the evidence of the baptism.

Today many ask if speaking in tongues is necessary. Here are three possible answers. First, James talks about the power of the tongue, comparing it to a ship's rudder and to a fire originating in hell! Perhaps surrendering the control of the tongue to the Holy Spirit is the ultimate surrender of ourselves to God. We put our trust in God that, once we let him be in control of our mouths, what comes out will be all good.

A second reason is given by Paul in I Corinthians 14. Faced with the insurmountable task of trying to change ourselves, Paul has exciting news for us. He tells us that praying in an unknown language is a means for building ourselves up. We allow the Holy Spirit to do for us what we can't do for ourselves. In fact, the Holy Spirit intercedes for us because we don't know how to pray for ourselves (Romans 8:26).

A third reason might be that God needs the use of our voices to enable him to accomplish his will in the earth. It is a matter of Law. Satan, the God of this world and the prince of the power of the air, is not going to give God permission to speak words of power. Legally, God has to speak his will through us and work through us. John Wesley remarked, "God does nothing but by prayer, and everything with it." Acts 4:24–33 gives a prayer prayed in unison by the disciples. The request they made suggests that it was this prayer that enabled God to turn loose great power on the disciples and begin the conversion of the world.

As important as speaking in tongues is, it is not something you have to do. It is something you get to do, something you are expected to do, and something that has tremendous benefits for you. You need the baptism if you want the power. I chose to speak in tongues because I wanted those benefits. I also wanted the bells and whistles, even ecstasy, like some people seemed to experience. I got none of that. All I got was two words that continued to echo in my mind: *trust* and *believe.* I was frustrated when it did not happen to me like I wanted it to happen. Frustrated, I began speaking what I called gibberish, just as a child speaks make-believe words. That is what it sounded like to me, make believe words.

It did no good to ask God about it. All he said was "Trust me." Well, I reasoned, God did promise that "he who asks, receives." I knew God wasn't a liar. Logically, that meant that when I asked for it, I got it. My gibberish solution was to pray, "Holy Spirit, I don't know if this is just gibberish or if it's real. But I command you in the Name of Jesus to turn it into a prayer language, and intercede through me, for me. Build me up like Paul said it will do." To this I added, "God, if you're not a liar, you've got to deliver."

One day I had a long drive. I decided to put this tongue speaking to the test. I spoke the gibberish sounding words for several hours. When I finished, all I felt was exhausted and hoarse. Even though I felt nothing, something had happened! That day marked the beginning of major spiritual breakthroughs in the churches I was pastoring. It was such an abrupt change I could trace it back to that day. The Holy Spirit had indeed interceded on my behalf! God was teaching me to trust regardless of whether I had "feelings" or not. We must take God at his word. Ours must be the attitude of "God said it. I believe it. That settles it."

That encouraged me to keep doing what I was doing and trusting God. But what I wanted didn't stop there. I wanted a road map for my life and all the decisions I would have to make. Like most people, I didn't get one. What I got was an understanding. In my own experience guidance has almost always come in the form of a growing conviction that I should do this or that or the other thing. After high school, I worked in a factory for a year. I listened to the other men talk. I considered the possibilities for advancement and became more convinced than ever that I needed to go to college.

Besides, my high school history teacher told me that if I didn't go to college right out of high school, I never would. That made me mad. I was determined to prove him wrong. By means of these little nudges, God moved me along although I didn't have the slightest clue that he was doing so. Psalm 27:4, 5 helps us see how God guides when we don't know he is guiding.

> Delight yourself also in the Lord, and He will give you the desires and secret petitions of your heart. Commit your way to the Lord <roll and repose each care of your load on Him>; trust (lean on, rely on, and be confident) also in Him and He will bring it to pass. (AMP)

Becoming a pastor was not a desire of my heart! But God had other plans. A friend talked me into teaching a Sunday school class. Then he insisted I could earn extra money by preaching at a little country church where he had preached when he was in college. He kept pestering me to do it until I did. All I had to do was come up with a sermon each Sunday. I did love to talk even when I didn't know what I was talking about! But the deal included eating dinner at Mrs. Linn's before the drive back to college. I did not know that this was God's doing. God had caught me in his trap! God set me up! He won me over into doing the very thing I had said I didn't want to do; become a pastor.

At the University of Iowa, I had become friends with Bill and Bob. Bill's dad was in the hospital. I volunteered to take him to visit his dad. Bob went with us but wanted to stop first at his sister Helen's dorm to see his parents, who had come to visit. For some reason, Helen, who I had never met, did something that day that she had never done before. While shopping, she saw a little gift she thought her mother would like and bought it. While I was sitting with Bob and his family, Helen gave the gift to her mother. When her mother asked why, Helen answered, "Because I love you." I have no explanation why that one little act grabbed me like it did. But instantly I was hooked on this girl who would one day become my wife. God had set me up!

The above illustrations show how Holy Spirit guidance for me has come in small steps of which I was unaware. Only in looking back could I see the pattern. Your experience will be different. In time, I learned that words would rise up from deep within my mind. I wasn't sure what to do with them, but I had vowed that I would do whatever God told me to do. That meant I had to find a way to test the word to be sure it was from God. The increase/decrease prayer has always worked best for me. I would pray,

"Father, if this is of you, please increase my desire to do it. If it is not of you, please decrease my desire to do it." Then I wait to see what happens.

God never explains to me what he is doing. My job is to obey and watch. For example, in one church I was serving, the people always came forward in groups, kneeling at the railing to receive communion. One day the thought came: "Pray for each individual with laying on of hands." For me that was a scary thing to do. I had to wrestle with the idea before I agreed to do it. That Sunday as I stood before each person, I listened and then spoke whatever words came to mind. I heard myself say things I hadn't planned to say and wondered if I was out of my mind doing this. I had no choice but to trust God. Later, much to my amazement, many people told me that God had spoken to them and it was the guidance, or confirmation, or inspiration received in their blessing that they needed! They wondered how I could have known. God had let me be a part of what he was doing.

As you become more and more conformed to the image of Jesus, your faith grows. We are to do as Jesus did and follow the leading of the Holy Spirit. What Jesus saw the father doing, he did. We also are to do what we see the father doing. Jesus came that he might destroy the works of the devil (I John 3:8). That is now our mission. Jesus is the firstborn of many brethern and you and I are counted among the many (Romans 8:29; John 1:12). God created you for glory (Isaiah 43:7). He chose you in Christ before the foundation of the world (Ephesians 1:4; Revelation 13:8, 17:8). He loves you just as much as he loves Jesus (John 17:23).

The same Spirit, the same power by which God spoke worlds into being by a word, and raised Jesus from the dead, now dwells in you (Mark 11:23; Romans 8:11). To aid you, the Father has sent the Holy Spirit into whom you can be baptised if you ask (John 14:26). When you confessed your faith in Christ Jesus,9,,,,,,,,, you were given a recreated human spirit (I Corinthians 6:19). This baptism, as pictured in Acts 1:8, is for empowerment.

> His intention was the perfecting and the full equipping of the saints (His consecrated people), <that they should do> the work of ministering toward building up Christ's body (the church) (Ephesians 4:12 AMP).

Here is a list of some qualities you will be exhibiting as a brother or sister of Jesus when you release the Holy Spirit to work in you.

1. As God creates by the word of his mouth, so too, your words have creative power.
2. As God is love, you are to be love.
3. As God is perfection, you are to be perfection.
4. As God is joy, you are to be joy.
5. As God is abundant life, you are to be abundant life.
6. As God is light, you are to be light.
7. As God is goodness, you are to be goodness.
8. As God is Jesus, you are to be as Jesus is.

CHAPTER 24

Don't Deceive Yourself

Boy! Did I know how to throw a good tantrum! I would lay down on the floor, howl, and scream. It never worked. I was trying to get my own way. I wanted to do what I wanted to do. I wanted to have what I wanted to have. Every time my, mother let me have it -- a bucket of cold water in my face! In later years I tried other tactics, like sulking, grouching, and bellyaching. They never worked either.

As a child, I was acting out the idea that I am the master of my fate, I'm the rugged individualist who does it his way. Civilization applauds rugged individualism and the self-made person. We applaud because those people have initiative. If you don't have the initiative to achieve anything, you never will. The way of the tantrum is not showing initiative.

The attitude of "wanting to do everything my way" can lead to great danger. The danger is self-deception. God created us with a free will, meaning we have the ability to make choices. We want to be our own gods; in control of our own lives, making our own choices, relying on our own wisdom. Self-deception comes when we ignore God and think we can do it better without him. The extreme of this is seen in study courses designed to teach us how to become an "Ascended Master". These courses teach the belief that we don't need God because we are gods.

Initiative is good. It is absolutely necessary in acquiring God's best for our lives. God's plans are the best. When the Hebrew people were captured and taken captive to Babylon, God told them he would bless them there: "For I know the plans I have for you, declares the LORD, plans for wholeness and not for evil, to give you a future and a hope" (Jeremiah 29:11 ESV). That promise applies to us. He holds good in his hands, waiting for us to take it. To possess it and make it truly ours, we must exercise our wills, our initiative, and reach out and take the good he offers. Jesus put it this way:

> "Keep on asking and it will be given you; keep on seeking and you will find; keep on knocking <reverently> and <the door> will be opened to you. For everyone who keeps on asking receives; and he who keeps on seeking finds; and to him who keeps on knocking, <the door> will be opened." (Matthew 7:7-8 AMP)

God's plans for us do not violate our free will. God is saying that as our creator he knows us better than we know ourselves. He knows how we can best achieve our heart's desires. When we ask Jesus to teach us, when we submit our wills to his, when we seek his guidance, we learn how to pray and how to use the power and authority that are ours as children of God.

Satan knows this. That is why he encourages self-deception. That is why he lies and says we don't need any other god than ourselves. He tells us that if we follow his occult teachings, we will become ascended masters just like Jesus. He does not want us to find out who we are in Christ and what we possess in Christ, and for good reason. Jesus has already turned us into ascended masters. Paul explains:

> But God, being rich in mercy, because of the great love with which he loved us, even when we were dead in our trespasses, made us alive together with Christ—by grace you have been saved—and raised us up with him and seated us with him in the heavenly places in Christ Jesus, (Ephesians 2:4-6 ESV).

We have been raised up with Jesus. We are seated in the place of power with Jesus. We had nothing to do with it. We couldn't earn it. We couldn't study, go through physical or mental disciplines, to achieve it. In fact, it is utterly impossible for us to achieve it on our own by any means whatsoever. It is God's free gift.

> For it is by free grace (God's unmerited favor) that you are saved (delivered from judgment and made partakers of Christ's salvation) through <your> faith. And this <salvation> is not of yourselves <of your own doing, it came not through your own striving>, but it is the gift of God; Not because of works <not the fulfillment of the Law's demands>, lest any man should boast. <It is not the result of what anyone can possibly do, so no one can pride himself in it or take glory to himself.> (Ephesians 2:8-9 AMP)

Satan does not want you to know what being seated with Jesus means. For one thing, it means we are seated with Jesus in the place of power; God's right hand. It also means that what God has put under Jesus' feet is also under our feet. "And He has put all things under His feet and has appointed Him the universal and supreme Head of the church… (Ephesians 1:22 AMP). Satan is under our feet.

Satan does not want us to know or believe that he is under our feet. He relies on our laziness, our reluctance to study God's Word. He works hard to keep us ignorant of the power and authority we possess. His demons constantly attack us. But, when we practice walking in newness of life, covered by the Blood of Jesus, that covering is an impenetrable shield covering us. All we have to do is resist; "Resist the devil <stand firm against him>, and he will flee from you." (James 4:7 AMP)

A lot of the suffering we endure could be prevented by using our authority. Satan attacks us in three areas. These are spirit, soul, and body. Man is a spirit, who has a soul, and lives in a body (I Thessalonians 5:23 KJV). When we are born again our human spirit is recreated by the Holy Spirit (John 3:5; 2 Corinthians 5:17). The new life flowing from our recreated human spirit begins to impact our soul and body, bringing wholeness to the mind (soul) and body. This coming to wholeness, or healing, does not happen without our help. Paul tells us to bring the body under subjection (I Corinthians 9:27), and to be transformed by renewing the mind (Romans 12:2). We are, as Paul instructs us, to work out our own salvation with fear and trembling "For it is God which worketh in you both to will and to do of his good pleasure" (Philippians 2:12 KJV).

God is at work in us, both to will and to do. Just as a car cannot change directions unless it is moving, if you want God to direct you, keep moving! If it is your desire to be guided by God, and if you have given him permission to bring about his will in your life, he will. You will discover his hand at work when you look backward with hindsight, and as you move forward in trust.

CHAPTER 25

Walking Like Giants

Satan gave us a misleading cliché. We use it with abandon and ignorance. It is that God can do anything. That is not true. God cannot do anything. Why? Because it would break the law. On a cosmic scale, all the laws of how things work are never changing. The universe is based on law and order. Two molecules of hydrogen and one molecule of oxygen will always make water.

Adam's lease was a legal document in effect for 6,000 years. God could not alter, cancel, or change its terms while the lease was in effect. It was the law. If God started breaking his own laws, all that he had created would disintegrate into nothing. That is why Satan knew that if he could steal the lease, the earth would be his for 6,000 years and Adam's race would be his slaves. Using deceit, Satan stole the lease, gained control of the earth, and enslaved Adam's race.

Unknown to Satan, God had embedded in the fine print of the lease, clauses that would instantly go into effect if Adam lost the lease. It was then, Satan discovered that God had a plan. That plan was bad news for Satan. Furious, he began to spread his deception that said God can do anything. Why? To try to turn us into unbelievers. If Satan can trick us into believing God can do anything but won't, or plays favorites, we'll get disillusioned. We'll get angry. Instead of a God of love, all we'll see is a God of wrath who is unfair.

If we're disillusioned, two things happen. First, we want nothing to do with God. Second, we rebel. We refuse to pray. Our love for him turns to hate and distrust. This deception causes people to blame God for all the evil Satan himself is generating. We blame God for storms, earthquakes, hurricanes, tornadoes, and sickness. Insurance companies label natural disasters as acts of God instead of acts of Satan.

The lease Satan held in his hands was full of loopholes. It gave God the legal right to intervene in the behalf of any individual, or nation that called upon his name. It must have been a black day indeed, when Satan heard Jesus tell his disciples,

> "Behold, I give unto you power to tread on serpents and scorpions, and over all the power of the enemy: and nothing shall by any means hurt you" (Luke 10:19 KJV).

In one of his letters John explains why God sent Jesus into our world:

> For this purpose the Son of God was manifested, that he might destroy the works of the devil (I John 3:8 KJV).

In I Corinthians 2:8, Paul notes how ignorant Satan and his fellow rebels were. For, if they had known that Jesus' death would redeem the human race, they would not have crucified the Son of Glory. Satan mistakenly thought that by killing Jesus he had ended God's redemption plans. He didn't realize that killing Jesus would complete it!

Another reason God cannot do everything is because we are in a partnership with God. God will not do for us what we have been told to do, and been given the power and authority to do. For example, we cannot pray, "God save so and so," because he already has. What is needed now are laborers to reap the harvest (Luke 10:2). That is what we need to pray for, realizing that we may be one of the harvesters. This is true for all matters where authority has been put in our hands: (Luke 10:19, 21; Mark 16:17-18). Tornadoes, hurricanes, and unusual weather patterns are all under Satan's control (Ephesians 2:2). Jesus only took authority over the storms that threatened to swamp their boat (Mark 4:39). He scolded the disciples for not doing it because they had the authority to calm storms that threatened them. He gave us the authority to speak to our storms.

We can tell the tornado, "in Jesus' name, pass over us and do not put so much as a shingle out of place." We can tell a hurricane "No, in Jesus' name, you're not coming in here." By the same token, we can ask the rain to come and water our crops. Isaiah commanded the rain to cease for three and a half years over an entire nation. He was speaking for God (a man had to speak it out) to discipline God's chosen people (I Kings 17). Since Jesus only took control over weather that directly threatened them, we can conclude that that is how to use that authority. A lady in one of the churches I pastored caught this truth, and commanded the rain to fall on her farm. It did. It fell on her farm and on no one else's!

While it would be fun to walk through a hospital and heal everyone, it will never happen. Why? Mark records the reason when he tells what happened in Jesus' home town. Mark says Jesus could do few mighty works there because of their unbelief (6:5). People are not automatically healed just because you pray for them. Something else is needed. That something is faith to be healed.

The presence of faith on the part of the Syrophenician woman made it possible for the Syrophenician woman's daughter to be healed (Mark 7:26-30) and the Centurion's servant to be healed (Matthew 8:5-13). Over and over again, Jesus said to the one being healed, according to your faith be it unto you (Matthew 8:10; 9:2, 22; 9:29; 15:28).

Just imagine that it is a very hot day. Someone asks if would you like a hot fudge sundae? Immediately you begin to picture it! A great big scoop of French vanilla ice cream topped with gobs of hot fudge, finished off with nuts, a giant mound of whipped cream, and a big red cherry on top. Can you imagine how delicious it will taste, with the cool ice cream and the oh-so-good hot fudge? Doesn't it make your mouth water just to think of it? That sundae wouldn't taste half so good if you didn't eat it first in your imagination. Mouthwatering anticipation makes it taste ever so much better.

It's exactly the same with healing. In prayer, mouthwatering anticipation has another name. It's called day dreaming. Don't confuse this with wild flights of fancy, such as dreaming of going to Mars. What are your real day dreams? What dreams are you hoping, with all your heart, will come true?

Mark relates the story of a man who dreamed a dream, and made that dream come true. I don't know the dreamer's name. Everyone called him

Tim's son. I don't know what happened, maybe sickness or an accident. But Tim's son had lost his sight. There were no schools for the blind. No welfare programs. No job training. Life was hopeless, the future bleak. Tim's son would never see a sunrise nor the breathtaking colors in a sunset. He would never look upon the face of a loved one or see joy in children's eyes. His life was a begging cup, and coins from strangers.

One day, while he was sitting in his begging spot, Tim's son heard strange stories about a teacher. A teacher who taught with the ring of authority, whose reputation spread like wildfire. It was said that the teacher healed great numbers of people who were suffering from all kinds of disease. It was said that wherever he went, in villages, towns, or farms, they laid down their sick right in the roadway and begged him that they might just touch the edge of his cloak. And all those who touched him were healed.

Tim's son began to dream. The more he dreamed, the more he lived and breathed and ate his dream. He visualized every detail. He dreamed of the teacher coming. He saw the teacher passing by where he was sitting. He saw the teacher stop. Heard the teacher call for him. Saw himself seeing. One day, a great crowd came strolling past. There was laughter, shouts of joy, and people praising God. "What is it? What's happening?" Tim's son asked. "Jesus is passing by!" they told him. The teacher had come. Immediately Tim's son shouted out,

> "Jesus, Son of David, have pity on me!"
>
> Many people tried to push him aside and told him to shut up. But Tim's son shouted all the more, "Son of David, have pity on me!"
>
> Jesus stood quite still and said, "Call him here." So they called the blind man, saying, "It's all right now; get up, he's calling you!" At this Tim's son threw off his coat, jumped to his feet and came to Jesus.
>
> "What do you want me to do for you?" Jesus asked him.

> "Oh, Master, let me see again!"
>
> "Go on your way then," returned Jesus, "your faith has healed you." (Author's paraphrase of Mark 10:46-52)

Tim's son recovered his sight at once. His dream had come true. Not by chance. Not by luck. Not by fate. But because he had dared to dream, and dared to answer three questions that set his dream free to come to pass. The first question he answered was: What do you want Jesus to do for you? (What is your soul's sincere desire?) Tim's son knew exactly what he wanted: "Oh, Master, let me see again!" That desire, that dream, was a pure dream. It was true to his nature. Tim's son discovered that it was as the Psalmist wrote: "I will give you the desires of your heart." (Psalm 37:4 Author's paraphrase)

The second question Tim's son had to answer was: "What is hindering you?" Is there anything standing between you and the answer to your prayer? There might be a block you never expected. Tim's son had to face fear. He had to face losing the security of a beggar. He had learned to live with blindness. He was poor, but there was security in knowing that by begging he would always have food, clothes to wear, and a place to sleep. If Tim's son could see, he would lose that security. He would lose the pity of family who met his basic needs. He'd have to get a job and earn a living. All he knew was begging. Who would hire a man with no job skills? It's scary to go into an unknown future with no security. Many give up their dreams because they are too afraid. Tim's son chose to give up fear and security in order to see again. He chose to follow Jesus into the future that God had for him.

The third question Tim's son had to answer was: "What is your point of contact?" A point of contact is something that enables you to release your faith. Tim's son knew what his point of contact would be. He had rehearsed it over and over in his mind. Maybe he couldn't see to get up and go to Jesus, but Jesus could see him. He made seeing his point of contact. He thought, "If Jesus sees me, and calls for me, I know I'm going to see again." It was just the right sort of point of contact for a blind person.

Tim's son also knew that sitting passively by would not get the job done. Having settled on his point of contact he acted almost ferociously.

How different the story would have been if he had sat there with his fingers crossed, saying, "I hope he sees me. I hope he sees me. Oh God, make him see me." Not only would the story be different, there wouldn't have been a story! Once Tim's son knew what his point of contact was, he went after it with everything he had. Tim's son teaches us three questions of prayer: What do you want Jesus to do for you? What is hindering you? What is your point of contact?

You might be tempted to say, that was then, this is now. Jesus has ascended into heaven. He's not coming by anymore. That may be true, but it is also un-true. Jesus may have gone, but the power to heal is still here. Before Jesus ascended into heaven, he gave believers the authority to use his name. We are about to see how much power is in Jesus' name.

It was a warm day in early summer. During the past few weeks there had been lots of excitement, celebrations, and feasting. It all centered about the old historic church. Visitors had come from far away. Many were still in town. Visitors often came with extra money to spend. Souvenir vendors, anxious to help them spend it, could be seen everywhere.

There were some other people who could also be seen. They were the kind of people the city fathers and the tourist bureau wished they could hide. These were the crippled, the blind, and the beggars. They always seemed to sit in the path where the visitors had to pass.

Two young men, Rock Johnson and his cousin, John, had been in the city for several weeks. They had been staying with friends, taking in all of the excitement, even being part of it. It was about three in the afternoon on this summer day and one of the important daily events was about to take place at the church. Rock and John were going. They made their way along the crowded streets, dodging donkeys and peddlers hawking their goods. They stepped over and around the beggars.

They arrived at the entrance and were just about to go in when something caught their attention. It was a cripple, a beggar. Something about the man was different. A chill ran up and down their backs. The beggar asked for money. Rock and John stopped and looked at the man. Rock spoke.

"Look at us!"

> The cripple looked. Hope and expectation were on his face. Perhaps these two, out of all the rest, would be generous. Perhaps tonight there would be food on the table.
>
> "I don't have any money," said Rock.
>
> Hope and expectation faded from the cripple's face. Were these two going to ridicule him? Give him a lecture about not blocking the public entrance?
>
> "But I do have something to give you," Rock added.
>
> Hope came back into the cripple's face. Then the most unexpected, the most wonderful, the most glorious thing imaginable happened! Rock reached out, took the cripple's right hand, and said, "In the name of Jesus Christ of Nazareth, rise up and walk."
>
> Instantly his feet and ankle bones grew strong. He leaped up, stood, walked. And walking and leaping and praising God, he entered the church with Rock and John. Immediately the people began to crowd around. "What happened?" they wanted to know. "Hey, don't look at us!" Rock exclaimed. "There's nothing special about us. But I'll tell you who is special. It's Jesus! And I'll tell you what made this man strong. It's faith in the name of Jesus. It's by the name of Jesus that this man stands here before you whole." (Author's paraphrase of Acts 3:1-16)

The name of Jesus? Suddenly something new had come. They had proclaimed baptism in the name of Jesus. Now the disciples were declaring that not only was there salvation in no other name, there was power to heal in the name of Jesus. We have been given authority to use that name. By the power of that name, signs and wonders are being wrought today, even as they were then. In one sense, the name of Jesus is like the ring of power in J.R.R. Tolkien's story of *The Lord of the Rings*[1]. The power is resident in the ring, not in the wearer. However, the ring of power doesn't automatically work just because you've got the ring. In Tolkien's story, Gandalf the wizard explains that it takes practice and time to learn how to control the ring.

In a sense, that is true with the name of Jesus. The name of Jesus is not a magic word. It is a word of authority, a power of attorney. If I have been sent to another country as an ambassador, I can only do what I've been assigned and authorized to do. If my country is a dominant power in the world, my authority will have that power behind it when I use it. When I use the name of Jesus, I must be absolutely convinced of the power and authority behind that name. My power and authority to use the name of Jesus is defined and described in the scriptures. The Scriptures are quite explicit on how to use the name of Jesus. To know intellectually is not enough. I can read every book that has been written about flying an airplane, but that doesn't make me a pilot.

The name of Jesus operates by faith. Faith is not intellectual assent. Faith is a firm persuasion, a conviction, based on hearing. Faith is a way of life, a way of living. It saturates your whole being. It resides in your heart. This is accomplished by saturating your mind with more faith based thoughts than worldly based thoughts. How many hours a day do you spend filling your mind with the garbage of TV, newspapers, novels, gossip, secular music, etc.?

> Finally, brothers, whatever is true, whatever is honorable, whatever is just, whatever is pure, whatever is lovely, whatever is commendable, if there is any excellence, if there is anything worthy of praise, think about these things. (Philippians 4:8 ESV)

Probably the most effective method for transforming head knowledge into heart knowledge is to confess the word. An excellent technique is to personalize the power promises. For example, Jesus promises in Matthew 18:18, "Whatsoever ye shall bind on earth shall be bound in heaven: and whatsoever ye shall loose on earth shall be loosed in heaven" (KJV).

Rewritten as a confession of faith, it might go like this: "Jesus has given me the power of attorney to use his name and all the authority and power behind his name. That which I bind on earth is bound in heaven. That which I loose on earth is loosed in heaven. In the name of the Lord Jesus I bind the principalities, the powers, the rulers of the darkness of this world and render them powerless and ineffective against me."

Learn to use, not misuse, the creative power of words. Proverbs 6:2, tells us: "Thou art snared [trapped] with the words of thy mouth, thou art taken with the words of thy mouth" (KJV).

This reminds us of the power of our words. This fact is emphasized again in Proverbs chapter 18 verse 21: "Death and life are in the power of the tongue: and they that love it shall eat the fruit thereof" (KJV). Peter reminds us that it was by the spoken word of God that the heavens and the earth came into being, and are sustained (2 Peter 3:5-7). Many Christians fail to realize the power of their tongues.

Over the years I've found most people could tell me all about their diseases. My disease this and my disease that. Some knew more about their diseases than the doctor did. They could tell me exactly how the disease would progress. But not one word could they tell me about who and what they are in Christ, or about what the word says about their authority and rights as children of God. Consequently, all day long they confessed the negative and got the negative.

A friend was hospitalized in Sioux City, Iowa. While there, her roommate, a young nursing student, told her how the name of Jesus had protected her. The young nurse was in her home. It was a warm day and she had the window open with the screen locked in place. Her door was locked. She went into her bathroom to take a shower. While she was taking her shower, a man broke through the screen, unlocked the door, and came in. He went into her bathroom with the intention of raping her. This was a young woman who had been learning about the authority she had to use the name of Jesus. She was beginning to understand who she was in Christ and what she possessed in Christ.

When she became aware of the presence of the rapist, her immediate response was to use the name of Jesus against him, against the evil that was driving him. In the name of Jesus, she commanded him to put his clothes back on. In the name of Jesus, she marched him back into the living room where she called the police. So overcome by the power of that name was the rapist that he repaired the screen he had broken, while he waited for the police. What a difference the name of Jesus makes! Imagine the impact that name had on the rapist. Imagine the excitement that would be stirred up at the supermarket, or at the mall, if you were to reach down like Peter and John and say to the cripple, "Silver and gold have I none; but such as I have give I thee: In the Name of Jesus Christ of Nazareth rise up and walk" (Acts 3:6 KJV). Imagine the impact as you exclaim to the bystanders: It is through faith in the name of Jesus that this man has been made strong and perfectly sound.

CHAPTER 26

The Blessings of Dreaming Large

Glenn Clark, founder of the Camps Farthest Out and author of many books on prayer, urged us to dream large[1]. Faith is a prerequisite for all prayer. Without faith it is impossible to please God (Hebrews 11:6). Once you understand that God is for you, and you place your faith in him, you also begin to discover that his dreams for you are greater than your own dreams. Jesus said, "I came that they may have and enjoy life, and have it in abundance (to the full, till it overflows)" (John 10:10 AMP). Paul wrote, "With God on our side like this, how can we lose?" (Romans 8:31 MSG).

Couple those thoughts with these.

> Thus says the Lord, Who makes a way through the sea and a path through the mighty waters … "I will even make a way in the wilderness and rivers in the desert" (Isaiah 43:16, 19 AMP).

> Lean on, trust in, and be confident in the Lord with all your heart and mind and do not rely on your own insight or understanding. In all your ways know, recognize, and acknowledge Him, and He will direct and make straight and plain your paths. (Proverbs 3:5-6 NIV)

We start out believing those words and confessing them. But I'm not sure we know what we are doing. That is because those promises are future oriented. We do something first, then God does something. We're at the doing something first stage. That is where Ferris and I found ourselves. Having left college, I was no longer exempt from the Draft. The army sent me to Germany. I was glad to go because I had studied German in college. The town near our base provided many opportunities to mix with the people. I ate Christmas dinner with a family that had fled from Poland when the Russians came. I learned how to play chess with another family. I attended a tent revival and enjoyed a circus. I was invited to show some slides to a German church group. But that is not the story I want to tell.

Once a year members of the military were allowed to attend the armed services beautiful interfaith retreat center at Berchtesgaden, Germany. My friend, Ferris, and I quickly took advantage of the opportunity. It was March and the snow still lay thick on the mountain slopes. But spring was in the air. The presence of God was in that place, bathing it with peace and joy. The retreat speaker was an army chaplain who had been stationed in the Holy Land following World War II.

The Chaplain thrilled us with his stories. He described the villages and countryside where Jesus had walked and taught. He told of floating down the Jordan River on a rubber raft. He told of the Sea of Galilee, the fishermen, the place where Jesus taught and Peter caught the big draft of fish. He told how the sudden storms come up. He described the ancient city of Jerusalem, the temple area, the Church of the Holy Sepulcher, Golgotha where Jesus hung on the cross, and the Garden Tomb from which Jesus rose from the dead.

We listened totally immersed in the wonder of the places he described; walking each step with him and looking into each old ruin through his eyes. Ferris and I looked at each other and asked, "Wouldn't it be great to go the Holy Land?" Could we do it? We began to think of all the options open to us.

The Air Force had planes that flew all over. If there was space available, we could fly anywhere for free. We could catch free rides to the Holy Land and back! We talked. The more we talked the more excited we got. We decided to ask God if we could go and if he would help us. Would he arrange it so that we could get there and back? It was only a matter of a little scheduling, or so we thought.

We became so excited about the idea that there was nothing to do but go for it. We prayed, "Father, may we go to the Holy Land? Would you work out our plane connections so that we can go? We don't have the money for a commercial flight and we don't have very much leave time coming. So we'll need your help. In Jesus' Name. Amen."

Guess what happened after we prayed. Nothing! There wasn't the slightest hint that God had heard or answered. But we were excited. We wanted to go. We knew it was possible. We read books about the Holy Land. We told everyone who would listen that we were going. No, God still hadn't said yes. But we had made a decision. We were going to act as though God had said "Yes!"

Some people thought we were whistling in the dark, telling us that it would never happen. But we weren't taking any chances. We were going to be standing there with our bags packed and ready to go when the door opened. We continued to pray. We continued to plan. We found out what things we needed to do in order to take our trip, and started doing them. It seemed natural to us to follow James's advice.

> What doth it profit, my brethern, though a man say he hath faith, and have not works [corresponding action]? . . . Even so faith, if it hath not works [corresponding actions], is dead, being alone. (James 2:14-17 AMP)

We acted as though God had said Yes loud and clear. We set a date. We applied for leave in August. We made a list of every country we might want to visit and got permission to visit those countries. Lastly, we made the ultimate commitment; we got our shots, some for diseases we didn't know existed!

True, opportunities for discouragement abounded. There was the paperwork, the red tape, the passports, the clearances, and doubters who kept telling us it would never happen. Plus, we still had no word from God. To top it off, even though our leave was scheduled to start at midnight

Sunday night, someone scheduled me for guard duty that very same Sunday night!

It was Tuesday night before we finally left and headed for the train that was to take us to Frankfurt, Germany. With passports and visas tucked safely away we headed for the Rhine Main Air Force Base. They gave us no encouragement. Not to be daunted, we picked up our bags and caught an Air Force bus going to the nearby Wiesbaden Air Force Base. We put our names on the waiting list and sat down. We waited and waited. We wanted to catch a ride on a plane going south. Nine p.m. came and went and there were no planes flying south. Finally, we gave up for the night, sleeping in beds the Air Force provided.

The next day we went back to the Wiesbaden Air Force Base and waited, and waited, and waited. We continued to pray. We continued to get nothing but silence. The day dragged on. The planes were flying every direction but south. We prayed some more. We waited some more. Finally, we prayed something like,

"God, we are all prayed out. We don't get any answer from you. It seems to us the best thing to do if there isn't a plane going south by six p.m., is to take the first plane going north to England."

We had done everything we could think of to do on our part. With that prayer, a sort of peace settled over us. Finally, about 7:30 p.m., we caught a flight to London. It was late at night when we landed. The bus took us to the Servicemen's Hotel. In the lobby of the hotel, we noticed a bulletin board. On it were listed the departure times and destinations of Air Force planes leaving London. Seeing nothing of interest, we went to our room.

We hadn't entirely given up on our dream. We had dreamed so long and hard, and prayed so much about it, that the sight of that bulletin board had revived our hope. Again we prayed. Again, no word from God.

The next morning, Friday, we rose early, ready for a good breakfast and a full day of sightseeing. Then it happened! As we passed through the lobby on the way to breakfast, we looked again at the bulletin board. There it was! A plane was leaving Saturday morning for Nouasseur Air Force Base in French Morocco, North Africa! The moment I saw that sign, God dropped his "Yes!" into my heart. I knew that I knew that I knew that God had given us our trip to the Holy Land! Now we knew why we had to delay our trip while I pulled guard duty. He needed to delay our starting. Now we knew why he had closed all doors except the one going north. Because we had to go north, in order to go south! As a bonus, he threw in a tour of London.

Faith is not a set of beliefs to be possessed. Faith is to trust in, to rely on, and to have a firm conviction of the truth of God's Word that results in corresponding deeds and actions. Faith requires action. Later, the Spirit told me that Ferris and I had given our faith life by acting on it. We believed God could arrange the trip. That belief became faith when we put action to it and began acting as though God had said yes. If we had not acted, if we had not said that we were taking the trip as though God had given an audible yes, faith would not have come alive and there would have been no trip.

We were calling those things that be not, as though they were. We were speaking them into being by our words and actions (Romans 4:17). Ferris and I based our prayer on our knowledge of God's Word, such as "Delight thyself also in the LORD; and he shall give thee the desires of thine heart" (Psalm 37:4 KJV). We committed ourselves by doing all the things necessary to take our trip. We trusted God. We did not realize that we were asking God to cause hundreds of people, including the United States Army and Air Force, to arrange their schedules just so that we could go to the Holy Land! If we had really understood what we were asking God to do, I'm not sure our faith would have been up to it! God met us where we were in our naïve faith.

Walking through the only doors that are open is a must. What if we had refused to go north? We must be open to God's guidance and avoid the mistake of dictating to God what to do and how to do it. Because we didn't know the details of how God was arranging the trip, we had to be constantly open to any guidance he gave. Throughout the trip, it kept us open and watchful. All the parts were in place. Air Force planes were flying all over the areas we would be passing through.

Time was our only real problem. We needed God's help if we were to make the trip in the short twenty days of leave time we had coming. To our way of thinking, what we were asking God to do was something we could easily see him doing. Our believing level could handle believing that. Thus, we were free to have faith. That applies to anything you are praying about.

Get it settled in your mind that what you are asking God to do is something you can easily see him doing. If you can see it, you can vision it.

That Saturday morning, back at the Servicemen's Hotel, we were ready and waiting long before the bus left for the airport. We were starting to get suspicious that God had planned more than plane connections for us. So we weren't surprised to find our plane landing in France for supper. It was a short stop, but our feet had touched French soil! Our destination, the Nouasseur Air Force base in French Morocco, was fogged in. So we landed at a base fifty miles inland. We slept under the airplane's tail.

As we prepared to leave Nouasseur, we discovered more of God's surprises. We had been told we would have to pay for our lodging and meals. No one would take our money! When we boarded our plane for Tripoli, no one would take our money for the inflight meal! When it came time to depart Tripoli for Cairo, Egypt, no one would take our money to pay for room and board!

Our plane landed in Cairo. We were directed to customs where our luggage was examined. We had just cleared customs when God surprised us again! A man stepped up and asked if he could share a taxi ride with us into Cairo. "It will be cheaper if three share it," he said. Imagine our joyous surprise to discover that this gentleman, Charles L. Benton, director of business and finance for the University of Maryland, a Baptist and a Christian, was going to Jerusalem too!

Mr. Benton was an experienced traveler. It was agreed to do everything together because it would be cheaper for all of us. Not only did this prove to be a wise decision, but Mr. Benton was a most enjoyable companion. God had arranged for a guide to help two naïve solders who would have had a tough time trying to making it on their own. Mr. Benton helped us see much more and do much more than would have been possible by ourselves!

In Jerusalem, we told our guide, Zaki, that we needed to leave Jerusalem on Monday. He learned that a Catholic Nun was going to Beirut, Lebanon by taxi on Monday morning and arranged for us to share the ride with her. Another blessing from God. For only five dollars apiece, we traveled all day through that countryside, passing through Damascus, and on to Beirut. We had no specific destination in Beirut. Our cab driver suggested letting us out in the center of the city where it would be easy for us to get directions.

We stepped out of the taxi, unloaded our bags, and the taxi drove off. Before we could even ask ourselves what to do now, a man had his car do a U-turn and screech to a halt in front of us! He explained that he was a hotel owner and wanted to take us to his hotel. We told him we wanted to catch a ride on an Air Force Plane heading towards Italy or Germany. He explained that the pilots of an Air Force plane were staying at his hotel and he would introduce us. You can hardly blame us that our first response to this was one of disbelief.

The stranger offered identification. And when we made a quick prayer check, we knew we were to go with this man. Imagine; God had arranged for the pilots of an Air Force executive plane to stay at this man's hotel, then sent this man out so that he would be driving by at just the exact time when we arrived! The hotel owner took us to his hotel, introduced us to the pilots, and gave us each a single room, a delicious supper, and breakfast in our rooms, all for only $4.50 apiece!

We left at six the next morning. Touching down first in Athens, Greece, our plane landed in Rome, Italy. We had enough money left to tour Rome and to pay for our train ride home to Straubing, Germany. We went on a trip of over 6,000 miles. We flew 5,558 miles. All for less than $150.00 apiece. It was a gift God gave us because we were willing to put our faith in him and to keep trusting, even when it seemed the trip was impossible.

Our story combines many lessons in faith. You might find it helpful to review it and make an outline of each step we took and what we did. The first step was believing God could do it. That is where you need to start. You must be convinced that God not only can do it, but will do it for you. You must believe that God will do what he has promised to do. Believe it and confess it. If we hadn't believed it, hadn't confessed that God was doing it, our unbelief would have blocked God. You must leave the details of working it out in God's hands and not try to tell him how to do it. You must be open to the unexpected and all the unexpected extra blessings he throws in.

CHAPTER 27

POWER IN - POWER OUT

The imagination is the seed bed for all we do. Everything we do is first conceived in the imagination. Do you feel hungry? Your imagination pictures that dessert in the refrigerator. Your mouth starts to water. You imagine yourself getting that dessert and eating it. Then you do the thing you have imagined. Do you want to go somewhere? Your imagination pictures how you will do it. Then you do it. Some things happen so fast we think they are instinctive responses, such as slapping a mosquito. It's an automatic response only because we've trained ourselves to respond that way. James says it works that way with evil, lust, greed, and envy. It first originates in our thoughts. We meditate on it and nurture it until it matures into action (James 1:15; see also Psalm 7:14; Isaiah 59:4). Jesus put it bluntly:

> "You brood of vipers! How can you speak good, when you are evil? For out of the abundance of the heart the mouth speaks. The good person out of his good treasure brings forth good, and the evil person out of his evil treasure brings forth evil. I tell you, on the Day of Judgment people will give account for every careless word they speak, for by your words you will be justified, and by your words you will be condemned." (Matthew 12:34-37 ESV)

We can harness and train our creative imaginations to help us grow our faith and our confidence in the promises of God. For example, in your imagination see yourself using the name of Jesus against Satan and his demons. Watch them flee in terror as James said they would (James 4:7). Let it become second nature to you. Form the image in your mind of the good you desire, and then speak it out, believing that what you say will come to pass, and you will have what you say (Mark 11:23). In so doing, we are following God's example. God created by first forming an image in his mind and then speaking it out.

> By faith we understand that the universe was created by the word of God, so that what is seen was not made out of things that are visible." (Hebrews 11:3 ESV)

> God ... calls into existence the things that do not exist. (Romans 4:17 ESV)

Because the power of the imagination is so great, Satan tries every trick in the book to get us to use it for evil. But we have this confidence, as James tells us, that God will help us use our imaginations rightly. "If any of you lack wisdom, let him ask of God, who giveth to all men liberally, and upbraideth not, and it shall be given him" (James 1:5 KJV).

The imagination played a key part in the Fall. Satan appealed to the woman's imagination when he tempted her to disobey God. In her imagination, she began to see herself eating the fruit. She saw herself enjoying its taste, savoring its beauty. She saw herself becoming wise, and being able to make wise decisions like God. Only after she had pictured herself in an exalted position attained by eating the fruit, did she eat (Genesis 3:1-6).

Job is a dramatic example of the negative use of the creative imagination. Job was a good man, upright, a God fearing man who avoided evil. But Job allowed his imagination to run away with him, causing him fear and worry. He began to imagine his children doing all kinds of evil things, even cursing God. For this reason, Job was constantly offering sacrifices on behalf of his children. At one-point Job cried out, "The thing which I greatly feared is come upon me, and that which I was afraid of is come unto me" (Job 3:25

KJV). When Job got his creative imagination straightened out God was able to bless him with more than he had lost (Job 42:12).

James tells us how our negative imagination brings forth death:

> Let no one say when he is tempted, "I am being tempted by God," for God cannot be tempted with evil, and he himself tempts no one. But each person is tempted when he is lured and enticed by his own desire. Then desire when it has conceived gives birth to sin, and sin when it is fully grown brings forth death (James 1:12-15 ESV).

There are many Christians today who are ignorant of who they are in Christ, and what they possess in Christ. Instead of grasping the good news that they are victors in Christ, they see themselves as powerless, tossed about by every whim of Satan and every gust of adversity. Their outlook on life and their own self-image, is totally negative and defeatist. Their personal lives are a mess. Their children are rebellious. Sickness and poverty and misfortune constantly assault them. These Christians are bewildered and discouraged, and can't understand why they suffer so much.

As the quality of fruit reveals what the tree is really like, so the fruits of the Christian reveal what the Christian has been putting into his mind and heart as food for his creative imagination (Matthew 7:15-20). The fruit of the impotent Christian proclaims to the world that that Christian is governed by a negatively fed creative imagination. Jesus explained that our outward words and deeds are determined by the treasure we have built up on the inside, in our hearts. If we have been filling up the storehouses of our creative imaginations with negative and destructive input, our lives will be impotent, powerless. The fruit will be diseased, scrawny, and wormy.

This means that the key to success, the secret of the presence of power in a Christian, is the good treasure in his heart. God works with the good treasure to enable the Christian to be an overcomer, to reign as a king in life. If you want to be an overcomer you must build up the good treasure in your heart. Use your imagination the way God designed it to be used. Think of your mind as a computer. When a computer is first assembled, it can't do anything. Nothing will happen until you first load an operating system, providing a way for the computer to handle the information you put into it. Then you have to put information into its memory and tell it what to do with that information. If you want to play games, you must first load a game program. If you want to produce an animated movie, you must first load video animation programs that will enable you to produce your movie.

Without information, and a program telling the computer what to do with that information, all the computer does is take up space. Our minds are like a computer. Just as all that a computer has to work with is what you put into it, so too, all that God has to work with is what you put into your mind. A computer has only so much memory space, so much room in which to store information. If you fill up the computer's memory with the wrong information, the computer will give wrong answers. The program may lock-up and the computer stop running.

It's the same with our minds. If the information you put into your mind is useless, erroneous, or even bad information, you will not get the results you want in life, and your life may lock up! Computers need programmers. That's someone who writes the code that tells the computer what to do. Once the program has been written, the programmer then debugs, cleans up, his program so that it will do exactly what he wants it to do. He knows that you can't write a story with a math program. The computer can do only what it is programed to do. Without the correct kind of information, or data, it can't do anything.

Information is fed into a computer through input terminals. The main inputs are the keyboard, scanners, memory. Likewise, information is input into your mind through input terminals, which we call the five senses. Reflect back over your average day. Of all that you saw, of all that you heard, of all that you said, what percent of your input was of the positive things of God? What percent of the hours of TV you watch each day build you up, edify you with the positive things of God? What do you read? Does your reading edify and build you up in your most holy faith? When you converse with others, when you talk about your circumstances, when you talk about your family, your children, your mate, how many of your words are positive words that edify and build up? Or do you, in disobedience to God, just keep repeating bad stuff, defeatist stuff, negative stuff, with the excuse that you are just telling it like it is?

Because the imagination is such a powerful tool, we need to examine it more closely and learn how to use it. Just as all a computer has to work with is what is put into it, it is also true that all God has to work with is what you put into your heart computer. Some people have difficulty understanding this. They want God to be more powerful than he really is. This may startle you, but God is not all powerful! God cannot do anything he wants to do anytime he wants to do it. For example, he can't get you saved or make you tithe! God deliberately limited his own power when he made man, and put man in authority over this earth. God delegated some of his own authority to man, and he cannot legally take it back.

Listen again to what John Wesley said: "It seems God is limited by our prayer life--that He can do nothing for humanity unless someone asks Him." God's method of creating and acting is by speaking the word (2 Peter 3:5). His word has within it the power to accomplish what God wants it to do (Isaiah 55:11). But a man must first speak it out. When God put man in authority over this earth, he gave explicit orders that we were to do the same things he did. In essence God said, "Adam, if something goes wrong, don't call me; you fix it. I've given you all the power you need to visualize and speak things into existence the way I do" (Mark 11:23).

God, in speaking man's authority into existence, by that same word, made it legally impossible for he, himself, to step in and usurp that authority back from man. For that reason, the only way God can legally work in the earth is when a man, who has that authority, asks him. It is not a question of God's willingness or unwillingness to help us. It is a matter of our taking the limits off God; of providing him with a legal way of intervening on our behalf, or on the behalf of a loved one, or another for whom we are interceding. Those limitations will remain in effect until Adam's lease is up.

What would happen if God went against his own word? Because of the tremendous creative power in his words, if God violated his own word, everything would disintegrate. Hebrews 1:3, tells us that Jesus, through whom and by whom all things were created, is "upholding all things by the word of his power" (KJV). We can praise God that he never changes, and that his word is settled forever (Psalm 119:89; see also Colossians 1:16).

Satan, from whom men ran in terror, now runs from us in terror! The puniest, most anemic Christian has authority over Satan in the name of

Jesus (James 4:7). But if the puniest Christian does not know this, he will not use the name of Jesus and Satan will not run from him. Satan will try to keep him ignorant, miserable and imagining all manner of bad things. He floods his eyes and ears with all manner of violence and evil as seen in movies, TV programs, daily news, and threats of catastrophic attacks by our enemies. Satan wants every Christian to believe that evil triumphs over good. While you may think that you can take it all in and it will not affect you, calculate the ratio of how much non-edifying material you feed into your brain compared to that which is edifying. Is it enough to combat Satan's blatant propaganda and unleash the power of God?

Let's suppose you've just read Mark 11:23. Jesus says that if we believe it, we can have what we say. You decide you are going to start saying that you've got a new job that pays double the pay you're getting now. There are two requirements in Mark 11:23 that must be met. First, you cannot doubt in your heart. Second, you must believe that what you say will come to pass. The Greek work for doubt, *diakrino*, means lack of faith, rather than weakness of faith. To not doubt means to have faith. How does faith come? "Faith comes by hearing, and hearing by the Word of God" (Romans 10:17 KJV).

How do you hear? You hear by saying, by confessing God's Word over and over and over and over and over and over and over. You keep repeating the promises of God until it moves from head knowledge to heart knowledge; until you know that you know that you know. When it slips from head knowledge to heart knowledge, you will know, and nothing will ever be able to shake that knowledge. Prayer has to be preceded by confession and faith if it is to have power. As you work at hearing the word and the promises, you automatically begin building images in your imagination, images of living in those fulfilled promises. You see yourself overcoming. You see yourself walking in prosperity. You see yourself walking in divine health. You see the work of your hands prospering. In fact, you build a whole new self-image.

The second requirement is to believe. It means to have confidence in, trust in, rely on. Belief in this sense is not mere intellectual agreement. It is a way of life. It means obedience. It is an all or nothing thing. It's something like the discussion between the pig and the chicken. The chicken suggested giving a gift of bacon and eggs. To which the pig replied, for you that is just a gift, but for me it is total sacrifice. Some of us just offer eggs when total sacrifice is required. Believing is total sacrifice. Believing is to be working "out your own salvation with fear and trembling" knowing that God is working in you, giving you both the will to do it and the power to do it (Philippians 2:12, 13). Believing is to act like you believe your words will come to pass. It is to live in the midst of a miracle on the brink of disaster.

I grew up in rural western New York State, a little over 100 miles from Niagara Falls. In the last half of the nineteenth century and the first half of the twentieth century, walking across the Falls on a tight rope, or going over the Falls in a barrel, were the dare devil stunts of the day. In 1911, a British relative of mine, Bobby Leach, was the second person to go over the Falls in a barrel. He put his faith in a steel barrel he designed. It cost him two smashed knee caps, but he was able to convert his experience into a small fortune.

The Great Blondin did much better. He built his fame by walking on a tight rope across the Falls in 1859. Whether or not it is true, there is a fascinating story told about Blondin. One day he pushed a wheelbarrow across on the tight rope. When he reached the other side, he was surrounded by an enthusiastic crowd. He asked the crowd if they believed he could wheel the wheelbarrow across with someone in it. Of course the crowd went wild, shouting yes, yes. To which he responded by asking for a volunteer. The crowd suddenly became quiet. No one volunteered. No one had enough faith to get into the wheelbarrow. How often do we shout yes, yes, and then draw back when it's time to step into the wheelbarrow?

There is a big difference between having faith in Blondin's skill and having faith in God. Blondin could always make a mistake, or be caught off guard by a vicious gust of wind. But not so God. God, as he always does, would simply make a way where there was no way, and not bother with the tight rope at all (Isaiah 43:16). Let's make this a little more personal. Imagine that you have your own personal Niagara Falls to cross. What will yours be? Is it a terminal illness? God will not take you out on a tight rope where the next step might end in a disastrous fall. God simply makes a way where there is no way. Are you drowning in debt? God will make a way where there is no way. You can't have a Niagara Falls so devastating that God cannot make a way if you will put your faith in him and his wheelbarrow. God always makes a way. Can your faith pass the wheelbarrow test? And totally trust him?

When Ferris and I acted like we had faith, it was not a life or death choice. We did it because we had everything to gain. We did it because it seemed the logical thing to do. Our preparations, our getting into the wheelbarrow, is what we would have done if we had heard a great big voice from heaven shout yes. That is what God expects; actions corresponding to our faith statement. But not foolish, or foolhardy actions. To give your car away as an act of faith because you want a new car is foolish. You will end up doing a lot of walking! Instead, help someone who needs a car buy a car.

Acting out your believing produces powerful benefits. Before you can act out your believing, you must first form an image of the answer in your imagination. We "saw" ourselves taking that trip. We saw ourselves taking each step in proper sequence. As we studied, we imagined ourselves seeing each of the things we read about. The result of this imagining was to build the vision of that trip in our bellies, our innermost beings. As we kept acting, we kept building and strengthening that image. In other words, your imagination is a most powerful tool. What you constantly visualize in your imagination is what you get. Your imaginings are added to the treasures in your heart.

When God uses your spirit as a lamp to search your inward parts, what does he find? If your innermost parts are full of the word of God, and God inspired imaginings, nothing can stop you. You will have given God the building material he needs to make you victorious, an overcomer. But if you've put in 99% garbage (such as TV soap operas, smutty magazines, books and words of unbelief) into your innermost parts, God has nothing to work with, and you will live a powerless, defeated life. God wants to bless you, but if you don't give him anything to work with, he can't. So, what are you putting into your imagination, the most powerful computer ever created?

CHAPTER 28

HOMEWORK: EXPERIMENTING WITH PRAYER

Laughter, joy, and delight in each other is the order of the day when our family gets together. Our children have fun sharing old times and bringing each other up to date on their lives now. Our grandchildren look forward to playing together. How did this come to be when so many families have the opposite experience? It had nothing to do with being good parents; which we often were not. It came as a blessing from God in spite of our failures as parents.

In our youth, we had both received Jesus as our Lord and Savior. When we married, we asked God to take over our marriage and guide us in the ministry to which he had called us. From the time our first child was born, we began to claim the promise of Isaiah 54:13, "All your children shall be taught by the LORD, and great shall be the peace of your children (ESV). We took our children to CFO camps where they witnessed firsthand the power of God at work. They learned for themselves that what dad preached was real.

Laughter, joy, and delight in each other is God's pattern for the family. When you got saved, you got a new family. Your new father is God. Your new brother is Jesus. Your helper and tutor is the Holy Spirit. Prayer is family talk. That means that the times we spend in prayer should be times of laughter, joy, and delight in each other, as well as the serious moments when we seek their help and guidance. Have you ever just sat quietly and enjoyed God? The Westminster Shorter Catechism states that "Man's chief end is to glorify God and enjoy him forever" (c. 1648 A.D.).

Another reason for joy in prayer is the joy of calling those things that be not as though they were. Abraham joyfully imagined the son who was yet to be born, through whom would come a countless host of blessed people (Romans 4:16-18). Talk with God about the joy that will come when the sick person is well, the need is met, the unsaved are saved. Glenn Clark told about a prayer meeting that had more power when a bubbling young girl was with them. When he asked what she did, she said she imagined the joy the healed one would have.

As you think about praying with joy and laughter, turn your prayer tree into a multi-page list. Use a separate page for each item. This will enable you to do some sorting and arranging. On the top of each page put the following on separate lines: Date, Subject, Description, and the prayer promises that apply. Finally, list anything you can do to sow seeds for the kind of harvest you want. For example, if you need a job, sow job seeds by doing odd jobs for others for free. At the end, write out a confession of faith for the prayer.

Words create. How many people do you know who confidently confess that they always get a bad cold in the spring and in the fall? They always get what they confess, don't they? Since what we confess is what we possess (Proverbs 18:20-21), it is much more profitable to confess that God is working and to act like he is working. We disbelieve the testimony of our eyes and feelings until the testimony of our eyes and feelings comes into line with the Word of God.

Family talk requires listening to what each other is saying. Father God is always speaking to us. We have to work at training ourselves to hear his voice. As children, we became good at tuning-out our parents' voices. We also become good at hearing sounds we want to hear, like money dropping on the floor or sidewalk. When I was growing up, we were suspicious of people who said God had spoken to them. We didn't rule out the possibility. We agreed it could happen. It happened to the Old Testament prophets. But our mixed up ideas about God caused us to be more comfortable with the belief that God speaks to us through the Bible. As a result, we did not try to hear God speak.

Once we understand that God does talk to us, and wants to talk to us, we need to find out what his voice sounds like. Thunder on the mountain like in Moses's day is pretty scary. I like it better when God comes as a person, as He did when He talked to Abram. But that is not the way he talks with us today. Perhaps the best description of how God talks with us today is how he spoke to Isaiah, as recorded in I Kings 19:12: "And after the earthquake a fire, but the Lord was not in the fire; and after the fire <a sound of gentle stillness and> a still, small voice" (AMP).

God speaks with us today in a still small voice. Just as we learned to recognize the sound of a coin falling on the pavement, we must learn to recognize God's still, small voice amidst all the louder noises ringing in our ears. The good news is that it can be done. How? By obeying the oft repeated words: Shut up and listen! We're not used to being quiet. We're not used to sitting around doing nothing. The moment everything gets silent around us, all manner of thoughts and ideas flood our minds crying for our attention.

You are listening for a still small voice. It takes quiet to hear. It takes concentration and practice. You may want to lay prostrate on the floor, sit in a comfortable chair, or lay on your bed. The only words you need to say are, "Speak Father. I am your redeemed child through the blood of Jesus. I am listening." Don't be concerned with the myriad of thoughts that flood into your mind. Let them pass through and don't dwell of them. Concentrate on

> Casting down imaginations, and every high thing that exalteth itself against the knowledge of God, and bringing into captivity every thought to the obedience of Christ" (2 Corinthians 10:5 KJV).

Satan's demons will also try to distract you with their constant babble. Learn to tune them out. Keep bringing your mind back to a listening mode. You may even fall asleep. But, once you've trained your mind to hear God's voice, you will recognize it and respond immediately wherever you are. Try to spend at least one hour a day listening. Break it up into segments. You may get discouraged. But it's the only way to develop sensitivity to God's voice. Keep it up and you will be rewarded.

Keep in mind that the Bible is our authority for faith and practice. If you do not know what the Bible says you can easily be led astray. The

Bible is your safety net. If the ideas and thoughts that come to you are not supported by God's Word, they are not of God. When in doubt ask God to prove, with scripture, that it was him speaking. Listening takes time, but it pays great dividends in faith.

Lest this seem a drudgery, remember that prayer is having fun. It is a joy to have prayers answered and to learn how to get every prayer answered. It is a joy to bless others by your prayers. Joy removes from prayer the negative connotations of work, of disappointments, and frustration. Joy puts it into the realm of going from victory to victory. That is a great confidence builder. In all true prayer what is important is not the destination, but the journey. We may desperately want a prayer answered, a need met. But what then? Do we breathe a sigh of relief and forget prayer until the next crisis? Too many of us do.

Do not be discouraged when it seems your prayer is not answered. Father Edgar Sanford tells the story of Jennie[I]. Jennie was a young woman who was desperately ill. She did not know God and needed him badly. Father Sanford met with her to teach and pray with her for almost a year. Jennie improved and was able to be about the house again. Then, while Father Sanford was away on a preaching mission, Jennie died. When she knew she was dying she dictated a letter to Father Sanford. She asked him not to feel sad. While she did not find the health they had been seeking, she found something far greater, far more important. She had found her God whom she had lost. Now God was very dear to her, and she would never lose Him again.

When prayer stops being a continual asking, and begins to be *being* and *knowing*, and *loving*, it also becomes prayer without ceasing. Ask a small child to share his dreams. What would he like to be? To do? Imagine that you are truly interested in what the child says. You enter into it, talking together about his dreams. That is what prayer without ceasing is when sometimes you are the child and God is the adult, and other times it is you who listens as God shares his dreams.

When you are the child talking to God as people's needs touch your heart, that is prayer without ceasing. When you minister to God by praising and thanking and listening to His needs and dreams, that is prayer without ceasing. It is just something you do all the time, because your mind is going all the time. [When praying for someone in joy you ask, "Oh, Jesus, touch them and make them well." You reach out your hand and touch, like you want Jesus to do.] When you sense that God's heart is breaking, you can reach out and hug God. This is family. This is prayer unceasing. Epaphras labored fervently in prayer for the Colossians (Colossians 4:12). In other words, he was "seeing" them mature and strong and triumphant. He praised God that it was so, rejoicing in their joy.

PART E

The Territory of Redeeming Love

Dear children, let us not love with words or tongue but with actions and in truth. (1 John 3:18 NIV)

CHAPTER 29

THE POWER OF LOVE AT WORK

You'd hardly think of love as an essential tool of the successful salesman. Yet it is that love that keeps each sale from being a battle of wills, leaves the customer happy, and ensures that the salesman will be welcome when he returns. The power of love, and what it can accomplish, is so great that some have suggested that love is the energy out of which all things were created. The salesman quickly learns that if he first sells himself by loving his customer, selling his product is much easier. Likewise, we discover that the more we love God, the easier it is to pray with power.

The principle of loving held true when I performed magic. In preparation, I would follow the example of great magicians from the past. They would affirm over and over, "I love my audience". When my audience realized that I really did like them, we started to have fun together. I enjoyed hearing laughter and gasps of wonder as an audience was swept along in the fantasy I wove.

But I have wished, as all of us have wished, that I had real magical powers, like in the stories about wizards. I would use my powers to change things that needed to be changed, to do some tedious or boring task, or take a girl on an exotic date. The problem is that in all the stories told about wizards we learn that only those born with the *gift* can be wizards. Being born with the gift, however, doesn't make one a wizard any more than having things to sell makes one a salesman. One had to go through a long apprenticeship to a master wizard. There were books to study, tedious work, and tests to pass. There were no short cuts. You had to be born with the gift and the gift had to be developed.

Wizards and magic and gifts are the stuff of fairy tales. But those things pale in comparison to the amazing truth that each of us has been born with a greater *gift*. It happened the instant we were born again. The gift is the authority to use Jesus' name. We have been commissioned to use Jesus' name to do all the works Jesus did; miracles, healings, and authority over Satan and his demons. This gift is activated by faith and powered by love. It does require study and training. The givers of the power; the Father, the Son, and the Holy Spirit, teach us how to use it. Bear in mind how we are related to these givers of power. This awesome, almighty creator God, is also our father, our daddy. Jesus, who reached out to us in love and died our death, is our brother. The Holy Spirit, our teacher, comforter and intercessor, is dwelling in us to help us.

We learned that God has turned us into the right stuff, and there is no condemnation in us (Romans 8:1). Now it is time to let our new family train us. First, we will examine our weapons and see what they can do (2 Corinthians 10:4-6). These are weapons of offense. We are to be winning battles and driving the enemy back. The Lord is coming soon and we must set as many people free as we can. This is praying with power.

CHAPTER 30

AMBASSADORS WITH AUTHORITY

We have been commissioned to be Christ's ambassadors. The commissioning is for a specific purpose, a specific mission we are to undertake and complete. When Paul wrote to the Corinthians he referred to this commissioning saying, "we are ambassadors for Christ, God making his appeal through us" (2 Corinthians 5:20 ESV). Jesus gave this commission to us just before his ascension.

> God authorized and commanded me to commission you: Go out and train everyone you meet, far and near, in this way of life, marking them by baptism in the threefold name: Father, Son, and Holy Spirit. Then instruct them in the practice of all I have commanded you. I'll be with you as you do this, day after day after day, right up to the end of the age. (Matthew 28:18-20 MSG)

The words of commissioning are repeated again in Mark 16:15-20, John 17:18; 20:21-23, and Acts 1:8. What is this authority we possess? How do we use it? What do we show and prove we have it? E.W. Kenyon, in his book *The Wonderful Name of Jesus*[1] tells of a conversation he had with a lawyer. In the course of the conversation the lawyer asked about the meaning of the above words in Matthew 28. He wanted to know if those words actually meant that Jesus had given us the right to use his name. Kenyon turned the question around and asked the lawyer to explain the meaning of Jesus' words.

To which the lawyer replied that if the meaning of the words had not changed, and meant today what they meant when Jesus spoke them, then Jesus really did give the church the Power of Attorney to use his name. Kenyon concludes that according to the lawyer, Jesus has given us the authority to use his name. The scriptures bear witness to the fact that this is true. In Luke 10:17, "the seventy returned again with joy, saying, Lord, even the devils are subject unto us through thy name" (AMP). This showing of power is repeated over and over in the Acts of the Apostles where, when the name of Jesus is spoken, miracles occur. "Be it known unto you all, … that by the name of Jesus Christ of Nazareth, … doth this man stand here before you whole" (Acts 4:10 KJV)

Paul will be our primary instructor as we learn about our authority and our assignment as ambassadors. A word of warning! Beware of vain philosophies that can confuse us. To some degree, every philosophy arises out of the philosopher's personal experience. The most brilliant philosopher to come on the scene was Saul, a native of the Roman town of Tarsus. The depths of his knowledge and study were recognized by Porcius Festus, the Roman governor of Judea, who said, "Paul, you are mad! Your great learning is driving you insane!" (Acts 26:24 AMP). Paul also spoke of his educational background:

> I am a Jew, born in Tarsus of Cilicia but reared in this city. At the feet of Gamaliel, I was educated according to the strictest care in the Law of our fathers, being ardent <even a zealot> for God, as all of you are today." (Acts 22:3 AMP).

As with all philosophers, something happened to Paul that set him apart and shaped his teaching. Most philosophers base their philosophies on a *eureka* (I have found it!) moment. With Paul it was different. The enlightenment that happened to Paul swept away all his philosophical beliefs. He came face to face with Being itself, and with Knowledge, and Conduct as taught by that Being. It forced him to shed all his years of theological and philosophical training and thinking. Two important concepts Paul had to relearn, and which the world's philosophies have not learned, is the Biblical meaning of *free will* versus *predeterminism* (predestination).

Free will, the teaching of the Bible, is that we have the freedom to make choices without outside coercion, or force. Our abilities and interests come from our genes. What we do with them is our own free choice. We cannot blame environment or heredity for our decisions or the choices we make.

I was free to be what I wanted to be. I could have chosen to follow one or more of several different professions: a pilot, a scientist, politician, a magician, the list goes on. With all those possibilities, I ended up choosing none of them in order to say yes to God, and do the thing I had said I would never do, be a pastor. It was my decision, freely made.

Free will sounds good, but it does have a down side. It means that I must accept responsibility and blame for all my bad or destructive choices and actions. I cannot claim to be the innocent victim of events beyond my control. As I explained before, my psychology professor blew that idea out of the water when he said that while my parents may have provided the environment, what I did with it was my own contribution! His answer didn't help either when I complained that my mother threw water on me when I was having tantrums, and he said "Good for her." The up side is, that if old choices don't work, I can make new choices.

But wait! Paul also writes that we were predestined, "chosen and appointed beforehand," to be adopted as God's children (Ephesians 1:11 AMP). That seems to imply that my life has been predetermined and I don't have free choice. This confusion is removed when you put this verse alongside John 1:11-12,

> He came unto his own, and his own received him not. But as many as received <take hold of> him, to them gave he power <authority> to become the sons of God, even to them that believe on his name" (AMP).

What is predestined is what will happen when you receive Jesus as your Lord and Savior. It's like chocolate ice cream. The ingredients that are used to make chocolate ice cream predetermine that it will be chocolate.

It will always be chocolate every time it is made with those ingredients. It is predestined to be so. Predestined, as Paul uses the term, means that if you make Jesus your Lord and Savior certain things will automatically happen. You will be instantly adopted as a son or daughter of God. You will instantly be given the authority to use the name of Jesus. Have you made Jesus your Lord and Savior? The choice is yours to make with your free will. What will happen if you don't choose Jesus is summed up in the concept of perishing (John 3:16).

Your ambassadorial appointment, with the power of attorney to use his name, is what you got when you chose Jesus. It is a part of the package. It is not earned. It is not deserved. It's what you get automatically. Since we've been given this authority, the question is how to use it. Paul writes this about Jesus' name:

> Therefore <because He stooped so low> God has highly exalted Him and has freely bestowed on Him the name that is above every name, That in (at) the name of Jesus every knee should (must) bow, in heaven and on earth and under the earth, And every tongue <frankly and openly> confess and acknowledge that Jesus Christ is Lord, to the glory of God the Father" (Philippians 2:9-11 AMP).

Jesus' name, the name greater than any other name, is a name of power. It is the one name the devil and his demons fear. Every knee must bow before the name of Jesus. Every sickness or disease or problem, has a name. That name must bow before the name of Jesus. That is the first lesson about our authority to use the name of Jesus. That authority is the authority to command sickness to leave, to command demons to leave, to command lame men to stand and walk, to command withered hands to grow out, to command issues of blood to dry up, to command wind to die down and storms to pass over us and seas to become calm.

Jesus said that whatever we saw him do, we will do, and even greater things, because he was going to the Father.

> "I tell you the truth, anyone who believes in me will do the same works I have done, and even greater works, because I am going to be with the Father. You can ask for anything in my name, and I will do it, so that the Son can bring glory to the Father. Yes, ask me for anything in my name, and I will do it!" (John 14:12-14 NLT)

It takes more than head knowledge to use this authority. Jesus made it clear when he kept saying "according to your faith." You get faith by immersing yourself in the word so much and so often that it slips from your head down into your heart, and becomes heart knowledge. There is no short cut. Our own life experiences teach us that. Diligent practice is the key to anything you want to achieve. If you took music lessons, the one word you probably grew to hate was, practice. Competence and mastery require practice. There is no escape from it. But, once you became competent, you began to fully enjoy your music. When the truth of the power and authority of the name of Jesus finally slips down into your heart, you become an unstoppable dynamo, an overcomer.

It even influences your giving, for you realize the truth:

> "Give, and <gifts> will be given to you; good measure, pressed down, shaken together, and running over, will they pour into <the pouch formed by> the bosom <of your robe and used as a bag>. For with the measure you deal out <with the measure you use when you confer benefits on others>, it will be measured back to you." (Luke 6:38 AMP)

If you are bothered by the idea that you may not be good enough to use your authority, look again at the story of Balaam, told in Numbers chapters 22 and 23. When King Balak asked Balaam to curse the Israelites, Balaam reported the vision God gave him. In the vision God told Balaam that he has not beheld iniquity in Jacob, neither has he seen perverseness in Israel (Numbers 23:21).

From our perspective we saw just the opposite. But the scriptures testify that God does not hold our sins against us. He wants only to bless us for his name's sake (I Samuel 12:22; Psalm 23:3). God is love. His love is there to bless us. But we have a tendency to block his love by our actions and our words. We have to learn that God wants to bless us and allow it to happen. As his adopted children we even have a legal right to his blessings. We're family. It's part of the package. The only thing stopping us is our own stubbornness and unwillingness to believe what God said. We say we believe God heals, but don't believe he will heal us. We say God blesses financially, but he won't bless us. Etc. Every time we say something like that we are calling God a liar. How dare we heap such insults on God! God doesn't lie. God said it and that settles it!

The word of your testimony makes you an overcomer. When an overcomer pleads the blood of Jesus over a situation, or lays down a bloodline around people and things, Satan and his demons flee. The overcomer knows that there is power in the blood and is not hesitant to use it against Satan and all his scheming.

> For the accuser of our brothers and sisters has been thrown down to earth — the one who accuses them before our God day and night. And they have defeated him by the blood of the Lamb and by their testimony. And they did not love their lives so much that they were afraid to die. (Revelation 12:10, 11 NLT)

It is one thing to read that we have authority to use the name of Jesus and another to actually wield it, or be ambassadorial. In any new venture, we need a starting place to help us get the feel of it. Considering the long list of things Jesus did, and which he said we would do also, is there a good starting place? I wouldn't recommend trying to walk on water! Feeding the multitude with a few fish and a couple loaves of bread would be stretching our faith too far, as would be raising the dead. I've a better suggestion. Remember what Paul wrote about the name of Jesus?

> That is why God has now lifted him to the heights, and has given him the name beyond all names, so that at the

> name of Jesus "every knee shall bow," whether in Heaven or earth or under the earth. And that is why "every tongue shall confess" that Jesus Christ is Lord, to the glory of God the Father. (Philippians 2:9-11 PHS)

Let us begin living in the power of his name.

CHAPTER 31

Living in the Power of His Name

Many years ago, H. T. Webster created a character named Casper Milquetoast. Casper was a man who always spoke softly and always got hit by a big stick. He became so popular that his name entered into general usage to mean weak and ineffectual. Various American dictionaries define it as meaning someone of

> "an unusually meek, bland, soft or submissive nature, who is easily overlooked, written off, and who may also appear overly sensitive, timid, indecisive or cowardly" (2016 Wikipedia, the Free Encyclopedia).

This is also descriptive of how some Christians live their Christian lives! The Milquetoast Christian is full of excuses: Doesn't want to make waves, doesn't want to stand out or be noticed, believes it takes too much effort to live up to it, not good for social status, could hurt business, ignorance. The list goes on. God told Hosea "My people are destroyed for lack of knowledge" (Hosea 4:6). Charles Haddon Spurgeon (1834-1892) tells a story of the harm being a Milquetoast Christian can do to you. He went to call on an elderly lady in her home. She was bedfast, suffering from malnutrition. As he talked with the woman, Spurgeon noticed a framed document hanging on the wall.

He studied it a moment and then asked the woman if it was hers. "Yes," she answered. She had worked as a maid in the household of some English nobility. Before her employer died, she gave her the document. The elderly lady had served her employer for nearly half a century and was very proud of the fact that her employer and given her the document. She had it framed, and it had been hanging on the wall ever since her employer had died ten years earlier. Spurgeon asked the woman if she would let him take the document and have it examined more closely. The woman, who had never learned to read and felt too timid to think it might be more than a piece of paper, gave her permission.

The authorities had been looking for the document. It was a bequest. The English noblewoman had left her maid a home and money. But the maid, who could not read and was too timid to have the document read to her, was living in a little one room house built out of wooden boxes. She was starving to death. And yet she had on the wall, a document that gave her the authority to be well cared for and to live in a fine house. It belonged to her. But it did her no good until Spurgeon helped her use it.

We possess a legal document of far greater importance than the maid's bequest. Regrettably, it has gone unread and misunderstood. Jesus tried to explain it to us. But the devil has blinded our eyes so that when we do read, we do not see. Our ears, overwhelmed with a cacophony of noise, hear but do not understand. We walk around like Casper Milquetoast. We run around as victims, ignorant of the fact that Jesus has put in our hands industrial sized power with the strength to crush every evil, every need, every disease, and every storm. Whatever we use it on yields to its power, the power of the name of Jesus.

As long as no one stops him, Satan can cause all manner of natural disasters, such as flooding nuclear plants in Japan, and sending tornadoes to rip through cities. He is the prince of the power of the air (Ephesians 2:2). He can use unsaved people to spread epidemics, cause strains of bacteria to become impossible to treat, and oversee the poisoning of the world's water. He can enter into the hearts of men and turn them into machines of hatred and violence and greed. Today, the situation appears to be getting worse and worse. Some would say, hopeless. But, actually, it isn't! The good news is, if we will take the bequest off the wall and start using it, Satan can be stopped! How do I know? I know because I have God's word on it.

> Therefore <because He stooped so low> God has highly exalted Him and has freely bestowed on Him the name that is above every name, That in (at) the name of Jesus every knee should (must) bow, in heaven and on earth and under the earth, And every tongue <frankly and openly> confess and acknowledge that Jesus Christ is Lord, to the glory of God the Father. (Philippians 2:9-11 AMP)

Jesus told us, "I tell you the truth, anyone who has faith in me will do what I have been doing. He will do even greater things than these, because I am going to the Father" (John 14:12 NIV). Those were not just empty words. The word *truth* means that you can absolutely trust what he says next. Jesus states that there is only one condition to be met. That condition is to have faith in him. That is exactly what you did when you believed in your heart and confessed with your mouth that God raised Jesus from the dead and were, thereby saved, according to Romans 10:9-10. Return to that confession and you are well on your way to confronting Satan with the power of Jesus' name.

Once we meet that condition, Jesus declares we will be able to do what he has been doing! What has he been doing? He walked on water. He calmed the storm. He raised the dead. He cast out devils. He commanded the sick to be healed. He commanded crooked limbs to be made whole. He commanded the deaf to hear and the blind to see. He preached the Good News of God's love. He fed the multitudes. He did not say we might do these things. He said we will do those things. He has already declared that he did what he saw the father doing, and said what he heard the father saying. He didn't make things up. He spoke only what God spoke. So, in reality, it wasn't Jesus saying we will do them. It was God saying we will do them!

What is your decision going to be? You must take your stand that God is not a liar. If God is not a liar, then when he says we will do the things Jesus did, we will. He did not say we will undo the works of Satan in the future. We are to undo them now. He said that when we believe in him, at that moment and from then on, we will undo them.

If you were Satan, what would you do to keep it from happening? You would try to get us to do what got him in trouble. Rebel. You rebel when you refuse to believe what God has promised. You rebel when you substitute your wisdom for God's. You rebel when you brag, I did it my way. Before doubt or pride overtake you, please be aware of Satan's big lie. He wants us to believe that it is by our own power that miracles happen. We need to get ourselves out of the picture as quickly as we can. We're halfway there when we realize we aren't the ones doing the greater things. Peter made this clear in Acts 3:1-16. He asked,

> "Why are you looking at us as though we had some power by which to make this man walk? It wasn't any power we possess. It was faith in Jesus' name that made this man strong" (KJV).

Peter understood that they were the delivery men, not the source of miracles. The source was the name of Jesus. Satan wants us to think we are the source, the originator of the miracles. Not only does that get our pride mixed up in it, it also opens us up to all kinds of self-blame when the miracles don't happen. Both are very effective tools in disarming us. We bemoan not having enough faith. Or worse yet, we conclude it doesn't work, so why try again. Whereas, the truth is we have failed to use our authority to render Satan powerless, by not letting the name of Jesus do its work.

Satan's goal is to turn us into non-assertive Casper Milquetoasts. In that way, he has nothing to fear from us because we aren't doing anything. Whereas, he is deathly afraid of the power and the authority of Jesus' name. How do we take back this territory Satan has stolen from us? We start by finding out everything we can about our authority to use Jesus' name. We turn to Acts 2, Mark 16:17, 18; John 14:12; and Philippians 2:10. There are many other relevant passages, but these are representative. There is mighty power in the name of Jesus.

- ➢ Salvation comes only by calling on the name
- ➢ Faith in the name brings healing
- ➢ Healings, signs, wonders done through the name
- ➢ Cast out devils by authority of the name

- Speak in new tongues,
- Protection from deadly things by the power of the name
- Lay hands on the sick and they recover by the power of the name
- Do even greater things than Jesus did through the power of his name

It all boils down to the fact that Jesus has given us the authority to use his name. In fact, he actually commissioned us to use it. That is the power of the ambassador. When we speak, it is as though Jesus was right there doing the speaking. Jesus wouldn't put up with the devil's acts and defiance. Why should we? We've got the power. It's just a matter of speaking up and using it and not being a Casper Milquetoast.

My starting point for experiencing the power of Jesus' name was in binding demons. In his book, *The Screwtape Letters*[I], C. S. Lewis relates a series of letters written by a senior demon, Screwtape, to his nephew, Wormwood. Screwtape is trying to train Wormwood to take advantage of every little human imperfection, blowing everything out of proportion. The goal is to undermine faith and promote sin. You might picture it as an imp on your shoulder, whispering in your ear, telling you why you should be angry, or suggesting someone slighted you, or making you believe people are making fun of you.

Making you jealous or envious and nursing hurt feelings, is a really good one if he can pull it off. He especially loves church services where he gives you all kinds of reasons to find fault with the choir, with the sermon, with how someone is dressed up or underdressed, or with not being properly thanked for doing something. The list goes on and on. You get the idea. Our goal is to stop the demons in their tracks on this level.

In the late '60s, we started a Christian coffee house. The young men who were helping us were Spirit filled. I told them to get as many of the youth saved and Spirit filled as possible. When you start winning people for Christ, the demonic powers get very upset and turn up the heat. They use every vile and evil method they can to stop you and defeat you. Playing fair is not in their vocabulary. They were doing their best to stop us winning youth to Christ.

It all came to a head one night when we were to have a meeting of the

Official Board of the church. Word came to us that two men were coming to the meeting to cause trouble. One of the two young men who were working with me, Joe, had had a lot of experience starting Christian coffee houses. He also had had a lot of experience taking authority over evil spirits and binding them in the name of Jesus.

When he heard about the trouble that was brewing, he said, "Let's just bind the evil spirits, and they won't be able to make any trouble." I hadn't heard of that before, but I was eager to learn. We went into the meeting room and prayed a blessing over each chair, adding the following: "All you evil spirits, in the name of Jesus Christ we take authority over you and in the name of Jesus Christ, we command you to be bound dumb and silent in and around every single person who comes here tonight."

In addition, Joe had us go to each door of the church and pray like this: "You Guardian Angels of our Lord Jesus Christ, in the name of Jesus we command you to place a wall of protection around this church, and in the name of Jesus, by your fiery swords, keep every spirit that is not of our heavenly Father from entering this church." The result was the dullest board meeting I have ever attended! The two men came, but weren't able to say one word against us or against what we were doing!

I was intoxicated with the sense of power that that gave me! It was fun to take authority and see what happened. One night while I was driving, I began to think about some people and the trouble they were causing. As I thought about it, resentment boiled up in me, and all I could think about was that resentment. Then, all of a sudden, it popped into my mind that the resentment I was feeling was way out of proportion to the situation that had caused it! Then the thought came, "Do you suppose that I am being harassed by a spirit of resentment?" With that thought came the answer, "yes." Next came the instruction to bind that spirit of resentment. So I said out loud, "You spirit of resentment, in the name of Jesus I bind you dumb and powerless in and around me." That was all it took. No sooner had I spoken those words than the resentment left instantly. I felt like I was standing on the top of a mountain and that all the demonic forces had to obey me! Since then, I have learned that the battle with the demonic forces is more involved than that. But I knew success. And I knew that I had the authority to use the name of Jesus.

It is important in dealing with demonic forces that one be absolutely confident he has the authority for doing so. That means you take no guff and you speak with absolute authority and conviction. You are not binding them by your own power, but by the power of the name of Jesus. Demonic forces cannot stand the sign of the cross, the communion elements, or the name of Jesus. They must give way in the presence of them. Our scriptural authority is in passages like: Matthew 16:19; 18:18; 28:18-20; Mark 16:15-20; James 4:7; Ephesians 6:10-17; Luke 10:19; I Peter 5:8-9; and I John 5:8.

These are only a sampling of verses describing our authority. It is always good to speak these verses out loud when doing spiritual warfare. Not only do they remind us what our authority is, it is a defense against demons trying to tell us we don't have the authority. If demons can bluff us into giving up, they will. Don't give up! Get mad! The more we work at getting this knowledge from our heads down into our hearts, the bolder we become in using our power of attorney.

A neglected, but powerful, use of our authority is in house cleaning! The Church of England has long had a simple service of exorcism to clear the demons out of your home. Demons love to take up residence in our homes. We're not talking about things that go bump in the night or ghostly figures prowling around. Ours are the garden variety of demons that love to get involved in our arguments, get us mad and then say things we're sorry for later. Sometimes the atmosphere gets so thick you can cut it with a knife.

I first came across this handy cleansing service in the book, *Steps to Prayer Power,* by Jo Kimmel.[2] Some of the ideas I am sharing come from her book. About the same time as I came across this service I also learned about cleansing a house from Lee N., a regional director of the Full Gospel Businessmen's Fellowship International. What I share from Lee are things he told us in several talks I recorded. Lee had gotten involved in the occult when he was selling insurance and stocks and bonds. He learned how to exert power over potential customers, causing them to buy what he was selling. He could not do this in homes where there was any evidence that they were practicing Christians.

Through a series of experiences, Lee got delivered from the occult. He then began to witness about the evils of the occult and how to deal with it, speaking from his firsthand experience. The demons did not like this and tried to stop him by having witches and warlocks (yes, they are real) overpower him at his meetings. But every time they tried to manifest, he would bind them dumb and powerless in Jesus' name, often leaving the witch or warlock unable to move or speak. Lee began to study the authority of Jesus' name over demons and demonic activity. People would come to his home to get delivered from demonic influence of one kind or another. When they left, they left the demons behind.

If Lee forgot to command the demons to leave his house and leave the country, the demons would start messing with Lee, after the manner of poltergeists. Lights would flick on or off, an organ would start playing. Lee would bind them and send them away. Demons like to infest our homes as unwanted guests. Lee discovered that by setting his mind to be sensitive to a demonic presence, he could go through a home, and wherever he found them, he could command the demons to leave. After commanding the demons to leave, the Holy Spirit was invited to come in and dwell in the home, which he always does. The home becomes a place of peace that people can sense the moment they enter the door. Lee offered to go through our house and cleanse it.

He walked slowly around each room with his hands held in front of him, palms up, saying, "All spirits that are not of my heavenly Father, in the name of Jesus I command you to leave this room and leave this house, and go 6,000 miles due west." (That was to keep evil spirits from staying around to bother somebody else.) As Lee went through our home, he found places where he detected the presence of evil spirits. When he was done, we immediately sensed a difference in the atmosphere of our home. There was an atmosphere of peace and harmony that hadn't been there before. We noticed that our children fought less and enjoyed each other's company more. Lee said that, for some reason, demons seem to like attics and furnace rooms.

Jo Kimmel told us about using a glass of water. She said to hold the glass of water in your hands, and ask God to bless it. Imagine his blessing streaming into it. Then dip your finger into the water and draw a small cross with a circle around it. Put it on all the walls, doorposts, and corners of all mirrors. I combined Jo Kimmel's glass of water with the procedure that Lee Nystrom used. If you are going to cleanse every nook and cranny of your home, it doesn't really matter whether or not you can sense the presence of evil spirits. They have to obey the authority of the name of Jesus and leave. But you might discover, as I did, that you can sense their presence. To me it was a sense of an unseen resistance, a feeling of malice in the air.

You would think with all the sermons and all the prayers and all the singing and all the praises going up, that churches would be free of all demonic influence. Lee said, No! Demons love churches, too. We were preparing for a Lay Witness Mission. Our preparation ended with a 24-hour prayer vigil. My wife had signed up to go to the church to pray in the middle of the night. Other times when she had been in the church alone, my wife felt uncomfortable. It was as though some unseen malice lurked in the building. She was not looking forward to being in the church alone in the middle of the night. That evening I went through the church, combining Lee Nystrom's method with the glass of water cleansing of Jo Kimmel. I found several hot spots in the church. I commanded all spirits that were not of my heavenly Father to leave in the name of Jesus. Then I used the water, making the sign of the cross inside a circle, and claimed that room for Jesus. The proof that the church was cleansed was going to be how my wife's prayer time went. When I asked her, she said that there was a beautiful presence of peace in the sanctuary.

> NOTE: It isn't all that hard to spook yourself out! It isn't hard to make yourself believe you are seeing things and feeling things that aren't there. So don't start seeing demons under every stone or peeking out of every cupboard. Once you feel competent of your authority, the demons may run before you get to them. Demons can't stand Jesus' name. Apparently, the more you proclaim it and command using it, the more pain it causes.

Jo Kimmel adapted her glass of water cleansing to cleansing people. That does not mean the people are demon possessed. Demons like to seek out footholds in our physical bodies and our minds (See Ephesians 4:27 AMP). This service builds protection around any such areas. You begin with a glass of water, asking God to bless it, and imagining his blessing coming into it. In the same manner, you draw a cross and make a circle around it. You do this to the forehead, saying "I cleanse you (say the person's name) in the name of Jesus." Do this again at the back (nape) of the neck, the solar plexus, and the base of the spine. Finally, you set the glass down and lay hands on the person's head and thank God for cleansing him/her, and ask Jesus to fill him/her with his love and wholeness.

CHAPTER 32

LEARNING LOVE

The Bible proclaims that God is love (I John 4:16). It also states that we were created in his image, the image of love. What does it mean to be created in the image of a God who is Love? It means our basic nature, prior to the Fall, was love (I John 4:8). We were love made flesh. While this was lost at the Fall, where we received Satan's nature, when we are born again we receive a recreated human spirit. That recreated human spirit is a restoration of the love image that was lost. Love is the true nature of a born again person because love is God's nature. Love is not weakness. Neither is love painless. My dad insisted that he loved me, which he really did. But that did not lessen the sting of his razor strap across my bottom when I was naughty or smart-mouthed him back!

Love was the atmosphere, the climate, the air man breathed prior to the Fall. Love was how man related to and interacted with all of creation. Love was how man related to God. Man was not God's slave, God's robot. Man was partnered with God in the business of ruling this earth and developing all its vast resources in and by love. It was a partnership based on love and trust. In that same way, love was the way all creation related to God. The angels and all the host of heaven were also products of God's love, created to be powerful instruments for God to use in carrying out his love plans.

The love partnership worked until the day something went wrong. As we've already seen, one angel, the most powerful, perfect, intelligent, and most beautiful of all, perverted and mutilated love. Perverted and mutilated love is ugly. It does ugly things to us. It poisons us. It throws our mind and emotions out of kilter. Our bodies suffer from its poison. We can be its victims when it is imposed on us. Or we can be the perpetrators when we impose it on others. In I Corinthians 13, Paul describes the many facets of the God kind of love. A finely tuned engine develops all manner of problems and requires costly repairs when impurities are mixed with its fuel. So does man need all kinds of repairs when his love fuel is mixed with the impurities of perverted and mutilated love. The chart below shows what love changes into when it is perverted.

Pure Love	Perverted Love
Merciful and self-restrained	angry, cruel, violent
Good, kindly, gracious	ugly, unfriendly, stingy
Generous, supportive	burns with jealousy
Courteous, friendly, thoughtful	vain-glorious, braggart
Unpretentious, lowly	puffed up, conceited
Elegant, graceful, becoming	unseemly, rude, bad-natured
Unselfish, giving	plots against, insists on its rights
Never exasperated or angered	quick tempered, intolerant
Keeps no record or memory of wrongs	remembers and broods over wrongs
No delight in suffering and unrighteousness	malicious delight in evil done
Is glad when truth prevails	rejoices in lies and gossip

It goes without saying, that the life of the body is in the blood. Lose the blood and the body dies. If the blood becomes corrupted, the human body becomes very sick and can die. It works the same way with the soul. The life of the soul is love. When love was corrupted at the Fall, the soul (mind) became sick (Isaiah 1:5). Our ability to love God, others, and ourselves was corrupted. We could no longer become and do what we were designed to be and do. While the biological, medical, and social sciences give us insights into how amazing our bodies are, only the Bible, our manufacturer's handbook, gives us knowledge about our true created nature. It tells how and why we were created. It tells how our bodies were designed to work. It explains what went wrong and what God has done to repair us.

Do not, under any circumstances, misinterpret what this means as it applies to you. God does not love in general. He loves in particular. He knows and loves each of us individually. David expressed this beautifully.

> O LORD, you have searched me <thoroughly> and have known me. You know my downsitting and my uprising; You understand my thought afar off.
>
> You sift and search out my path and my lying down, and You are acquainted with all my ways. For there is not a word in my tongue <still unuttered>, but, behold, O Lord, You know it altogether.
>
> You have beset me and shut me in—behind and before, and You have laid Your hand upon me. Your <infinite> knowledge is too wonderful for me; it is high above me, I cannot reach it.
>
> Where could I go from Your Spirit? Or where could I flee from Your presence? If I ascend up into heaven, You are there; if I make my bed in Sheol (the place of the dead), behold, You are there. If I take the wings of the morning or dwell in the uttermost parts of the sea, Even there shall Your hand lead me, and Your right hand shall hold me.
>
> If I say, Surely the darkness shall cover me and the night shall be <the only> light about me, Even the darkness hides nothing from You, but the night shines as the day; the darkness and the light are both alike to You. For You did form my inward parts; You did knit me together in my mother's womb.
>
> I will confess and praise You for You are fearful and wonderful and for the awful wonder of my birth! Wonderful are Your works, and that my inner self knows right well. My frame was not hidden from You when I was

> being formed in secret <and> intricately and curiously wrought <as if embroidered with various colors> in the depths of the earth <a region of darkness and mystery>.
>
> Your eyes saw my unformed substance, and in Your book all the days <of my life> were written before ever they took shape, when as yet there was none of them.
>
> How precious and weighty also are Your thoughts to me, O God! How vast is the sum of them! If I could count them, they would be more in number than the sand. When I awoke, <could I count to the end> I would still be with You. (Psalm 139:1-18 AMP)

This means that God knows your name and loves you just as you are. You must have a firm conviction and assurance, deep down inside of you, that you are the beloved of God. That conviction and assurance is your birthright. The Bible testifies that, from the beginning of time God had you in mind. It makes no difference if you were a wanted child or an unwanted child; if you were conceived in love, or lust, or anger, or rape. It makes no difference if you were raised in a godly loving home or in a strife filled, hate and sexual perversion infested house. God planned for you to be and you are the beloved of God. Knowing that you are the beloved of God, knowing it in every fiber of your being, sets you free. It sets you free for love and joy, for dreaming and becoming, for living the life of overflowing abundance that Jesus came to give (John 10:10). This freedom, that comes from knowing, is your birthright. If you need help knowing, begin or continue confessing the affirmations given in Part A.

We were at a CFO Camp when the speaker, Barbara Ann Chase, asked a question that shocked us. She said, "I want you to ask God, 'What do you think of me?'" None of us had dared to ask it before. We were afraid, afraid of the answer. As long as we didn't ask it, we could keep hoping God really did love us. Now the question had been asked and we were afraid. Oh sure, we could quote the Bible verses that said God loves us. But deep down inside we weren't sure he did. We knew what we were really like. It wasn't that we weren't saved. We'd confessed our sins and asked Jesus to come into our hearts. We'd felt cleansed, forgiven, new. But soon we fell back into old sins and even new ones. Time after time we had disappointed ourselves. We had done things we shouldn't have done and said things we shouldn't have said. Things we should have done we didn't do. At times we could not love ourselves. How could God possibly love us?

The question had been asked. We were afraid to hear the answer. What if he despised us? What if he couldn't stand the sight of us? What if he threw in our faces everything bad about us? We were afraid God would reject us. What had brought us to this point of listening anxiously for an answer we were afraid to hear? The speaker had just led us in prayer. Before we knew it, we had asked God the Forbidden Question. Anxiously each of us awaited the answer. Sounds of weeping broke out across the room. A holy awe enveloped us.

Barbara asked, "What did Jesus say to you?"

"He called me his beloved child," said one woman, through tears of joy.

"I heard him say, 'I'm glad you're my son.' But I thought that couldn't be so. It had to be my imagination," said a man who had been convinced God couldn't love him.

And so it was throughout the audience. At first, we tried to dismiss the words that surfaced in our minds as wishful thinking, as our vain imaginings. But the words did not dismiss. The speaker assured us that the first words we heard really were Jesus' words. Each had received a word of love, a word of affirmation, from God. The Forbidden Question had been asked and the answer was love.

We see the power of love in our prayer groups. It has nothing to do with liking or disliking anyone. For example, everyone attending a CFO Camp is assigned to a prayer group. The people in each group are often strangers to each other. But when we pray, compassion rises up within us as we intercede for each other. In those moments, we are harmonizing together (Matthew 18:20). We are literally bearing one another's burdens. When the prayer time is over, we go our separate ways.

This illustrates two key facts about prayer. The first is that love energizes faith. Without love there can be no faith, and prayer without faith is nothing more than a sounding brass (I Corinthians 13:1). Faith comes from believing God, and God is love (Romans 12:3b; I John 4:16). Paul makes this clear in his letter to the Galatians:

> For <if we are> in Christ Jesus, neither circumcision nor uncircumcision counts for anything, but only faith activated and energized and expressed and working through love" (Galatians 5:6 AMP).

In his letter to the Hebrews, Paul reminds us that

> without faith it is impossible to please him: for he that cometh to God must believe that he is, and that he is a rewarder of them that diligently seek him (Hebrews 11:6 KJV).

The second key fact is that love does not mean being buddy-buddy with someone. When you love with the God kind of love, it doesn't matter who the person is with whom you are praying or for whom you are praying. You can pray with power with someone who is your total opposite in personality and likes and dislikes. The fact that we pray together doesn't mean we have to hang out together.

Love also opens our eyes. Have you ever found yourself observing a person and wondering what happened to that person to make them behave the way they do, or believe the way they do? That means that you have recognized that there is a person behind the behavior you see and words you hear, an inner man. It is the inner man that we love. We must never confuse the outward behavior we may dislike with the inner man. It is this inner man of whom Paul speaks in his letter to the Ephesians:

> May He grant you out of the rich treasury of His glory to be strengthened and reinforced with mighty power in the inner man by the <Holy> Spirit <Himself indwelling your innermost being and personality> (Ephesians 3:16 AMP).

There is something that can kill love and rob our faith of power. It is the nasty things we do with words. James mentioned this when he wrote:

> If anyone appears to be "religious" but cannot control his tongue, he deceives himself and we may be sure that his religion is useless. . . . We use the tongue to bless our Lord and Father and we use the same tongue to curse our fellowmen, who are all created in God's likeness. Blessing and curses come out of the same mouth — surely, my brothers, this is the sort of thing that never ought to happen! (James 1:26; 3:9, 10 PHS)

Because your recreated nature is love, you can use that love to bless your neighbors and win them to Christ through prayer. When you do pray, be sure you pray in the right way. Ed Silvoso tells how to pray, and how not to pray, for the people in your neighborhood. He had been walking around his neighborhood praying for the people in each house. One day, in the middle of his walk he, had a conversation with God in which God taught him how to pray for his neighbors. The Lord spoke and said,

> "Ed, I am so glad you have not witnessed to anyone!"
>
> Surprised, Ed replied, "Why, Lord?"
>
> And the Lord said, "I do not want any of your neighbors to know that we are related! You see, I love them, I weep for them, I constantly extend my hand of mercy toward them since I make the sun rise over righteous and unrighteous alike. You, on the contrary, are constantly testifying for the prosecution, condemning them. I did not come to condemn them, but to save them!"[1]

The Lord is saying, it's the things you say when you pray. You are either cursing or blessing. We think we are only stating facts, not cursing the person. When, in reality, what we think are only facts are actually curses. It happens when we say things like, "The lady across the street is always drunk by 10 AM. She is going to die of cirrhosis of the liver." We are actually cursing her to repeat her behavior and to die of cirrhosis of the liver. When we say, "Those rowdy teenagers are a pest and a danger to our neighborhood. They drink and text while they drive. One of these days they are going to kill someone or be killed," we are cursing them to continue to be pests and a danger and to die. Perhaps one of the evilest things we can say under the guise of just stating facts is something like, "My next door neighbor is a pervert and he is going to burn in hell."

To keep your faith working, always pray down good on each person. Never, ever, mention the bad things from that time on except in the past tense. Let your words be "He or she used to be or do, but God's got his hands on 'em now." Ask God to meet that person's needs, to bless that person with all good things, to go before and with that person in all that they do that day so that they will have good success. Then think of the joy that will be theirs when they make Jesus their Lord. Your benefit from praying in this way, in the power of Jesus' name, will be tremendous.

> ... so that Christ may dwell in your hearts through faith—that you, being rooted and grounded in love, may have strength to comprehend with all the saints what is the breadth and length and height and depth, and to know the love of Christ that surpasses knowledge, that you may be filled with all the fullness of God. (Ephesians 3:17-19 ESV)

CHAPTER 33

LOVE REDEEMS THE PAST

Remember Dick's story? It ignited a desire in me to attend a School of Pastoral Care. It was my senior year in college. I'd always wanted to try acting. I used to joke about it and say I'd had acting experience – I once had my arm in a cast! That year an opportunity came. I tried out for a part in a college play. I got it! About that same time, the dates came for the School of Pastoral Care. It was to be held at the same time as the performances of the play. I wanted my chance to act. I decided not to go to the School of Pastoral Care.

I was sitting in church the next Sunday, when a most unusual thing happened. A great inner turmoil rose up in my spirit. At the same time an inner voice seemed to say, "Resign from the play. Go to the School of Pastoral Care." It was a strange experience. I fought it at first. But it was so strong I had to give in. The professor who was directing the play was in church. I told the inner voice I would speak to him after the service. As soon as I made that decision, the inner turmoil lessened. At the close of the service I caught up with the professor and resigned from the play. No sooner had I spoken, than the turmoil stopped. As you can imagine, with an experience like that behind me, I went to the School of Pastoral Care with much anticipation.

At the School of Pastoral Care, we sat spellbound as Agnes told Mary's story. Mary was the victim of a lie; the lie that says there's nothing wrong with cheating a little, or stealing company pens, or telling a little white lie, or stirring up strife, or gossip, or tale bearing, or sexual playing around. There's a lie that says this is a new, modern age, free from all those old crippling do's and don'ts that robbed us of our freedom. People try to deny it, but when you are born again, your conscience is activated. Your conscience and your body know the difference between right and wrong. When you do wrong, your conscience accuses you. If you ignore your conscience, your body may cry out.

That is what had happened to Mary. Mary would become very ill each month at the beginning of her menstrual period. At first it had been mild, but with the passing of each month it got worse. Mary was examined, examined again, and reexamined. Nothing showed up in any of the tests and examinations. Finally, her Gynecologist said, "Mary, we cannot find anything organically wrong with you. There is no physical reason to account for your sickness. I am going to send you to Dr. S. He is a very good psychiatrist. Perhaps he can help you."

Mary went to see Dr. S. As they talked Mary confessed that she had been having sexual affairs. "But that's perfectly alright," she quickly added. "Everybody does it. That couldn't possibly have anything to do with my...."

"Mary!" said Dr. S, interrupting her, "Your sexual affairs are wrong! Your body knows they are wrong. Every month it is crying out to you that you are sinning against God, against your fellow man, and against yourself. It will keep crying out until you admit you are wrong, confess your sins, and receive forgiveness and cleansing." Mary's defenses broke. Sobbing, she admitted she knew it was wrong. She had tried to convince herself it was okay. But deep down she knew it wasn't. What could she do? Dr. S told her how Jesus' blood can wash us clean of all our sin. If we will confess our sins, he is faithful and just to forgive us.

Because Dr. S did not feel that it was ethical for a psychiatrist to lead a patient in a prayer of confession, he told her to go to her pastor and ask him to hear her confession. She went to her pastor. Instead of declaring her forgiven, he just patted her on the back and said, "Oh, we all make mistakes. It's okay. Don't worry about it." In desperation Mary went back, sobbing, and told her story to Dr. S. Dr. S, moved with compassion for this young woman who was so desperate, kneeled on the office floor beside Mary and led her in a prayer of confession. Then, using his authority as a Christian, he pronounced her forgiven (John 20:23; I Peter 2:5). Mary rose from her knees a transformed person. Gone was the anguish, the near panic. Her beautiful face shone with joy, her outward beauty now mingled with an inner beauty. Deep within, Mary knew that she, too, was a forgiven beloved of God.

As Agnes talked about Mary, hope rose up within me. God wants to set us free from all the dirt and sin that drags us down. He doesn't want to condemn us. He wants to set us free. He wanted to set me free. He was showing me how I could be set free. Some would say I was foolish to feel weighed down by sin and guilt. After all, hadn't Jesus carried all my sins to the Cross? Hadn't I gone forward at Jack Wirtzen's Word of Life Rally and asked Jesus to come into my heart and life? That was true. I did have a recreated human spirit. But my beliefs about myself had not been transformed. I knew what I was like. I was painfully aware of all my failures and shortcomings. I knew how far short I came from measuring up to the goal of my high calling in Christ Jesus. I did not feel worthy of Christ and I didn't see how he could find me acceptable.

But joy was awakening in my heart. At home I had always believed I had to measure up to my imagined standard of perfection to be acceptable to my parents. Now I was beginning to understand, to sense in my heart, that the only standard God wanted me to measure up to was to admit that I needed him and that without him I would continue to have troubles. He wanted to make something wonderful of my life. All I had to do was let him do it.

Agnes described two ways God has given us to deal with our hearts. The first she called "Prayer for the healing of the subconscious mind," which is nothing more than the forgiveness of sins; sins we have committed and sins that have been committed against us. It is true that when we are born again we receive a recreated human spirit. But a recreated human spirit does not solve all the problems. The soul (heart) and body have to be brought in line with the word of God. That is why Paul tells us to be transformed by the renewing of our minds (Romans 12:2). For some of us, before that renewal takes place, things get short-circuited. Our minds begin condemning us for our failures. (Satan loves this because it provides him a foothold from which to torment us with his evil whispers.) We do things we know we shouldn't do. Our minds try to tell us that we are forgiven and loved, that all we have to do is confess our sins and we will be forgiven and cleansed. But self-condemnation rises up in us and writes us off as a perpetual failure.

That is how I felt - like I was looking at a feast but was too unworthy to take a single bite. I wanted to feast. I went to where the feast was. I kept hoping things would change. Then, Agnes spoke and hope arose in me. She told how to pray for people with mental and emotional troubles. She said, "Do not say to them 'I know God can help you.' Say, 'I can help you.' Tell them they don't have to do anything. They don't have to rely on their own belief. They don't have to make any effort, or try to work up enough faith. Say, 'My faith is sufficient. The Lord knows you don't have enough faith.' Speak firmly and surely. Don't pussyfoot around."

I thought, "That's for me! I'm going to make an appointment with Agnes." I did. In spite of how easy she made it sound, I still found it was a scary thing to do. What if it didn't work? What if God really did reject me? It would shatter me. I had not yet learned that God is not a liar and that what he said he would do, he will do (Numbers 23:19). When I went into the room at the time of my appointment, I told Agnes my fears.

"It will work," she replied with quiet authority.

"Does this depend on my faith?" I asked, fearfully. "Because if it does, forget it. It won't work."

"It does not depend on your faith," she answered.

"Should I be praying while you do this?"

"No," Agnes assured me. "Just let your mind wander wherever it wants to." She stood behind me, placed her hands on my head and began to pray. She asked Jesus to go into my subconscious mind, into the deepest depths and hidden places, and heal whatever was causing the trouble. Next, going back through my life stage by stage, she asked Jesus to open the windows of my memory rooms and let in the fresh air and sunshine. He opened closets and swept out the dirt and hurts he found there. She ended the prayer by having Jesus go back to the time before I was born, before I was conceived, and deal with what was going on between my parents and with the trauma of birth.

A lightness filled me, accompanied by a deep peace and the knowledge that God really did love me! I also felt led to use the second way God has for dealing with our hearts; the confessional. The process was simple. I would make an appointment with her husband, Rev. Edgar Sanford, and ask him to hear my confession. I divided my life up into five year sections (I was 25). I wrote down all the sins I could think of for each five-year period. I took the list with me to the confessional. I wasn't a big sinner. I hadn't murdered anyone, robbed a bank, had an affair, and that sort of thing. I was not a wicked person. The only sins I could think of were little petty ones, the kind nobody thinks are sins because everybody does them. And yet, never in my life have I had to do anything as hard as read that list in front of Rev. Sanford as I knelt at the altar!

As I knelt, trying to read that list out loud, I kept thinking, "I can't believe this! I'm not confessing to murder or robbery. Why is it so hard to confess them?" My list of sins was symbolic. I was disclosing my whole being to God in what I had perceived as all its rottenness. I was letting God see me as I saw myself. I was still afraid God would turn his back on what he saw. I still had not gotten I John 1:9 through my mind; he doesn't condemn, he cleanses. I struggled through the list. I waited for the ax to fall. But no ax fell. In a quiet, authoritative voice, as though he had not heard one word of my confession, Rev. Sanford spoke.

"By the power and authority invested in me as a priest in the church of Jesus Christ, I pronounce you forgiven."

And I was! My little list had symbolized all my sins, and God had forgiven every one! It felt like a hundred-pound load had been lifted off my shoulders! I felt clean! Really clean! God had forgiven me! He really did love me! I knew that I knew that I was the beloved of God. Later God showed me that Jesus had born all my sins to the Cross two thousand years ago. What happened to me at that confessional was that I finally forgave myself! In forgiving myself I became free to receive the love and forgiveness God already had for me. But there was a price to pay for what God had done for me! "Share it," he said. "Help others know that I love them too."

Share it, I did. Here is just one example of sharing. The 1977 Conference on Charismatic Renewal in the Christian Churches was being held in Kansas City, Missouri. A group of us chartered a bus and went. It was an exciting time. During the day we attended various workshops and at night we all gathered in Arrowhead Stadium for a tremendous Spirit led meeting.

When the meeting ended, we found our way back to our bus and drove to Lawrence, Kansas where we stayed in a college dormitory.

So many exciting things happened during the day that we couldn't go to bed until we had shared it all. So it was that on this particular night we were gathered in a lounge, talking and sharing. One of the young women, Julie, went out to call her mother. She returned with tears in her eyes. "What's wrong? What happened?" we asked, expecting to hear of some tragedy back home.

"I just had a fight with my mother. She won't believe anything. She said I was stupid for coming," Julie sobbed.

As Julie spoke, a spirit of compassion rose up within me and I knew that Jesus wanted to minister to Julie. "Julie, what kind of relationship do you have with your mother?" I asked. Julie began to tell of the many hurts. She wanted so much to be close to her mother. But it seemed like arguing and fault finding was all she ever got from her mother. Something had happened in the past between Julie and her mother to cause a barrier to be erected. "Julie," I said, "let me pray for you. Let me ask Jesus to walk through all those old memories and hurts and heal them. He'll set you free to love your mom."

Julie sat in a chair. I had others stand around her and lay their hands on her head and shoulders. Then, I knelt in front of her, her hands in mine. And I began to pray for the healing of her memories. I asked Jesus to remove the hurt from this last talk with her mother. I asked him to walk back through every memory room, back through childhood and birth, back to the moment of conception. The Holy Spirit guided the words I prayed. When the Holy Spirit was finished, I looked up at Julie's face. The joy of the Lord radiated from it. Tears of hurt had become tears of joy.

Another young woman, seeing what happened to Julie, asked to be prayed for. We prayed for her. The same thing happened. The old hurts were gone and joy was on her face. We were rejoicing in what God had done, when a young man stepped into the room. "Will that work over a distance?" he asked. Unknown to us, this young Jewish man had been standing in the doorway watching as we prayed. He saw the transformation that came over the two young women. He could tell by what he saw that prayer for healing of the memories worked. He shared this story:

"Last Fall my mother was viciously raped. She is a Christian. She has forgiven her attacker. She has done everything she knows to do. But she can't get rid of the fear. And she keeps having nightmares. Will this prayer work for her?"

We didn't know because we had never tried praying in proxy for anyone before. However, we didn't know any reason why it wouldn't work. So we had this young man sit in a chair and we gathered around him to pray. I instructed him to sit with his palms up, as though he were holding his mother up to Jesus. He was to keep this picture in his mind and to keep saying, "Jesus, this is mom." I asked Jesus to go back through every part of that ugly rape experience. I asked him to rebuke the terror, to put peace in her heart, to take her and hold her, and heal her as though the rape had never happened.

About three weeks later I received a very short note from the young Jewish man. "It works," he wrote. His mother was set free as we prayed. God really does care. He is ever present with his healing power to transform us by the renewing of our minds. Jesus came to give us life; life in overflowing abundance. He bore our pain for us. He took all our sins and failures upon himself and bore them to the Cross. We do not have to bear them any longer. In place of death, he gives Life. In place of sadness, he gives Joy. In place of poverty, he gives prosperity. In place of sickness, he gives health. You cannot earn it. It is a free gift, freely given to all who will accept it. Why? Because you are the beloved of God.

It is so very important that you know in every fiber of your being that you are the beloved of God. You can trust God. He won't reject you. He loves you very much. He wants you to know beyond the shadow of a doubt that you really are his beloved. Take courage from these stories. If you need help, don't hesitate to find someone who can pray with you like Agnes and Rev. Sanford prayed with me.

You are the beloved of God, as Isaac Watts and John Wesley sang.

> Were the whole realm of nature mine,
> That were an offering far too small;
> Love so amazing, so divine,
> Demands my life, my soul, my all!
>
> (Isaac Watts)

And can it be that I should gain
An interest in the Savior's blood?
Died he for me, who caused his pain?
For me, who him to death pursued?
Amazing love! how can it be
That thou, my Lord, shouldst die for me?
Long my imprisoned spirit lay,
Fast bound in sin and nature's night;
Thine eye diffused a quickening ray;
I woke, the dungeon flamed with light;
My chains fell off, my heart was free,
I rose, went forth, and followed thee.
No condemnation now I dread;
Jesus, and all in him, is mine;
Alive in him, my living Head,
And clothed in righteousness divine,
Bold I approach th'eternal throne,
And claim the crown, through Christ my own.

(John Wesley)

You are the beloved of God! From the beginning of time he had you in mind! God's love is utterly amazing! In Romans 16:25-26, Paul speaks of "the revelation of the mystery, which was kept secret since the world began, but now is made manifest" (KJV). What is that mystery? It is a mystery of love! Stand in front of a mirror. Look yourself in the eyes. Now say out loud to yourself, "I am the beloved of God! From the beginning of time God had me in mind!" Was it easy to say? Did you shout? Once it was hard for me to say it. But not now. Because now I know God's love secret.

The great God, the creator who laid the foundations of the earth, before he began his work of creating, laid plans for you and me to be with him forever in his kingdom of love. Even before he had created us, he loved us. Ephesians 1:3-11 is a celebration of the mystery of his love. God is a wonder! Before he began to create the world, before even the first man was made, God loved us! He knew what would happen when he created us. He knew how dirty and sinful and stinky we would become. But he loved us even then, and in love and kindness and favor he deliberately chose us for himself! Can you envision the wonder of that? He knew the depths to which we could sink if we gave ourselves to evil. And yet it was his will, that regardless of how deep the pit of our evil, his love would be there with the promise of life for all who would accept it. (Ephesians I:3-4)

Lee N. tells of the length and depth and breadth of God's love. A young woman in Minneapolis was so filled with demonic forces it took six months to set her free. She had two murder raps hanging over her in California, a couple felonies, plus time in prison. This woman had not sunk deeper than his love could reach. She said "Yes!" to his love, and found that she was a beloved of God.

Lee told us wonderful stories of God's amazing love as he worked with victims of Satan. A thirteen-year-old girl who had become a witch, who had sacrificed her own baby to the god of the obelisk and drunk its blood, had not sunk deeper than God's love could reach. She said Yes! to his love, and found that she, too, was a beloved of God. A high priestess of the Church of Satan, who gave herself to sins so inconceivable they cannot be told, had not sunk deeper than God's love could reach. Saying Yes! to him, she discovered that she was a beloved of God. You cannot stoop so low but that his love is deeper still. In my ignorance and pride, I tried to think that I was beyond his love. But, praise God, I discovered that his love is deeper still.

Yes, God in grace (his unmerited favor), out of that great love with which he has loved us, deliberately chose us for himself. By his own deliberate act, he gave Jesus, who took upon himself all our sin, all our sickness, all our failures, all our poverty, all our punishment, and went to hell for us. There was absolutely nothing we could do to even remotely earn or deserve his love. It is a free gift. And when we accept it, he immediately declares us utterly holy and blameless, without fault or blemish. Immediately he declares that we are his pride and joy, his beloved. We are his pride and joy because he has made us his kids! He set his will beforehand to adopt us as his children through Jesus Christ; and that well-pleased him and suited his will and desire.

What we have become brings praise and commendation to God because of his glory and grace, which he has lavished upon us in the beloved. And in doing this, he has also lavished upon us the wisdom of God and sound sense (practical insight). And he made known to us the secret of his will, his plan. It was this: according to his good pleasure, his merciful intention, which he purposed in himself, at the appointed time to head up all things in Christ, things in the heavens, and things on the earth. In Christ we have been made God's heritage, God's portion. (Ephesians 1:5-11)

Prayer is family talk. It is basking in the love father God pours upon us. It is confidence in his "covering our back" when we go forth and use the authority and power of Jesus' name. And it is the assurance that when we goof up there is instant forgiveness and a hand on the shoulder that says, "Let me help you keep from making that mistake again."

CHAPTER 34

LOVE REDEEMS THE PRESENT

Yes, God does have our backs, as the saying goes. We really need it because for some reason many Christians seem to have a difficult time following directions. Failure to follow instructions can lead to much frustration and false conclusions. This little quiz (author unknown) was posted on the internet. Get yourself a sheet of paper and a pencil. Sit down. Take the test. At the end compare your answers and see how well you did.

Directions Quiz – Read through ALL the numbered steps below before you begin. Read the directions carefully and do exactly as they say.

1. Use the back of this paper to complete steps 2 – 11.
2. Write your first name in the middle of the paper.
3. Draw a heart above your name.
4. Write your last name in bottom right corner.
5. Cross your last name out with two lines
6. Draw a picture of your favorite food underneath your name.
7. Draw a smiley face inside the heart you drew above your first name.
8. Raise your hand. When your teacher calls on you say "I am on Number 8!"
9. Draw a cow in the bottom left corner of your paper.
10. Label whether the cow is a noun, verb, or adjective.
11. Do not do steps 1 -10. Put your pencil down quietly and wait for others to finish.

How did you do? We get into trouble by not following instructions. We make wrong assumptions and then make wrong conclusions when things don't work as we had assumed they would work. We rush through steps 1–10 without first reading through to step 11. Failure to read through to step 11 in this test is what we often do in prayer. We miss the extremely important fact that God isn't going to do everything we ask! Why? For one simple reason. He told us to do it! You already knew this, although it may not have been stated so bluntly. A quick excursion through the Gospels makes this clear.

Jesus went around doing good. Healings and miracles abounded. While he spent many hours in prayer, there is only one recorded time when he asked God to do something. That one time was in the Garden of Gethsemane when he asked, "Father, if thou be willing, remove this cup from me: nevertheless, not my will, but thine, be done" (Luke 22:42 KJV). This prayer had to do with Jesus' commitment to do God's will. All other times, Jesus used his authority. He expects us to do exactly as he did. This is the same authority he expects us to use as his ambassadors. He chided the disciples for their lack of faith and resultant failure to calm the storm at sea. Satan may be the prince of the power of the air and storms may be under his dominion, but Jesus had given them power over the power of the enemy. Instead of cowering in the bottom of the boat they should have used their authority and calmed the storm.

When people "brought to him all who were ill . . . those suffering severe pain, the demon-possessed, those having seizures, and the paralyzed," he healed them (Matthew 4:24 NIV). He explained that they had the power to bind and loose. If two of them agreed about anything they asked for, "it will be done for you by my Father in heaven. For where two or three come together in my name, there am I with them" (Matthew 18:19 NIV). (See also Mark 1:25-27, 41; 4:39-40; 5:41; 7:33-34; 11:23-24; Luke 7:13-15; 10:17-19; John 14:12)

God will not do for us what he has given us the authority to do ourselves. He told us that we are to take authority over storms, demons, sickness, and everything that has a name, because every knee, every name, must bow at the mention of Jesus' name. Remember how the disciples came back and excitedly told Jesus that even the demons were subject to them in

Jesus' name? As you will see in the following examples, this fact is the key to this chapter.

Satan, the god of this world, is the storm god. But, we have the authority to rise up and command the storm, saying "In the name of Jesus don't you dare come in here". We speak in authoritative and demanding tones. That was the situation Dr. B. described when a tornado tore through Branson, Missouri. Her son pled the blood of Jesus over his house and commanded the tornado to pass over without causing even a shingle to flap. It did, while homes around him sustained damage. A visitor to Branson, who had just registered at a motel, pled the blood of Jesus over the motel and commanded the tornado to pass over the motel in Jesus' name. It did, and damaged a motel next to his. The devil will try to make you think this was just coincidence, hoping to destroy your faith. Tell him to go to hell!

Do not try to use your authority beyond what Jesus did. He calmed the storms that directly involved him and the disciples, not others. When your authority meets faith, you need only speak the word and miracles happen. When you share the word, signs follow for the benefit of those receiving salvation. You can also exercise your authority on the behalf of your family. Jesus did not command every demon everywhere to be gone. Healings that took place over a distance required someone who had the right to give him permission. The Centurion enabled Jesus to heal his servant at a distance by giving him permission, in faith. The Syrophenician woman gave Jesus permission, in faith, to cast the devil out of her daughter who was at home. A modern example is that of the Jewish son, in the story just told, who gave permission for his mom's memory to be healed of the trauma caused by rape.

Casting demons out, as in exorcism, is not the only way we can take authority over demons. I first heard of this from a veterinarian. No matter how wonderful you think your family is, you cannot escape conflicts between husband and wife, between parent and child, or between siblings. We are all different, all exerting our own individualities, which often leads to disagreements. What we don't realize is that Satan uses this as a playground for his demons. Demons do not play fair. They work tirelessly trying to blow up everything into arguments, anger, hurt feelings, you name it. The veterinarian discovered that you can identify the demons by the trouble they are causing and when you bind them dumb and powerless, the trouble instantly ceases.

Every time his kids got into an argument, he'd go where the kids couldn't hear him and then command, "You demons causing my children to argue and fight, in the name of Jesus I bind you dumb and powerless in them and around them, now!" Instantly the arguments ceased. He shared this with his kids, because they needed to know how to use it. When dad and son or daughter got in an argument, or mom and dad, or mom and one of the kids, someone would remember to bind and loose and end the conflict. We began using this authority in our family with great success.

In John 10:10, Jesus tells us that "the thief comes only to steal and kill and destroy." It is vitally important that we understand what that means in our everyday living. The demons have been turned loose to harass us at every turn and in every way. That is why Paul stresses the importance of putting on the whole armor of God. Satan's goal is to defeat us in the little things. Once you know this, you can minister to many people. One time a little girl came to me for prayer. She was troubled by some fears she couldn't get rid of. I sensed that a demon of fear was harassing her. Under my breath, so that she would not hear me, I bound that demon dumb and silent in Jesus' name and commanded it to leave her. The next day when I met her I asked her how she was doing and she happily announced the fears were gone.

Someone else taught us about interceding for people by "doing a page" on them. The prayer group asks the Holy Spirit for a list of the forces, demonic and otherwise, that are tormenting the one for whom prayer has been requested. The thoughts that come are written down. Obviously Satan will try to sabotage our efforts by tossing in some worthless names to mislead us. That was okay. We'd bind everything that came to us, figuring that in the mix would be the key forces that needed to be bound and cast out.

When the list was complete, we would go through the list and bind each demon, every negative emotion. Then we would go through the list again and loose the opposite force into the person's life. One night our prayer group received an emergency call from a mother of a young woman. This woman had spent several weeks in a psych ward. She had been home for a few weeks. But that afternoon she had gotten so bad they took her back.

Would we pray for her? We did the page, and bound and loosed. The next day the young woman was released and was well enough to get her own apartment in town. She had been set free of the demonic oppression.

Another way of redeeming the present is to release the Holy Spirit into what appears to be an impossible situation. That is what happened to Ordelphia, a CFO speaker who shared her story[1]. When Harald Bredesen's phone rang in the middle of the night, little did he know of the miracles that would soon come to pass. Neither did Ordelphia dream of the wonders that would come to pass through her. By his Spirit, God uses ordinary people to do extraordinary things.

Finding herself depressed, disturbed in her spirit, Ordelphia cried out to God in the middle of the night. God answered by giving her the strange impression that she should get out the Yellow Pages of her phone book and turn to the section titled "Clergy." She did and her finger went to a name she did not know. Marking it with her fingernail, she dialed the number. A man's voice said, "Hello." And Ordelphia sobbed, "I need prayer. I need help."

"Dear Lord Jesus, help my sister." The prayers rolled out. Hanging up the phone, Ordelphia went upstairs and went to sleep; an undisturbed sleep for the first time in many months. She woke up the next morning feeling as light as a feather. The problems had not disappeared. But they no longer had the power to oppress her. Throughout the day the lightness remained. The problems still did not depress her. She decided to call up the pastor who had prayed for her and thank him. But she couldn't find the phone book! A month later, when she wasn't looking for the phone book, she found it. By her fingernail mark she saw his name and address. That night she drove over to see him and thank him personally.

The pastor was Harald Bredesen. Harald, and the many people he had taken into his home, welcomed her with open arms, and "Thank you Jesus." Immediately, they all gathered for prayer. They had been praying every day for this woman who had called in the night. They had asked Jesus to bring her to them. Before she left that day, Ordelphia met Jesus as her baptizer in the Holy Spirit, although her prayer language did not come until nine months later. That was in June. Ordelphia went to Harald's every day that summer for his morning Bible study. When Harald asked if any had needs,

Ordelphia was always the first to respond. And everything she asked for, those people prayed down upon her.

Ordelphia taught brain injured, emotionally disturbed children. Each child she taught had some neurological impairment. That fall, Ordelphia went back to her classroom a changed person. Walking into her classroom before the students arrived, she prayed, "Jesus, heal my class." She had seven students. Remembering Oral Roberts teaching on a point of contact, she arranged each seat and prayed over each student by name. She touched each seat and claimed each child for the glory of God in the name of Jesus. Then Ordelphia looked at the children's records: paranoid, schizophrenic, non-reader, hyperactive, very disruptive. "Boy Lord! Praise God! I don't have to do it. You do." She claimed them all for Jesus. Next, she anointed everything in the room with oil. She put the sign of the Cross on every window. Lastly, she put oil on herself, asking God to make her the best teacher ever.

On March 17th that school year, she was driving up the Thruway on her way to school when her prayer language suddenly burst forth and flowed. She prayed in her new language all the way to school. When she got to school, she knew people would think she had flipped if they saw her. And so she snuck into her classroom. Harald Bredesen had given her a copy of the American Bible Society's translation of the New Testament, *Good News for Modern Man*. She had read it through several times and loved it. She had the book with her in her school materials.

Her students, who came on the little buses, started to arrive. The first child that ran into the room stopped short, and asked, "Gee, what happened to you this morning? You look so different!" "Oh, the Lord just gave me this new language to praise him," she said. "Oh, Roger, that's something you read about in the Bible," she added and handed him her copy of *Good News for Modern Man*. Now that was the wrong thing to do in a school that has nothing to do with God. But it didn't matter, because none of her students could read. She was teaching them by the association method. Roger might find one or two words he recognized. But there was no way he could possibly read it, to say nothing of understanding what he read. That day the kids looked at her, knowing there was something different. They were quieter. She didn't have to talk so much. She was having a good time teaching.

That night she soared home praying in her prayer language. And the next morning soared back to school. Roger came running up to her and he looked at her and said, "Teacher, the Lord has given me such insight!" Ordelphia's mouth just dropped open! She said, "Roger, what are you talking about?" He said, "This book you gave me. I've read it." Ordelphia couldn't believe that. Roger was reading very simple things like, "See Jane. See Jane run. See the balloon."

"What did you read?" she asked him. He opened the book and he looked up at her and he read, "When the day of Pentecost arrived, all the believers were gathered together in one place... They were all filled with the Holy Spirit and began to talk in other languages, as the Spirit enabled them to speak." And he read. And he read. And he read. Ordelphia listened, her mouth still open. When she came to herself, she opened a dictionary, something academic. She said, "Read Roger, right through the A's." She pointed to a word. He read, "Aardvark: an ant eater, a long nosed animal." Ordelphia did not know before what an aardvark was. But she knows now and will never forget! She picked up other books on her desk. Roger read from all of them at random.

Roger had been healed! Overnight Roger had become normal in every way; with one exception. His physical coordination had been very bad. But that day Ordelphia begged the coach to let Roger compete in the regular gym class with the other boys his age. After much protest the coach allowed it. And that day, in the regular gym class, Roger won the Gold Medal for first place in relays and high jumping.

A couple days later Roger was baptized in the Holy Spirit at Harald Bredesen's. Roger joined Ordelphia in praying. And by the end of that semester, her whole class got healed. One child who was legally blind was totally healed. Roger had been diagnosed as having only enough potential to finish grammar school, nothing more. He was twelve years old. After his healing, Roger went on to complete high school. He served in the Army. He has been to Germany. He is a beautiful Christian.

Ordelphia, an ordinary person, began to do extraordinary things. That happens when you spend time in family talk. We are Christ's ambassadors, reconciling the world to him. When Ordelphia put her hand in God's and let the Holy Spirit guide her, miracles happened. That very possibility is yours and mine today. Take your Father's hand, yield yourself to the Holy

Spirit, and you too will begin to do extraordinary things as the Holy Spirit works through you.

Carol, a young mother, had been discovering the authority she now had as a blood bought, Spirit filled child of God, to bind and loose according to Jesus' words in Matthew 18:18. At first she was skeptical of this spiritual authority. But she was willing to learn. One day her little girl seemed beside herself with fussing, crying, tantrums. It came into Carol's spirit to use her authority. "You spirit causing my little girl to be like this, I bind you in the name of Jesus. I command you in Jesus' name to leave her alone." Instantly the fussing and crying stopped. Her little girl looked up at her and smiled. Carol realized with a thrill that her little girl was free from that thing. She was free and she was happy and she looked at her mom with thanks. An ordinary person did an extraordinary thing through the power of the Holy Spirit that dwells permanently in her as a blood bought child of God, Christ's ambassador at work.

These aspects of our ambassadorial powers excite us. Even as you read, you are seeing in your mind opportunities to use them. I wish healing was as easy as that. It isn't always. This is illustrated in Jesus' own ministry. Near the sheep market in Jerusalem there was a pool. It was said that at a certain season an angel troubled the water. Whoever was the first to get into the water after it was troubled was healed of his disease. One day Jesus was walking by this pool. There were a great number of sick and crippled people there, waiting for the troubling. Jesus noticed a man who had suffered with a severe disorder for 38 years. He spoke to the man and told him to get up. The man did, being instantly healed (John 5:2-9).

Why weren't the others healed? Was it somehow connected with Jesus' experience in his home town of Nazareth where he could do no mighty works there because of their unbelief (Matthew 13:58)? Why was it only the man on the pallet, let down through the roof, who was healed? The text says very plainly that the power of God was present to heal (Luke 5:17). We can easily attribute the failure to be healed to unbelief. But what about those who do believe and still do not receive their healing? Jesus was always telling people, according to your faith be it unto you. Does that mean they didn't have enough faith? He didn't say that.

We can conclude unequivocally that God does not send sickness. He wants us well. Sickness is from Satan. This is the Bible's message. As far as having enough faith is concerned, Paul tells us that God has given to every man the measure of faith. Jesus said it only takes faith the size of a mustard seed to move a mountain (Matthew 17:20). How that faith is directed or fragmented, makes the difference. When you think of it like that, it changes the meaning we usually associate with Jesus' words, "according to your faith be unto you." It is not a matter of having enough faith, since we were all given enough. It is how we hinder or fragment or block that faith. Evangelists have reported cases of people telling them, "I know Jesus is right here with my healing, but I just can't receive it."

That is not the only thing that causes our faith to be fragmented. Someone once said that we have been vaccinated with just enough religion to become immune to it! Paul, the brilliant scholar who had outdistanced all his teachers, had to be hit with a force so powerful it forced him to lay aside all he had learned, "I count them but dung" (Philippians 3:8), so that he could apprehend the simplicity of the Gospel (2 Corinthians 1:12). Paul feared that, just as the serpent beguiled Eve through his subtlety, so our minds should be corrupted from the simplicity that is in Christ (2 Corinthians 11:3).

It seems that each of us must examine ourselves to ascertain where our faith is and to find out what we must do to defragment our faith. A characteristic of denominations is that each one attempts to uphold some truth that it believes others have forgotten, denied, or distorted. When you combine this with the teachings of individual pastors and authors, it tends to create confusion in our minds. Perhaps this explains why people who are not Christians seem to receive so easily. They've not had years of indoctrination. It was the indoctrinated Jewish officials who could not receive from Jesus. The humble poor believed and received.

Here is one possible way to defragment faith. First, arbitrarily affirm: God said it. I believe it. That settles it. Second, approach healing with bite size portions, or the smallest bit possible that you can believe for without doubting. Perhaps for the arthritic it is to see the swelling go down on one finger or movement to come back to the finger. For a heart attack, ask what is the one thing that needs to happen now? As each thing responds to prayer, move on to the next. Third, saturate yourself with healing scriptures and keep speaking them out loud so as to drive the truth from your head down into your heart. Fourth watch your mouth! Speak only what faith says. Faith says that by the stripes that wounded Jesus the sick were healed (I Peter 2:24). Choose life and speak life.

CHAPTER 35

Love Redeems the Future

In Christ we are redeemed out of the past and given new possibilities for the future. "For if a man is in Christ he becomes a new person altogether — the past is finished and gone, everything has become fresh and new" (I Corinthians 5:17 PHS). Toyohiko Kagawa, born in Kobe, Japan, became a most remarkable man because his future was redeemed. His father was a philandering businessman and his mother was a concubine. Both parents died while he was young. As a youth, he became a Christian. The rest of his extended family immediately disowned him. He nurtured the image of God with amazing results. Kagawa discovered that with God living inside him, he had entered into a partnership that could do far more than he, Kagawa, could have ever done by himself. In serving the people in the slums of Kobe, Japan, he lost most of his eyesight. Undaunted by his near blindness, he went on to write many books. He gave voice to the vision that drove and sustained him in these words:

> . . . today
> A wonderful thought
> In the dawn was given,

> And the thought
> Was this:

That a secret plan
Is hid in my hand;
That my hand is big,
Big,
Because of this plan.
That God,
Who dwells in my hand,
Knows this secret plan
Of the things He will do
for the world
Using my hand!
(From "Discovery")[1]

Kagawa let God use his hand. From it flowed several hundred Christian books. Because Japan is 98.4 percent literate, millions of copies of these books were sold to the entire Japanese nation. Using Kagawa's hand, God was able to reach into thousands of minds and hearts, and plant His thoughts there. It is amazing what God does with us when we let our inner image be transformed into the image of God. His resources become our resources. That is the secret of redeeming the future. We allow him to unfold the plans he has for us.

> "For I know the thoughts and plans that I have for you, says the Lord, thoughts and plans for welfare and peace and not for evil, to give you hope in your final outcome" (Jeremiah 29:11 AMP).

Redeeming the future also means to change directions and emphasis, following God's leading. This is not always easy. Sometimes he asks us to make decisions we really don't want to make. I had to go through that. It had to do with performing magic. I grew up with a love of magic. I enjoyed making people laugh. I joined the International Brotherhood of Magicians (IBM). Through the pages of its monthly magazine, I learned about all the great magical performers. In 1967, I became involved with Ring 24 of the IBM, ultimately becoming the president of that Ring.

My skills improved. I began performing for Boy Scout Blue and Gold Banquets, Church Groups, etc. The day came when I knew I was good enough that I could book shows to do in my spare time, and earn more money performing magic than I was being paid as a pastor. It was tempting. I had the professional skills and I knew how to get the show dates. One of my favorite illusions was an enlarging machine I built. It was a box that sat on a table, illuminated inside with ultra-violet light, complete with flashing lights and musical notes on its control panel. I would open the doors, show the machine on all sides. I would put an ordinary penny on a pedestal, so that it could be seen inside the box. I would close the doors, switch the machine on, and when I opened the doors there was a five-inch wide penny. In would go a small tennis shoe, out would come a large tennis shoe (complete with enlarged odor!). Finally, in would go a small Barbie doll, and out would come my daughter, dressed exactly like the Barbie doll, and more than filling the enlarging machine, which had appeared empty. It all happened out in the open.

My love affair with magic passed all the tests of being a good thing. It was loving. It harmed no one, and gave many people moments of laughter, fun, entertainment, and amazement. In no way did it compromise my work as a pastor, or so I thought. I always closed my performance with a Gospel object lesson. I also used the magic for object lessons on Sunday. It seemed to me the adults liked the magic and would listen to the children's sermon. But when it was time for the adult sermon, they didn't listen as well. So I always gave a child's version of the adult sermon.

Then unexpectedly, God began dealing with me. Extra income from the magic would relieve the financial stress on my family, and give us more money that we could use for God, or so I reasoned. A totally foreign thought began to surface in my mind. It was the thought that God wanted me to get totally free from all involvement in magic. I was to sell everything I had, except for a few things for children's sermons. I was to resign from the presidency of our magic club. As those thoughts continued to grow in me I said, "God, if this is of you, you've got to take away my love of magic, and relieve me of all regrets about selling it." Having said that, I loaded everything up and went to a distant city where a friend had a magic shop. I left everything with him. I got in the car and drove away. This was the big test. If this guidance had come from God, I would have no regrets, no second thoughts.

I was amazed as I drove home. I had no regrets! No second thoughts! In fact, God took away my love of magic so completely that I didn't even care about going to the magic club meetings! He hadn't said anything about not going to them. That is how God works in us both to will and to do, if we will allow him. Many things that claim our attention, that we desperately want to hang on to, may be very good in and of themselves. But when God says it is time to move on to something else, he gives new desires. Your task is to always be open to his guidance, willing to do whatever he leads you to do. There was nothing wrong with the magic, but the time came when God had future plans for me. That is how it will be with things in your life. Be open. Be sensitive. Be obedient. Let the future be glorious.

CHAPTER 36

HOMEWORK: DREAMING WITH GOD

As we join in family talk with our Father, our brother Jesus, and the Holy Spirit we discover that we can change our future by the dreams we dream. We begin by dreaming large. Dreaming large was your assignment when you drew your prayer tree. The next step was to add detail to those dreams as you transferred each one to a separate page. Next you were to write out each dream as a prayer request. You've been collecting scriptures that give you legal authority for making each prayer request. Lastly, you were to rewrite each scripture in the form of a prayer or a confession.

Do all in attitude of reverence and awe. The fact that we are now related as family does not diminish in any sense that God is almighty, creator, omniscient, and sovereign. Nor does it diminish the price Jesus paid to redeem us from death and from Satan's possession. It is by grace, and grace alone, that we have been given a place in God's family circle; a gift totally unmerited, and yet a gift filled with promises.

God has promised "In all thy ways acknowledge him, and he shall direct thy paths" (Psalm 3:6 KJV). And he has promised, "Delight yourself in the LORD, and he will give you the desires of your heart. Commit your way to the LORD; trust in him, and he will act" (Psalm 37:4 ESV). In order to claim those scripture promises, we need to complete one final step. That is to pray the increase/decrease prayer over each prayer request. Go through your requests one at a time. Think about it. Is it just a passing fancy, like a fashion fad? Is it a soul's sincere desire? Is it true to your nature? Once you are ready, ask God to increase your desire if it is good and right for you. If not, decrease your desire. This prayer has always worked well for me.

Satan will try to discourage you, suggesting that this won't work and you should give up. Satan will throw seemingly impossible obstacles in your path to stop you. That is why Paul tells us to put on the armor of God. Whatever else may be understood about God's armor, from Satan's point of view, when you are wearing it he is face to face with God. And when you use your power of attorney and start taking authority over Satan, he has no choice but to bow the knee and creep out of there as fast as he can. Be absolutely convinced that God does not lie. That

> Every promise in the book, is mine,
> Every chapter, every verse and every line,
> All are blessings, of his love, divine,
> Every promise, in the book, is mine.
>
> (Author unknown)

It is fun to set our minds on goals and dreams. Let prayer be fun. Let your imagination run wild with dreams. Talking those dreams over with your new family is fun. Within your list will be dreams God has given you, as well as your own desires. You are discovering God's Divine Plan[6] for you. Keep writing dreams as they come to you. With God guiding you, the impossible becomes possible. While you are dreaming, ask God what his dreams are, and pray for his dreams as you pray for yours. Put any dreams you have doubts about in the back of the notebook. You may come back to them later.

Try to discern God's guidance. Recognizing it when it comes is not always easy. One of the primary ways God speaks to us, apart from the Bible itself, is through the dreams in our hearts. Those dreams are not always clear to us because of the clutter we add. Our task is to remove the clutter and let those dreams stand out in clarity and purity. We all have some things we don't want to subject to the increase/decrease prayer. We just plain want them! We don't want God telling us No! We don't want God decreasing our desire for them! I've been down that road, too. For those things, I alter the prayer just a bit. I add; Replace my desire for this thing with a greater desire for what you have for me. Upgrading to his best is one of the special things that happens as you use the increase/decrease prayer. With it, you are submitting yourself, your hopes, and your dreams to God, and allowing him to direct your paths. With it, you are learning more about his blueprint for your life, which will always be greater than you had dreamed. This pleases God and is no burden to him. In fact, he told us to do it:

> Lean on, trust in, and be confident in the Lord with all your heart and mind and do not rely on your own insight or understanding. In all your ways know, recognize, and acknowledge Him, and He will direct and make straight and plain your paths (Proverbs 3:5, 6 AMP).

God, himself, will bring your dreams to pass! God works with you. He works as you work. It is a partnership. Mark put it this way, "And they went forth, and preached everywhere, the Lord working with them, and confirming the word with signs following" (Mark 16:20 KJV).

Paul writes that there are many kinds of prayer and rules that apply to each. We have God's word on it that all the promises of God are for you and will work for you. It has nothing to do with you deserving or not deserving, or doing anything to earn it. To say that it doesn't apply to you is to call God a liar. When Jesus gave you the power of attorney to use his name, he did not put any restrictions on it. He said when you use his name the devil has to flee, sickness has to depart, money has to come to meet your needs, and mountains have to get up and move. It has nothing to do with who you are, but with who he is.

I've said before and I say again, you must be convinced that your faith works. You arrive at that conviction by way of knowledge. You have no power of your own. Peter and John were adamant about that when they said that they had no power (Acts 3:12). What they had was the authority to use the name of Jesus. It was through faith in the name of Jesus that the cripple was healed (Acts 3:16). You don't have faith in your abilities or worthiness.

You have faith in the name of Jesus. Your faith works because your faith, your confidence, your trust, is in the name of Jesus, and not in yourself.

You've spent time getting to know this Jesus. You've studied his life. You've let all the words that tell about him sink into your heart. You've come to love him more than life itself. Your task now is to bring honor and glory to his name by using his name in the ways he said to use it.

PART F

The Territory of Prayer

Use every kind of prayer and entreaty, and at every opportunity pray in the spirit (Ephesians 6:18 GDS).

CHAPTER 37

God Is Not Like My Dad

When I was a child, there were voices I loved to hear; mom asking if I wanted to lick the cake batter bowl, dad reading stories, grandma and grandpa's cheery voices when we went to visit, my dad inviting me to spend the day riding around in his grocery truck, and my big sister inviting me to play with her. Those voices always meant good things. But sometimes those voices changed. I did not like to hear them then, for it meant something bad was about to happen --- to me! I had been naughty and I had to face the consequences.

At church and Sunday school they talked about hearing another voice, God's voice. The grown-ups said we should talk with God every day. But all they did was to talk at God, say Amen when they were done, and go on to other things. They never took time to listen. They didn't tell us how to listen. It wasn't like we could see him or call him on the telephone. They described God and mostly painted a good picture. But they never talked about God talking back to them or what his voice sounded like. They said God was a father. That sounded good because my father was good. But my father also had a temper and knew how to spank! Each time after he had spanked me, he would come to see me before I fell asleep to tell me he loved me. That helped with my picture of God. I knew in my head, although not in my heart, that no matter how bad I had been, God still loved me.

Knowing my father loved me did not lead to having an intimate relationship with him. He was a private person and did not share his thoughts with me as I wanted him to do. Years later, when I voiced my frustration to God over not having the intimate relations with him that I wanted, a picture came to my mind. The year after my mother died, I went alone to visit my Dad. I pictured how it would be, just the two of us, sharing the deep thoughts of our hearts with each other. But it was not to be. I don't know what caused him to do it, but my dad had closed the door to his heart. He was loving and proud of his family. But his innermost thoughts he kept to himself. Try as hard as I could, he would not, or could not, open up. We were together in the same house, but there was a wall I could not get past.

All was not lost, however, for my dad had written many poems and other things. What he could not share intimately with me, I began to discover in his writings. In them, I caught a glimpse of the man who was my dad. As I reflected on this, two things were shown to me. First, I was assuming God was exactly like my dad and that I could expect no more of him than I could of my earthly dad. Dad was a man of great promise who had never achieved his potential. That was how I unconsciously pictured God. Financially, my parents just got by. My expectation of God was to just get by. While my dad was physically present, he was fenced in by an invisible wall that kept people at a distance. He was a good man who could not let his guard down enough to form close friendships. I projected this image of my dad on to God, and expected no more of God than I did of my dad.

The second, and most important thing I was shown, was that just as I began to know my dad's heart when I read his writings, God also has revealed his heart in his writings. If I really wanted to know him, I had to study his writings. The Bible is God speaking directly to us through his writings. When we looked at how Jesus related to people, and saw how his followers knew him, we began to know him as his friends and disciples did. After his resurrection, Jesus went out of his way to prove to the disciples that he was still the Jesus they had always known. We've looked at God and learned that he is just like Jesus. In addition, we've discovered a document in his writings that tell us that God, the father of Jesus, loves us just as much as he loves Jesus, and has adopted us. We've now become his very own beloved children, co-heirs with Jesus. Our Father desires to give us good things just because he loves us.

My mind began to grasp the fact that Jesus is the same for me as he was for the disciples. That was part of my trouble; it was stuck in my mind.

I had to get it to go from my mind down into my heart. I felt awkward inserting myself into the circle of the disciples. But as I looked more closely at that circle, I became to realize that the circle was immense! I could not see the whole of it. And then, most amazingly, I saw that the circle was open towards me, and everyone was beckoning me to come! I may continue to feel awkward and shy, but now I know I'm wanted and welcome. That is what I've come to see in my mind as I read his writings. If you will let it happen, that is what you will also see in your mind.

But what about God? When I was very young, snuggling up in my father's lap was easy to do. But how do I snuggle up in God's lap now? I'm a grown man! As I grew older, I met many Christians I'd call saints. I began to hear them say, "God told me this." How could that be, I wondered? Does God really talk to people? I'd been told God speaks to us through his Word, the Bible, and I had certainly experienced that. They said he reveals his will in the Bible. Yes, I saw that. The Bible tells us to make our requests known to God and he will supply all our needs (Philippians 4:6). Was that what prayer is about? Making a list of requests and reading them to God? That's not how I treated my dad.

I saw, too, that living right also played a part because the Bible said that the prayers of a righteous man make tremendous power available (James 5:16 AMP). But that didn't answer the question. What were people talking about who said God spoke to them? When asked how, they always gave the same answer. "God speaks, but you have to listen."

If I had my way, I would have a cell phone inside me that would ring whenever God had a message for me. But it doesn't work that way. When God speaks it is easy to confuse it with our own thoughts. We may call it intuition, inspiration, or even our own wisdom. There is a way that helps us give God his rightful credit, but it is costly. It requires that we stop taking credit for ourselves, and begin giving God credit for everything for which we'd like to take credit. It's developing an attitude of gratitude.

You choose to willfully believe that God is guiding and speaking to you whether you are aware of it or not. You thank him in all things. When you fall flat on your face you say, "Father, forgive me if I got it wrong, or failed to do it right, or trusted in my own wisdom instead of your guidance." When things go right you say, "Father, thank you for guiding me and helping me." When that is your attitude, God becomes your strongest supporter and biggest fan.

All guidance must be tested to see if it comes from God. It is loving? Is it in line with God's character as creator and loving father? Does it bless everyone and hurt no one? Is it in line with the scriptures which are our standard for faith and practice? Does it bring God glory? Following God's guidance is not always a "walk in the park," as the saying goes. Sometimes it means you must trust when you cannot see.

CHAPTER 38

Listen for a Still Small Voice

My wife and I found ourselves in an unexpected situation in which we had to apply those tests every step of the way. Much of the time we had to trust God when it seemed to us that he remained silent, and we were about to fall off the cliff. He did not give detailed instructions or prepare us for what lay ahead. When God spoke to us it was more like an inner conviction. It was through impressions, convictions and words that rose up inside us. Almost always we heard "Trust Me" for an answer when we questioned him. We took wrong turns, but God always brought us through. He brought us through because our one goal was to serve him and be obedient.

It was the spring of 1985. God told us to leave the pastorate. I didn't hear a voice. The words were just in my head. He said "Leave now or you never will." From the time I first surrendered to the call to be a pastor, I knew I would not retire from the pastorate. I don't know how I knew. I just knew. We had already set up our own non-profit Shepherd Ministries, Inc. so that people could donate to our tape ministry. In our minds we planned to leave the pastorate after our children were grown. It made no sense to leave while four of them were still in high school and college.

Those words came as a bit of a shock. They were suddenly in my head and did not go away. I tried to pray them away, applying all the tests. But they wouldn't go. I also knew what "or you never will" meant. If there is such a thing in the pastoral ministry as a comfort zone, I was about to enter it. If I delayed leaving, I would probably never leave. I'd miss out on God's best. But to leave now, with no pre-planning, no place to live and no job; that's scary! With much trepidation, we applied for early retirement and looked for a place to live. We had visions of living on the street or having to move in with my wife's parents.

It was too late to qualify for a mortgage. They expect you to prove you have a job! I didn't have one. We drove around looking at houses that were for sale. We picked out the one we thought could most easily be adapted to our family. Then we prayed and waited on God to work it all out. He was silent, embarrassingly so, for us. Time was running out. God did not provide us with a down payment. We still had no place to go.

During this time, my wife had been talking to Ellie, a lady down the block. They wanted to sell their old two story yellow home. They were anxious to move away, but couldn't unless they sold their house. They were so anxious to move that they offered to move out the next weekend and move into their parent's basement in a nearby city. They had talked to their real estate agent and he told them that all we had to do was take over their mortgage payments and the mortgage would be transferred to us. We gratefully accepted their offer. They moved out. We painted walls and moved in.

The real estate agent was a friend of the owners. He assured them that the mortgage was transferable. It turned out that it wasn't. But by then the deed was done. They had moved out and we had moved in. Under no circumstances were they moving back. So for the next few years we sent the mortgage payment to them each month. Helen felt led to be a teacher at the Oasis Child Care center at the Assembly of God in Indianola. All the leading I got was to pray, study, and write. I searched for work I could do from home, to no avail.

Christmas time arrived, and with it, many letters asking for money. One letter caught our attention. It was from Becky and Daniel Beutler, owners of "The Lord's Own Tape Ministry" free lending library. They were asking for funds for the library. Their Christmas appeal letter ended with the question, "Are you interested in taking over the library?" Our interest literally jumped! Yes, we were interested. A small free loan tape library was already part of our ministry. We had visions of how the income from the Beutler's tape ministry would supplement Helen's income.

Maybe it was our imaginations working overtime, but we thought God was as excited about our acquiring the tape ministry as we were. At least, that is how it seemed when we prayed. We boldly asked God to give it to us. We were increasingly sure it was part of God's plan. It was like a "yes" had risen up from deep within us. In January, the Beutlers wrote, asking about our plans for the library. We answered, telling them about our non-profit corporation, and our own small free loan library. They approved and agreed that they were sure God wanted us to have their library. Would we please send them $10,500?

Ten thousand five hundred dollars! They might as well have asked for the moon. God, we asked, what is going on? We were so sure you wanted us to have the library. Didn't you give us the conviction that has remained so strong in us? We don't have the money and we don't know where to get the money. What do you want us to do? God remained silent. We had to tell the Beutlers that we didn't have the money and we didn't have any idea where to find it.

In July, a letter came saying the library had been purchased by a man from Chicago. The tape library was gone, just like the house we had prayed for was gone. In both cases, we were sure God had said, "Yes, trust me." And in both cases it seemed to our natural senses that our trust had been in vain. We could have given up, but instead we stubbornly clung to trusting God.

When Christmas time came round again, we received another Christmas letter from Daniel and Becky, again appealing for funds. The letter explained how they had borrowed money to pay wages and meet the expenses of the tape library. Because the library had closed in July, all income had ceased. Daniel was working part time as a school janitor. They needed our gifts. Their letter didn't say anything about the library, or about the man who had purchased it. On the remote possibility that the deal hadn't gone through, I sent a note with my gift. Were they still looking for someone to take over the library? If so, we were still interested.

Boy! Talk about riding an emotional roller coaster. We had been on high, thrilling to the idea that we were going to have a tape ministry to administer. Then we were at the bottom, with no prospects of getting the tape ministry, and with no guidance telling us what to do next. And then, suddenly we're racing back up! Becky called! The other deal had fallen through. They now knew for sure that we were the ones who were supposed to have the library. How soon could we raise the $10,500? Well, over the top and down to the bottom again.

This time I wrote to everyone on my mailing list. I explained the opportunity, and asked for contributions. I tried to find other sources of funding, but found none. Praying didn't seem to help. After all our efforts, we had raised a paltry $350! Meanwhile, Becky kept calling to find out what progress we were making. The more we talked, the more Becky shared her story. In the twenty years they had lived in Florida, they had foregone needed repairs on their home in order to keep the tape ministry going. They had had to hire people to process the orders. Often the gifts that came in were not enough to pay wages, and they had to borrow. Daniel got a part time job to supplement their income.

Without income from the tapes, they were desperate. It took all of Daniel's earnings and some of their social security to make payments on the last bank loan they had taken out to pay wages. What was left to live on ran out about 10 days before the end of the month. Friends and neighbors would stop by with a little money, groceries, or a meal. That was how they survived until the next social security check came.

Now the Florida rains were pouring in like a flood. The roof they had neglected was leaking like a sieve. They sat up all night emptying pots, moving things out of the way of the water. They stretched sheets of plastic to catch the water and funnel it out the window. They were desperate. They didn't know what to do. We were their only hope. We began to feel the weight of their need bearing down on us as they looked to us for help. We wanted to help, but $350 was far short of the $5,000 needed for just the new roof. Meanwhile, an idea was growing in my mind. The people who used the library needed to know the sacrifices the Beutlers had made, and thank them for their ministry. I would send that letter once Becky sent me her mailing list. To protect their clients, she didn't want to give me the list until we also had the library.

The Beutlers hired a lawyer to handle all the legal details of transferring the assets of their non-profit ministry to ours. Their lawyer talked them into asking only $8,000 for the library if we could get the money to them by the end of May. Try as hard as we could, we couldn't raise a single additional penny. If God wanted us to have the library, it was up to him. We were stuck. We waited, and the Beutlers waited. Then one day an unexpected package came. Becky sent the mailing list of all the library users! The moment I saw that list, I knew it had come so that I could write that letter.

I wrote the letter and sent it to all their borrowers describing how the Beutler's had sacrificed for the library. I described the need they now faced. I asked the borrowers to write a letter of appreciation and enclose a gift if they could. Once I had the letter ready, I bought stamps for the envelopes. It was then that I discovered that the $350 I had raised was just enough to pay for the envelopes and postage! Slowly I began to see God's hand at work in this. I saw the rest in what happened two weeks later.

Becky called. "What did you do!?" In one week, they had received $5,000! They were overjoyed. By the time the last gift arrived, they had received over $13,000! It took a year and a half to work it out, but when it was done, they were doubly blessed and the library was paid for. But that was not the end. We had to pay the shipping costs. Daniel was willing to pay the cost and have us repay him as we had the money. We paid him in full when we received a check from a stranger for $1,000. Together with the Beutlers (now deceased), we shared a miracle.

On January 4, 1988, the tape library and equipment arrived. There were over 4,000 reel-to-reel master tapes, 4,000 cassette master tapes, and over 36,000 cassette copies. We assembled the library shelves and used them as room dividers. We divided the large second floor room of our house into four bedrooms with shelves of tapes as the walls. That is where our children slept, each with a small area that was their own.

God blesses the people who are willing to let him use them. The couple from whom we got our home, who were willing to move instantly, were part of God's plans. Because of that, he did two things for them. Our local school system said their son had learning disabilities. They were sure the problem was the teacher and not their son. Six months after moving to the city, their son was in regular classes earning "A's." The second thing was the furnace. Had they stayed here, they probably would not have had the furnace checked for leaks. We did and discovered that it leaked poisonous fumes. Had they stayed here another year, their two children might have succumbed to the fumes.

We had witnessed miracles in acquiring the tape library. We had a house full of tapes when we had no money to pay for them. Why, then, hadn't we got the house we wanted? I was sitting at my desk, meditating, when I asked God, Why? Suddenly, as clearly as if a voice had spoken, I heard words rise up from deep inside; "This was the only house available with enough room for the library." I was stunned. That meant that before the call came to leave the pastorate, God already knew he was going to give us the library! He knew the house we needed in order to have room for it!

He hadn't told us his plans in advance. He made us walk it out by faith, trusting him. In that moment, God gave me a glimpse of the vastness and breadth of his plans. There was still more to come. People were not borrowing tapes like they once did. The Word was not getting out. Cassette players were giving way to CD players. The internet was providing people with instant access to information. People did not want to wait a week for the tapes to come, and then be bothered to return them. That is when we discovered God's final plan. He wanted us to build a website and put the messages from the tapes on the website where people could access them at any time to listen to them immediately, or download them to listen to later. We built the site and, almost instantly, the number of listeners exploded into the thousands, with multiple thousands of downloads each year. It was then we finally understood a little better the scope of God's plan when he said "Leave now or your never will."

My experience of hearing God's voice and setting my will to trust him regardless of outward circumstances will not necessarily be your experience. I share it to encourage you to keep trusting God and not to give up regardless of outward circumstances. Trusting is not always easy but it pays tremendous dividends.

CHAPTER 39

THE ONE CALLED TO YOUR SIDE

When I was growing up, praying in tongues had mixed press. Mainline denominations said it was an emotional excess and was not the speaking in tongues of the New Testament. I began to search the scriptures to see what they said. The Old Testament story of King Saul told how the Holy Spirit would come upon ordinary people and transform them for a task they were to carry out. The change lasted only as long as the task lasted. The Holy Spirit always came over, but not into the person involved.

Something different and exciting happened when Jesus came. The Holy Spirit now comes into us, transforms us, and remains in us. This work of the Holy Spirit is first encountered in the new birth, as Jesus named it (John 3:7). Legally we belonged to Satan. The penalty for sin is death. By belonging to Satan, we inherited Satan's destiny. There was no way to escape it (Romans 5:12). Death for us meant eternal separation from God in the lake of everlasting fire that was prepared for the devil and his angels (Matthew 25:41).

The only way to escape the fire was for someone to redeem us by taking our place. But that in itself was not enough. If left unchanged we would be like the thief freed from prison. He may have been freed, but he was still a thief. It was only a matter of time before he stole again. If left unchanged, it would only be a matter of time before we sinned again and landed back in Satan's possession. God had to do more than redeem us. He had to transform us into a new creation that Satan could never own. He does that by putting His Holy Spirit in us.

When we are born again, the Holy Spirit recreates our human spirit. We become new people in Christ (John 3:3, 5; 2 Corinthians 5:17). The apostle Paul illustrates this by his own life-changing transformation on the road to Damascus. Saul, the persecutor of Christians, died that day. In his place, Paul the Apostle was born by regeneration by the Holy Spirit (Titus 3:5). According to Paul, God, through his Holy Spirit, comes into us and makes his home in us. That is baptism by the Holy Spirit. It is similar to drinking a glass of water; it goes inside you. Paul explains; "Don't you realize that you yourselves are the temple of God, and that God's Spirit lives in you?" (I Corinthians 3:16 PHS).

Being baptized by the Holy Spirit is the common experience of all born again believers. The new birth experience of being baptized by the Holy Spirit (being born again) was not what Jesus meant when he told the disciples to wait in Jerusalem until they were empowered (Acts 1:8). Empowerment is not the same as new birth. Jesus told them to wait until it was time and then they were to jump into the water of the Spirit! They were to be immersed into the Holy Spirit. In so doing, they would receive dynamite power.

> "But you shall receive power (ability, efficiency, and might) when the Holy Spirit has come upon you, and you shall be My witnesses in Jerusalem and all Judea and Samaria and to the ends (the very bounds) of the earth. (Acts 1:8 AMP).

In the Upper Room experience, there were signs that accompanied their immersion in the Holy Spirit. There were wind, flames of fire, speaking in tongues, and, in the case of Peter, a boldness and fearlessness that he had never had before. There was also a release of power that grabbed the listeners and caused the people to ask what they must do to be saved. Three thousand souls were added to their number. And many signs and wonders were done.

In his letters, Paul explains the work of the Holy Spirit. The Holy Spirit apportions out to people gifts and job assignments, as needed, in the church. These are the Spirit's gifts. No one owns or possesses the gifts of the Spirit to use whenever he feels like it. But the Spirit can use any person to manifest any gift as he wills (I Corinthians 12:7-11). We also note that the Spirit bears fruits of love, joy, peace, longsuffering, gentleness, goodness, faith, meekness, temperance and righteousness (Galatians 5:22-23; Ephesians 5:9). If we are immersed in the Holy Spirit, the Spirit will begin manifesting these fruits in us.

In all the descriptions of individuals and groups receiving empowerment by the Holy Spirit, there is always the evidence of speaking in tongues. In our modern day, when we have allowed the sophistication of knowledge and scientific achievement to shape our thinking, the thought of speaking in tongues can be very troublesome for us personally. This is understandable for at least three reasons. First, many denominations whose origins included speaking in tongues, and signs and wonders, have now talked themselves out of it. They have relegated those manifestations of the Spirit to the days when they tended to be over-emotional.

The second has to do with our rugged individualist tendencies. We have prided ourselves in being a nation of rugged individualists. We celebrate the fortitude and resilience of the individual who is in control of himself as he strikes out to carve out a farm or establish a business. The one thing he does not tolerate is someone else putting words in his mouth. He controls his tongue. He does not like the idea of having words he doesn't understand coming out of his mouth. We don't want to be puppets on the end of someone else's string. Baptism in the Holy Spirit is asking me to trust the Holy Spirit to use my mouth to say things that I do not understand. In my head I know I can trust the Holy Spirit, but in practice it's sometimes scary.

The third reason has to do with Satan. You see, Satan hears and understands everything we say and plan. He likes to hear what we're talking about to God so that he can interfere and cause trouble. He is still the ruler of this world and he is going to do his best to make things go his way. He is outraged that God snuck a clause into the lease that lets God talk to men and help them. Our praying in tongues is one of his biggest headaches. He doesn't know the language. He doesn't know what the Holy Spirit is praying through us. Is it any wonder he does everything he can to discourage us from praying in the Spirit?

The Bible says praying in the spirit edifies us (I Corinthians 14:4), it builds us up in our most holy faith (Jude 20). It helps us in our weakness and inability to produce results (Romans 8:26). Regular, disciplined times of praying in the spirit gives God the opportunity to change us on the inside. The speed at which these changes take place depends on the individual, and on the amount of time spent praying in the spirit.

We all experience a great inertia towards change, towards doing those things needful to bring about the results we want. Things like the exercise program we never start or the pounds we never lose. There are other things on the inside that need changing, too. We were born into a sinful world with a sinful nature. Things happened that hurt us and we did things that hurt others. These sins and their fruits cripple us. We are like a tree whose roots are rotted even though the tree looks healthy. To be truly healthy, we must make the roots healthy. If our roots are healthy, our fruit will be healthy. Redemption makes it possible for us to become healthy.

One of the great benefits of praying in tongues is that it strips away the complications of sin by healing us on the inside, from the roots up, as well as in our mind and heart. Healing comes from being transformed by the renewing of the mind. Make the roots healthy, and the fruit will be healthy. For example, when you pray in the spirit, those things within you that cause you to lose jobs will be transformed. Pray in the spirit so that the root causes can be healed. I know it works because it worked for me.

My experience with the Holy Spirit is not the norm. But it has taught me some things. First, God meets us where we are. Somewhere in my childhood, I shut down my feelings because I was afraid of being hurt. I turned instead to the intellectual, to head knowledge. That put me at odds with what I really wanted. I wanted goose bumps and the sense of God's presence when I prayed. I wanted joy to bubble up within me. But my head kept getting in the way. I've learned that I have to set my will to believe.

My perfectionist nature concluded that the Christian life was the ideal. I made the intellectual choice to be a Christian assuming that that made me a Christian. I did those things my perfectionism thought a Christian would do. I was active in my church and youth group. In college, I joined Christian groups. I was living the Christian lifestyle. I didn't understand at the time that believing with my head was not believing with my heart, as Paul wrote in Romans 10:9.

It was not until I went to the Jack Wyrtzen Word of Life Rally that I realized the truth. When the altar call was given that night, I was suddenly under conviction. I seemed unable to stop myself from going forward. I repeated the sinner's prayer and heard the evangelist tell me I was forgiven. He said I was a new creation in Christ Jesus. I didn't feel anything and that left me confused and disappointed. I did not like being put in that position. It would have been so much easier to believe I was born again if I had had all those feelings I'd wanted. The joy. The goose bumps. The chills up and down my spine. But God said No! Since my head was my hang-up, I was going to have to deal with my head. I had to learn the principle that: God said it. I believe it. That settles it. To walk by faith is not to walk by sight or by feelings.

Four years later, I went to Agnes Sanford's School of Pastoral Care. She talked about inner healing and I realized I had a lot of stuff inside that was messing up my life and I needed to get rid of it. I asked her to pray for me. After my prayer for inner healing, I was invited by Agnes to meet with a small group in an upper room one morning. There they prayed for me to be baptized in the Holy Spirit. They all bubbled with joy as they prayed. I expected to bubble with joy, too. I felt nothing. I wanted to feel a prayer language rise up inside me. I was even hoping my mouth would start to move. I tried to let it go. I felt nothing. Then suddenly I got hit by a power that was so strong it was as though I had grabbed hold of a very high voltage power line.

I think God was saying to me, "You want to feel something? I'll give you something to feel that your mind will never be able to talk you out of!" That surge of power caused the muscles in my hands to contract so hard I could not move them or straighten them out. Agnes said I had been baptized in the Holy Spirit with power. She assured me the prayer language would come later. Even though I had come that close, I did not try to speak in tongues again. I let the experience lie dormant.

After becoming a pastor and serving as the associate pastor of a large city church, I was appointed to two small rural churches. At that time, a spiritual stirring had begun to cross the land. We came under the influence of Kenneth Hagin, Oral Roberts, Derek Prince, Frank Laubach, and Agnes Sanford. Our interest in the Holy Spirit was intensified. We began to actively seek the baptism with the evidence of speaking in tongues. Catholics were also being awakened to the Holy Spirit and the walls between us began to crumble. We began to mingle freely, praying together, sharing our faith together, and speaking in each other's churches.

It was during this time that a young man named Michael entered our lives and started us on an unexpected journey. Perhaps, I should begin by telling you about Geraldine Conway, who had taken Michael under her wings. Geraldine Conway was a remarkable woman. She proclaimed the gospel in many countries. She organized and financed several inspirational shows that toured military bases in Korea and VietNam. Geraldine is listed in Who's Who of American Women. She was a writer, counselor, and had made many radio and television appearances. She was much in demand as a speaker in churches, schools, colleges, evangelistic missions, retreats for ministers and laymen, conferences, women's clubs, and business men's groups.

We did not know it, but God was about to give our trust in him the biggest challenge it had ever faced. The Iowa CFO Camp had just ended. We were impressed with Geraldine, her spirit and how she taught. We longed to have someone like that spend a few days at our churches. We knew her schedule was full, but we asked anyway, just in case God had left a few days open just for us. There's nothing wrong with dreaming big dreams! Her schedule was full.

Michael was another story! Michael's father, a sports announcer on a radio station, wanted an athlete for a son. Michael was not an athlete. He was of slight, non-muscular build, with an artistic temperament. He was a very talented musician. He was everything his father detested. As a result, his father found it very difficult to love him, to say nothing of accepting his strange son. There was constant conflict between them. Michael's response to his father's rejection was to rebel and do things that irritated his father. He adopted effeminate mannerisms, dressing in non-macho clothes, used heavy amounts of make-up so he would "look good" when he played the organ in bars and night clubs.

Geraldine saw beneath his outward appearance and saw Michael's great talent and potential. She took him under her wings. As Michael grew in the Lord, he became a strong man of prayer. He was able to relate to young people who had been rejected by their parents, who were having problems at home, and were rebellious. At the Iowa CFO I had asked Michael to help me lead the junior high youth.

A couple days after the camp had ended, I received a phone call. "Matt, can you use Michael?" the voice asked. "Geraldine will be staying here for a few days speaking in several churches and Michael is bored. Geraldine said he would do a good job for you." I didn't have time to pray, ask my church board, or talk it over with anyone. She wanted the answer now. What do you do when you don't have time to talk it over with your Board? You do what I did. You listen to your inner witness. Mine seemed to be saying "Yes." So I said "Yes," and then began to wonder what I'd done!

The makeup Michael wore, plus his effeminate mannerisms, tended to offend a lot of adults. The young people found in him a kindred spirit. They loved him and accepted him just the way he was. He accepted them just the way they were. They saw in him someone who understood them and their problems. The adults eyed him with suspicion. He didn't fit any stereotype. He was what he was. I knew he would be controversial, but I did not know how controversial. With fear and anxiety, I brought Michael home. We set our wills to trust God. Our first test of trust came that very night. The county fair was on. Michael wanted to go and he wanted to take some of our youth with him. I loaned him our car and said, "Get them saved."

Night came. The time I thought they should have returned came and went. It got later and later. I tried not to worry. I did trust God. But my stomach churned! Michael came home, and he had won the youth to Christ. Trusting in that manner set the pattern for the whole week. At each meeting, I introduced Michael and then let Michael do what he believed God was telling him to do. While Michael did his thing, we sweated out trusting God to do his thing. It wasn't easy.

Michael was outspoken. He hated hypocrisy. He had the ability to discern who was a genuine Christian and who was false. He told people they needed to get right with God and get their lives in order. Young people saw that Michael was genuine. They listened, confessed their sins, received Jesus as their Savior, and were filled with the Holy Spirit. Criticism, objections, and rumors began to circulate. Some objected to this young man telling them they needed to get saved. Some objected to the young people getting saved and filled with the Holy Spirit. Some of those objecting became very vocal and began stirring up opposition in the church.

The more Helen and I trusted God, the worse things got. Some people became angry. It began to look as though everything was coming apart at the seams. It is often that way when you are trusting God. The more we trusted, the further things deteriorated. Finally, Michael called Geraldine and said, "Geraldine, you've got to come. Things are getting really bad. We need you to come and straighten it out."

Michael's plea was so desperate Geraldine cleared her schedule and came that Sunday. She spent the week with us. And God did his thing! Michael had been the appetizer, the forerunner, the stirrer-upper, preparing the way. Youth came from miles around. The school let Geraldine speak at a high school assembly. The church was packed with youth at a youth rally we had two days later, much to the surprise of those who said it couldn't be done. Adults who would never have stepped foot inside the church to hear an evangelist came to hear this woman and see this strange young man who had made such a stir. They got saved, too!

While Helen and I were still not praying in the Spirit at this time, praying in the Spirit was very much a part of what God was doing. Our desire intensified. Geraldine said we needed to follow up on what we had started. She recommended that Michael come back with Joe, who would help us set up a youth coffee house. Arrangements were made and Joe and Michael arrived. I told them to get as many of the youth baptized in the Holy Spirit as possible.

As told in an earlier lesson, when you start attacking the demonic powers, they use every vile and evil method they can to defeat you, never playing fair. With these events, our churches entered the move of the Holy Spirit in the Christian churches. People were being baptized in the Holy Spirit in all the communities surrounding us. We invited several different individuals and groups to come and share with us. Many of them prayed with Helen and me. Neither of us really trusted the words we were saying. In the meantime, we moved to another town, and became active in the Full Gospel Businessmen's Fellowship International, and the Women's Aglow.

Both groups met monthly at dinner meetings. When everyone was praying in the Spirit, or singing in the Spirit, we found it easy to join in with them. Since I had the authority to use Jesus' name, I started commanding the Holy Spirit, in Jesus' name, to intercede through me for the many needs of the people who requested prayer, and for whom I did not know how to pray. Jesus called the Holy Spirit the *parakletos,* which means "one who is summoned, called to one's aid as a helper, succourer, aider, assistant, a guide into all truth." That is what he is and what he does. The Holy Spirit can do for you only what you will allow him to do. Feel free to ask his help anytime. He will not let you down.

CHAPTER 40

ARGUING WITH MYSELF

"Desert Pete", written by Billy Edd Wheeler, is the story of a man who was crossing a cactus desert under a hot blistering sun. He sat down to rest and was amazed to see a water pump nearby. At first he thought it was a mirage. But when he walked up to it, he saw that it really was a water pump. Upon examining it, he discovered that there was a note stuck in a baking powder can. The note explained that the pump was old but worked. All you had to do was prime the pump with the water left in a bitters jar under a rock. The note went on to say:

> You've got to prime the pump. You must have faith and believe.
> You've got to give of yourself 'fore you're worthy to receive ......
> Have faith my friend, there's water down below.
> You've got to give until you get - I'm the one who ought to know.
> You've got to prime the pump, you must have faith and believe
> You've got to give of yourself 'fore you're worthy to receive
> Drink all the water you can hold, wash your face, cool your feet
> Leave the bottle full for others, Thank you kindly, Desert Pete
>
> (Used by permission)

On my grandpa's farm, we had three of those old pumps. The pump had a piston that went up and down inside a cylinder. The piston had a leather washer with a flap in it. When you raised the pump handle, it lowered the piston and the flap opened, letting the air escape. When you lowered the pump handle, it raised the piston and the flap closed creating a vacuum that sucked the water up. If the washer dried out, it wouldn't work. A little water poured on it would soften it up enough so that, with some fast pumping, it created enough suction to suck the water up. We kept a jar of water by each pump for priming the pump.

Little boys sometimes think the rules don't apply to them. Their minds race in a dozen different directions. They get in a hurry to get back to their next adventure, or bit of mischief, and take short cuts in their chores. Begrudging every minute they have to spend pumping, their child minds quickly reason that they don't need to take time to refill the priming jar because the washer won't dry out that fast. This, of course, leads to an unpleasant confrontation with Dad when he discovers the priming jar is empty.

This affair of the little boy with the priming water illustrates the fact that we have within us two natures, the flesh and the spirit. The flesh wars against the spirit. The little boy, who knew better, gave in to temptation, and chose selfish desire over responsibility (Romans 8:5-8). The stranger who found the pump in the desert faced the same kind of temptation as the little boy. Would he choose to satisfy his own thirst, leaving the priming jar empty? Or would he pour it in the pump, and pump like there was a fire? When he was done, would he fill it for the next person?

If the stranger didn't know about pumps, he was also faced with a second challenge. Could he trust Desert Pete? The stranger had to answer a tough question. Would he take a chance and have faith and believe? On the one hand, he had life giving water that his body badly needed. On the other hand, he was being asked to take a leap of faith and believe that what Desert Pete said was true. On the one hand was the sure thing of quenching his thirst. On the other was the promise of more than enough if he would first give up what he had. What would be the outcome of this debate with himself?

The gospels give us approximately 19 different accounts of Jesus healing someone in which we are also told what the illness was, what the ill person did, what Jesus did, what was said, etc. In each account, the faith of the sick person, or the faith of the one seeking Jesus's help for a sick person, was what made healing possible. Faith is the key. I have to make up my mind about God's truthfulness. Is God a liar? Is it true that God is the same yesterday, today and tomorrow? No other reason is ever given in scripture to explain why anyone is not healed. Who does Jesus say is responsible for poverty, sickness, and lack? Jesus says Satan is the source, the destroyer. John says Jesus came to undo the works of the devil. He needs our faith to do so.

As we stand by the pump and read Desert Pete's note, it is no longer about believing Desert Pete. It is all about believing God. Will I put my faith and trust in God's word, in God's promises? Will I give the last that I have, trusting his words? Those arguments will have to be settled before we begin to pray. Until we locate our faith, we will not know how to pray or be able to pray in faith believing, reaping a harvest of answered prayer.

Whatever we do, good things or bad, we first talk it over with ourselves. It might be to decide which flavor ice cream to get. Or how to pay for a new car, or a new washer and dryer. Or, devise creative excuses for procrastinating, such as I can clean out the garage any time, but I can only watch the game today. Or protest saying, "I said I'd do it, I just didn't say when." Or stubbornly insist, "Don't confuse me with the facts. My mind is made up." Or make the mistake of tossing the Bible aside saying the Bible is full of contradictions.

When we examine our thought life, we are not aware of any outside entity trying to influence us. We believe our decisions are our own. Consequently, we are surprised when we are told to beware of Satan. Satan focuses his attention on our thought life and on our weaknesses. The devil has a vested interest in messing with our heads in any way that will interfere with our Christian walk. There is a reason for this. When we got born again, that made us Satan's mortal enemies. Why? Because the born-again person has certain rights, privileges and powers including power over all the power of the enemy (Luke 10:17; Mark 16; Ephesians 6:11). We can bind him dumb and powerless in Jesus' name. We can command him to leave in Jesus' name, and he has to flee (James 4:7). We can undo his works in Jesus' name (I John 3:8).

This is not something Satan rejoices over. It has made him very angry. He is also wily and secretive and a deceiver, who can disguise himself as an angel of light (2 Corinthians 11:14). Satan's method of operation is to keep us ignorant of our power and authority to use Jesus' name. If we are ignorant, we are no threat. If we are afraid to use our authority, we will be no threat. To keep us powerless, he keeps breaking in on our little arguments with ourselves. For example, when I was a child I found a 22 caliber bullet that hadn't been fired. Common sense said give it to an adult. I did not hear common sense. Instead I had this insane idea of throwing it down on the pavement to see if I could make it go off. It was insane because it could have killed me. Satan said, go ahead, it won't hurt you.

I chose to believe Satan, and my guardian angel went into overtime. It was the same when I held a firecracker in my fingers to see what would happen when it went off. I place the blame on Satan, because Jesus blamed him: "The thief comes only to steal, kill and destroy" (John 10:10). I certainly had no intention of destroying myself. My conscience was trying to tell me not to do it. But I listened to the devil and did it. Paul warns us not to give any foothold to the devil (Ephesians 4:27). Jesus said "you will know the truth and the truth will set you free" (John 8:32 ESV). He also said that he is the truth (John 8:32).

In our minds, we encounter Satan as thief, killer and destroyer as he plants his destructive ideas and temptations in our thoughts. Having a bit of our ancestor Adam's rebellious nature, we fall for the temptations hook, line, and sinker. That is why we do wrong things. We can put a stop to that right now. When we are born again, we get a recreated human spirit, plus the Holy Spirit living in us (I Corinthians 6:19; 9:13). That means we have strong help and guidance built into us. To overcome that takes a stubborn and deliberate act of disobedience.

Do not underestimate the power of Satan's voice. Do not give Satan a foothold in your mind. He has been defeated. He must flee when you command him to do so. But he will not go and will not cease speaking as long as he thinks his voice has any power over you. It is a good thing to learn to laugh at Satan. He works in subtleties. For example, you want to get in the habit of reading the Bible every day. You decide the best way to start is first thing in the morning. You plan is to grab a cup of coffee, your Bible, and read for fifteen minutes. Satan puts the idea in your head that you are too tired to get up. You can read it before bed – all the time knowing that you won't. He knows that the more you read, the more you know. The more you know, the more dangerous you are to him. He will fight you in your thoughts every way he can to stop you.

This description of how Satan works is basic to understanding how to grow your faith, and trust, and believing. You need to fill your mind with the scriptures and faith building messages. Leave no room, no foothold for Satan, by squeezing him out with the Word of God. Follow the words of Desert Pete: "You've got to prime the pump, you must have faith and believe. You've got to give of yourself 'fore you're worthy to receive."

CHAPTER 41

Different Kinds of Prayer

If you grew up on a farm, one rule you were taught early in life was to use the right tool for the right job. That also applies to prayer. Our guide in how to pray is first Jesus, and then Paul and the other writers of the Epistles. We begin by stating some basic requirements. The first requirement is that we have to be convinced that God does not lie. "God is not a man, that he should lie; neither the son of man, that he should repent: hath he said, and shall he not do it? or hath he spoken, and shall he not make it good?" (Numbers 23:19 KJV).

If God does not lie, that means his words are true and that all the promises of God are for you and will work for you. This has nothing to do with deserving or not deserving it, of earning or not earning it. "This is the way it is" says God. "I do it for my sake, and not yours. Now deal with it!" (See Isaiah 43:25 Paraphrased). It is simply a matter of fact. God said it. You believe it. That settles it. "He that spared not his own Son, but delivered Him up for us all, how shall He not with Him also freely give us all things?" (Romans 8:32 KJV).

To say that God's promises don't apply to you is to call God a liar. When Jesus gave you the power of attorney to use his name, he did not put any restrictions on it. He said "When you use my name the devil has to flee, sickness has to depart, money has to come to meet your needs and mountains have to get up and move." It has nothing to do with who you are, but with who he is and the power resident in his name.

The second prerequisite is to know that your faith works. There is no recorded occasion when Jesus asked God to do the healing or perform the miracle. He always emphasized to those who came to him that it was their faith that got them healed. When their faith was not sufficient, he helped them to have faith. In his home town, he could do no mighty works because of their unbelief, their lack of faith. When you understand that faith is based on your confidence in the power of Jesus' name, you will also understand that building up your faith can be achieved by using a plan of growth.

The third prerequisite is respect. If you really love God, you will try your best to act in a way that pleases him and blesses him. You will not carelessly take him for granted or treat him as though he is your genii in a bottle. If I truly love my wife, I will not do or say things that will hurt or offend her. I will try to provide an environment in which she can blossom. To truly love God is to be part of the answer to the prayer, "Thy kingdom come, thy will be done on earth."

With those prerequisites in mind, develop your plan of growth. Pick one area you want to work on, such as healing, finances, job, etc. Break it down into the smallest part for which you can believe. For example, you want to pay off the bills you owe. Start with the smallest one because that will be the easiest one to believe paid. Say, "Bill, I declare you paid, in Jesus' name. Money to pay this bill, come to me in Jesus' name." James tells us that faith without corresponding action is dead. That means to do everything you can to pay it off. Use any extra money that comes to you; gifts of money, money from pop bottles, from cutting back on luxuries like pop or coffee. Do everything you can as your part. Never ever say negative things, such as, "We'll never get out of debt." The confessions of your mouth must always be, "I'm debt free."

Let's say you are a physical wreck. Your blood pressure is off the charts in one direction or the other. Your heart is weak. Etc. Ask your Doctor if he were to make a list of your problems in the order in which they need to be healed, what one would he put first. There is no way you can wrap your faith around all your problems. But you can apply your faith to the thing most needed. Say to the thing most needed, "In the name of Jesus I command you to become normal. You are my body, and you must obey me. Now become normal." Keep picturing it normal in your mind and thank God that it is normal. If you need to adapt a healthier life style, do that too. Never again confess the negative you have, but confess the health you are claiming,

It is critical that you remember that the source of power is the name of Jesus. When you bring the name of Jesus into your situation, the situation changes. Peter and John were adamant when they said that they had no power (Acts 3:12). What they had was the authority to use the name of Jesus. It was through faith in the name of Jesus that the cripple was healed (Acts 3:16). You don't have faith in your abilities or worthiness. You have faith in the name of Jesus. Your faith works because your faith, your confidence, your trust, is in the name of Jesus, and not in yourself. You've spent time getting to know this Jesus. You've studied his life. You've let all the words that tell about him sink into your heart. You've come to love him more than life itself. Your task now is to use his name in the ways he said to use it. Study how Jesus prayed and ministered and took authority. He is our teacher.

There are different kinds of prayer. Each has its own laws. Just as a mechanic must use the right tool for each task, we need to use the right prayer for each request. The following are descriptions of several kinds of prayer. Paul wrote,

> "Use every kind of prayer and entreaty, and at every opportunity pray in the spirit" (Ephesians 6:18 GDS).

The **PRAYER OF FAITH** is a prayer to change things that concern me, not others. "Now Faith is the substance of things hoped for, the evidence of things not seen" (Hebrews 11:1 KJV). The story is told of a missionary who was trying to translate the New Testament into a native language. He was stuck on finding a native word for faith. A messenger from another village came running into the hut. Exhausted, he flung himself into a chair to rest. As he did so, he uttered a word that meant he was entrusting his whole being to the chair to support him. That was the word the missionary was looking for. This is the first law of the prayer of faith.

To have faith in God is have the same confidence in God as the native had in the chair. The native trusted that the chair would support him and afford him the rest he needed.

You cannot see faith, but faith based on the word of God always gets results. James says that the sick person will be raised up if he calls on the elders to pray the prayer of faith over him (James 5:15). John says that "If we confess our sins, he is faithful and just to forgive us our sins and cleanse us from all unrighteousness" (I John 1:9 KJV) regardless of how we feel.

The second law of the prayer of faith is that the prayer of faith must be cultivated and nurtured because it is a growing thing. On that fateful day when Peter said, "Lord, if it is you, command me to come to you on the water," Peter did okay until he let fear overcome him. In answer Jesus said, "O you of little faith, why did you doubt?" (Matthew 14:28, 31 ESV). Little faith can grow into great faith when we take the time to nurture it.

The third law is that the prayer of faith must always be prayed according to God's will. The only way you are going to know God's will is to study God's word, and fill your mind with his word. Then you will know his will. It is a growth process. God does not expect you to be perfect before he grants your prayer prayed in faith. He meets you where you are.

The fourth law is that the prayer of faith is prayer for ourselves. You cannot pray the prayer of faith for another.

The **PRAYER OF INTERCESSION** has to do with the other person. The other person's will is involved. God cannot act against the person's will. Paul wrote in Galatians 4:19,

> My little children, for whom I am again suffering birth pangs until Christ is completely and permanently formed (molded) within you. (AMP)

Paul was not asking Jesus to save them. Jesus had already done all that he's going to do by carrying their sins to the cross. Neither do we ask God to save the lost because he has already done so. In fact, we are never told to ask God to save the lost. What is needed are workers to tell the lost what God has done for them, and help them to reach out and receive this free gift. We are told to pray for the lord of the harvest to send out laborers unto the harvest (Matthew 9:38).

We do what Paul did. We pray for whatever needs that individual has. We pray in tongues (in the Spirit) when we don't know how to pray (Romans 8:26). We pray for obvious needs, such as wisdom, protection, strength, comfort, finances, etc. We use our spiritual authority to bind Satan and his cohorts dumb and powerless around individuals and families. We cover them with the blood of Jesus. As an added precaution we ask the Holy Spirit to put a guard around that person's mouth so that they will not utter words that render our prayers null and void.

Prayers for the lost should be to hold back judgment. It needs to be made at the prompting of, and under the direction of the Holy Spirit. Abraham interceded for Sodom and Gomorrah. In Ezekiel 22; 30, 31 God looked for someone to stand in the gap and intercede. But found no one. God's desire was to avert judgment. When your heart is burdened for a loved one or a friend or neighbor, God is asking you to stand in the gap for them. To stand in the gap also means to model for them the difference Jesus has made in your life.

> And He said to them, "The harvest indeed is abundant <there is much ripe grain>, but the farmhands are few. Pray therefore the Lord of the harvest to send out laborers into His harvest." (Luke 10:2 AMP)

Because this is the Bible way to do it, this will get it done, provided the sinner is willing to open the door, as per Revelation 3:20. This biblical way is also the way to pray for another's needs. When there is need for employment, healing, finances, guidance, etc., we can ask God to send the people across their path who can help them. Paul put it this way:

> FIRST OF all, then, I admonish and urge that … intercessions … be offered on behalf of all men … For such <praying> is good and right, and <it is> pleasing and acceptable to God our Savior, Who wishes all men to be saved and <increasingly> to perceive and recognize

> and discern and know precisely and correctly the <divine> Truth. (I Timothy 2:1-4 AMP)

Jesus intercedes for us in John 17. Paul intercedes in Ephesians 1:15-20 and 3:14-19. As you pray these prayers remember that our responsibility is to pray, thereby enabling God to act. The results are not our responsibility.

The **PRAYER OF AGREEMENT** is agreeing together on a request being made in which God's will is known. It is based on Matthew 18:19 where Jesus said

> "Again I tell you, if two of you on earth agree (harmonize together, make a symphony together) about whatever <anything and everything> they may ask, it will come to pass and be done for them by My Father in heaven" (AMP).

To pray the prayer of agreement means to take God literally at his word. Which is to say, that if God doesn't do what he has said he will do, God is liar.

Look what happened when they harmonized together in Acts 1:14 and again in Acts 2: 1.

All of these with their minds in full agreement devoted themselves steadfastly to prayer, <waiting together> with the women and Mary the mother of Jesus, and with his brothers (AMP).

They were all with one accord in one place, in singleness of heart. In a mighty burst of power, the church was born. Scholars seem to agree that there are a minimum of 3,573 promises in the Bible from which to choose. These promises literally cover everything. As long as what you are agreeing on is in line with the word of God there are promises that cover it. These promises always have a man side and a God side. Do the man side first, and then God will do the God side.

Being that committed is easier said than done. While we are waiting for God to do his part, doubts, fears, anxiety, and the temptation to get out of harmony become troublesome. Satan always attacks you at your weakest point. If you are praying about a physical condition, he may make the symptoms get worse and worse. That is when you respond by saying over and over again, "______ and I agreed." Stand your ground and God will stand his. "Leave no <such> room or foothold for the devil <give no opportunity to him>" (Ephesians 4:27 AMP).

> Therefore put on God's complete armor, that you may be able to resist and stand your ground on the evil day <of danger>, and, having done all <the crisis demands>, to stand <firmly in your place> (Ephesians 6:13 AMP).

The **PRAYER OF WORSHIP AND PRAISE** focuses on God. Close your eyes and imagine, if you can, that you are in the throne room with God. You are covered by the blood of Jesus, and adopted as Jesus' sibling, a co-heir with Jesus. You approach the throne of your father who is also God. He speaks: "Welcome my child. What can I do for you? I love doing things for my children." You answer, "Sir, I don't want anything. I just wanted to sit by you and watch you run your creation."

God reaches out his hand and pulls you up to sit at his side, his arm around your shoulders. From there you look out upon the vastness of creation and marvel. What you see brings words of praise and adoration to your lips. You see his plan from the beginning, when he planned for you to be. You see his heart broken by sin and the price he had to pay for your redemption out of Satan's hands. You hear the heavens proclaiming his glory and singing his praise. You see him doing everything the law allows to win the lost back to himself. You sense his sorrow at those who reject his great love. You weep, too. Then the scene changes and you see the wondrous things he has prepared for those who love him.

What you have seen causes you to slip from his side and kneel at his feet. Words of praise and adoration flow from your lips. You hear a gentle laugh and feel a hand resting on your head as these words flood your mind: "I did it all for you! I'm so glad you like it."

> As they ministered to the Lord, and fasted, (Acts 13:2 KJV).
> And they, worshiping Him, went back to Jerusalem with great joy; And they were continually in the temple

> celebrating with praises and blessing and extolling God. Amen (so be it) (Luke 24:52-53 AMP).

Revelation 4:11 declares

> You are worthy, our Lord and God, to receive glory and honour and power, for you created all things, and by your will they were created and have their being (NIV).

Peter declares,

> But you are a chosen people, a royal priesthood, a holy nation, a people belonging to God, that you may declare the praises of him who called you out of darkness into his wonderful light (1 Peter 2:9 NIV).

We praise God because we need to, for our own sakes! Our praise makes miracles possible. Look at what happened at Antioch when they ministered to the Lord and fasted. The Holy Spirit told them to separate Barnabas and Saul and send them out as missionaries. Look at what happened when Paul and Silas, in prison, sang praises unto God. There was an earthquake and their bonds fell off and the keeper of the prison and his family got saved,

> About midnight Paul and Silas were praying and singing hymns to God, and the other prisoners were listening to them … The jailer called for lights, rushed in and fell trembling before Paul and Silas. He then brought them out and asked, "Sirs, what must I do to be saved?" (Acts 16:25, 29-30 NIV).

We believe in our hearts. It is our minds that give us fits. When we are praying the prayer of faith for ourselves, we may need to clarify it by saying we are praying according to the faith in our hearts, not by the doubts in our minds. The more we concentrate on extolling God's praises and rejoicing in what he has done and is doing, the more we reinforce the faith in our hearts, and weaken the doubts in our minds. I believe that part of what

Jesus meant when he said "Truly, I say to you, unless you turn and become like children, you will never enter the kingdom of heaven," (Matthew 18:3 ESV), is that children believe more easily and quickly, both in their hearts and in their minds.

As a little child of about four, I knew prayer worked. I'd proved it. My dad had just read to me one of Rudyard Kipling's *Just So Stories.* It told about a little boy like me living in an Indian village. It was very dry. Their corn was about to die for lack of water. The boy took a little stick, tied a wilted corn leaf on it, and stuck it in the ground so that the Great Spirit would see it and send rain. The Great Spirit did see it, and sent rain. Always after that, when they needed rain, the little Indian boy put out his rain stick and it rained. My dad came into the house a few days later and said, "If we don't get rain our garden will die". I asked my dad if I could put out a rain stick. He said yes. I did, and it rained a beautiful crop saving rain that very same afternoon. I did it again when we needed rain, and it rained.

The **PRAYER OF SUBMISSION** is a prayer of accepting the thing God is asking you to do, and committing yourself to obey. There is always a personal cost. To submit is to yield to the will of God who has given you specific instructions about what he wants you to do. When God asks you, and no one else, to do something, and you commit yourself to do it, that is the prayer of submission. This is the prayer Jesus prayed in the Garden of Gethsemane, a prayer of submitting himself to doing God's will, the thing for which he had been sent into the world.

> And going a little farther, He threw Himself upon the ground on His face and prayed saying, "My Father, if it is possible, let this cup pass away from Me; nevertheless, not what I will <not what I desire>, but as You will and desire" (Matthew 26:39 AMP).

Jesus had begun to experience all that it meant to fulfill the task God had set before him. It meant total separation from God, because God could not look upon sin. All he had left was the memory of his father's love and the fellowship they had shared together. Knowing this, we begin to understand why he asked, "Father, is there any other way?" There wasn't. Then we hear the words that mean life and hope and salvation for us, "Nevertheless father, not what I want, but what you want."

Every one of us may, at some time, hear God say, "There's something I want you to do." It may not be something we would have chosen to do. It will cost us. Perhaps it will cost the career we had laid out so neatly in front of us. Perhaps it will mean leaving the security of job and home and going where we are forced to rely 100% on God to supply our needs. Perhaps it will be to do things we never dreamed of doing, and were sure we had no talents for doing. When we finally agree to do what God is asking we pray the prayer of submission.

The **PRAYER OF CONSECRATION** is also a prayer of submitting to do God's will, but in a general sense. We've become new creatures in Christ. We have no specific word from God, but out of pure gratitude and love, we consecrate ourselves to obey his will and live his way the rest of our lives. We consecrate our homes to God and tell him he can use them in any way he wants; our doors are open. We might work at a local food pantry, provide transportation for those in need, etc. Having consecrated ourselves, we look for ways to serve others.

The **PRAYER OF DEDICATION.** We dedicate our children to God and commit ourselves to raise them in the nurture and admonition of the Lord (Ephesians 6:4). An outstanding example of this is Hannah's story. Hannah was barren. She poured out her heart to God and promised that if he would give her a son she would give him to the Lord. God gave Hannah a son. When he was weaned she took him to the prophet Eli. Hannah dedicated young Samuel to God (I Samuel 1:28). Samuel became one of Israel's greatest prophets.

The **PRAYER OF THANKSGIVING.** God loves a party. Joy and feasting are themes within the story of redemption. The kingdom of heaven is a treasure that gives great joy (Matthew 13:44). The faithful servant gets to enter into and share the joy, the delight, the blessedness of his master (Matthew 25:20). The unborn John leaped for joy in his mother's womb when Mary came to visit (Luke 1:44). There is joy in heaven over one sinner who repents (Luke 15:10). And God himself dances for joy over a sinner who repents (Zephaniah 3:17). Jesus said that he came that his joy would remain in us and that our joy would be full (John 15:11). For this we give thanks.

Prayers of thanksgiving are not obligatory responses for gifts received, or thank you notes we have to write for birthday and Christmas presents. Instead, they are a rejoicing in the midst of living in God's blessings. The Westminster Catechism says "Man's chief end is to glorify God, and to enjoy him forever." Prayers of thanksgiving are a rejoicing in and resting in and basking in all that God is, even though there may be turmoil all around us.

When being thankful, the first thing you notice is that God becomes very big and all your needs become very small. As you rejoice in God, and in his promises, your faith grows. You laugh at Satan and all the lies he is trying to feed you about how you are going under, how you are going to die, how you will never get out of debt, how you will never succeed, how you will never have enough faith and trust. Rejoicing opens your eyes and you begin to see that it is the father's good pleasure to give good things to those who ask him (Matthew 7:11). All the things that seemed like mountains to you become little bumps in the road. You rejoice that God is meeting all your needs right now. So great is our God.

An example of **UNITED PRAYER** is told in Acts 4:21-31. The day before, Peter and John had gone into the temple at the hour of prayer. A lame man sat there begging. Peter said to the lame man, "Silver and gold have I none; but such as I have I give thee (KJV)." Then, taking him by the right hand he raised the man up. Instantly healed, the man who had been lame went jumping and leaping into the temple. The Sadducees were not pleased, and had them arrested and jailed. The next day the whole official body of religious leaders met. They set Peter and John before them and asked them by what power or in what name they healed the lame man. Peter, sparing no details, told them that it was by the name of Jesus, and that there is salvation in no other name. The religious leaders let them go and told them not to speak in that name again.

They returned to the others and reported all the chief priests and elders had said to them. When the group heard it they all lifted their voices together in one accord, with one united mind, and said

> O Lord, it is You who MADE THE HEAVEN AND THE EARTH AND THE SEA, AND ALL THAT IS IN THEM, who by the Holy Spirit, through the mouth of our father David Your servant, said, 'WHY DID THE GENTILES RAGE, AND THE PEOPLES DEVISE FUTILE THINGS? 'THE KINGS OF THE EARTH TOOK THEIR STAND, AND THE RULERS WERE GATHERED TOGETHER AGAINST THE LORD AND AGAINST HIS CHRIST.' "For truly in this city there were gathered together against Your holy servant Jesus, whom You anointed, both Herod and Pontius Pilate, along with the Gentiles and the peoples of Israel, to do whatever Your hand and Your purpose predestined to occur. And now, Lord, take note of their threats, and grant that Your bond-servants may speak Your word with all confidence, while You extend Your hand to heal, and signs and wonders take place through the name of Your holy servant Jesus."
>
> And when they had prayed, the place where they had gathered together was shaken, and they were all filled with the Holy Spirit and began to speak the word of God with boldness. (Acts 4:24-31 NAS)

LISTENING PRAYER is the practice of just listening. Mothers train themselves to hear their baby's cry and to know what each cry means. A good mechanic can tell exactly what is wrong with a motor by the sounds it is making. Listening to hear God's voice is a matter of training ourselves to hear it. The first step is to learn exactly what it is you are listening for. If you were to tune each string of a piano to its precise number of vibrations, any music you try to play will sound bad. That is because the strings in an octave must be slightly out of tune by one beat per second or three beats per five seconds. The sound a piano tuner listens for is a mechanical sound, not a musical sound. When you are listening for God's voice, you are listening for an impression of a voice, not an actual voice. It may seem to come from way in the back of your mind, or down deep in your solar plexus. It may be so faint that you will have to concentrate, focus your thoughts, to hear it. What you hear, if it is from God, will always agree with God's written word.

The **VISUALIZATION PRAYER** uses pictures instead of words. Begin by asking the Holy Spirit to guide you, and bind Satan and his demons from planting suggestions in your mind. Then picture the person or situation for which you are praying. Picture Jesus coming and ministering as he wills. Watch what happens. When we are at a loss for what to pray, or how to pray, for an individual, or for our own needs, visualization helps us place this person or need into Jesus's hands, and to leave him or it there (I Peter 5:7).

The following two stories are included to help you understand, a little better, some of the laws of prayer in action. One is a delightful story told by a Southern lady. The second is an inspiring story told by Dr. George Washington Carver.

The story about Daisy illustrates how to pray for someone, and how not to pray. The story went something like this: Daisy came to work one Monday morning exasperated with her husband. "Miss Pansy," she said. "I wish you'd help me pray for old Joe. I'm worn out praying for that old man. I don't think my praying does any good."

Miss Pansy asked, "You pray without ceasing, don't you?"

"Yes I do," Daisy spoke right up. She told how she had learned to pray without ceasing during the 19 years they'd been married. She told how she even purposely woke up in the middle of the night to pray for him. But it wasn't working. Then she asked, "Miss Pansy, you know all about praying. You go to these places and teach about praying. Won't you pray for him?"

Miss Pansy answered, "Maybe I can help, Daisy. But first, tell me how you pray, and maybe I can help you pray right, with more effect. How do you pray for him?"

"I know that prayer by heart, backwards and sleeping and working," Daisy answered. "I pray, 'Dear Heavenly Father,'" and then went on to list everything bad about her husband that she could think of. When she was through with her list of grievances she ended by asking God to "please make him stop all that devilment before its everlasting too late for his never dying soul."

Miss Pansy was horrified and shocked! "Oh Daisy, you mean to tell me you talk to the Lord God like that about your husband?"

"Miss Pansy, I ain't telling God a thing about that man He doesn't know."

Miss Pansy then explained to Daisy that all she was doing was gossiping to the Lord about her husband. In fact, in all her nineteen years she had not actually prayed for him. Instead she had been talking against him.

"Well," Daisy answered, "I told you I need help."

"I'm going to tell you how to pray," Miss Pansy began. "But before I do you must promise me two things you'll do. First of all, promise that for 30 days you won't nag Joe about a thing." Daisy almost panicked, asking what she was to do to fill up all the time she'd spent nagging. Miss Pansy answered that she was to pray the prayer she was going to give her. The second thing Daisy had to promise was that she would not say "church" to Joe at any time during those 30 days. Daisy admitted that it didn't do any good anyway. He was always too drunk to go.

Next, Miss Pansy told Daisy to start her prayer this way: "Dear Heavenly Father I thank you for my good husband." Daisy was dumbfounded. That was like lying, she said. God knew he was a no account. But, even though praying this did not make sense to her, she agreed to pray like that, saying God would understand if praying like that wasn't right.

Miss Pansy gave Daisy a prayer to pray that went something like this. "Dear Heavenly Father, I thank you for my good husband. I thank you that you're his creator and he's your creature. I thank you that you're his father and he's your child. And I'm thanking you to my very toes that right this minute you have such good control of that child of yours that he's turning his thoughts towards the God that made him, and his feet towards your church house doors."

Daisy felt like this prayer was lying in God's face. But she agreed to pray it like Miss Pansy said. As Daisy left Miss Pansy reminded her to do this for thirty days. And if Daisy still needed help she'd pray with her.

That was Monday. The following Sunday afternoon about 3:30 Miss Pansy's telephone rang and it was Daisy. "Miss Pansy, I couldn't wait to come to work tomorrow morning to tell you the miracle happened." Joe had come home before dark. He gave Daisy his paycheck. He stayed home all-night. After breakfast on Sunday, he started ransacking the dresser drawers. When asked why, he said he was hunting for his Sunday shirt. He went to church with her. And after church, at the dinner table, he announced that it was time he started going to church.

The miracle is not that God stopped Joe from getting drunk and carousing around. The miracle is that he started Daisy on the path of obedience. We are commanded to love as Jesus loved, and not to condemn. He lifted people up and gave them new beginnings. Instead of condemning Joe into the old, Daisy was now calling forth the new, the good. When we begin to follow the path of obedience, to love and pray, our obedience may interfere with the path of disobedience somebody else is on. It gives God a line. Daisy was the closest heart to Joe, the one that loved him and cared the most. The miracle was that God could get her heart and her thoughts going his way so that they would not return unto her, void.

All too often, we just add on and build a prison around the person we are talking about. Every thought makes it just that much worse, establishes it like a plaster cast with many layers added to it. Daisy didn't know anything different. Some of us don't know anything different, either. For prayer to have power, we pray for and not against. We call forth the new.

Dr. George Washington Carver was a great man of prayer, as well as a great scientist. His discoveries of uses for the peanut transformed the agricultural economy of the South. Whenever Dr. Carver was asked to show the products he had produced from the peanut, he began by telling the story of how he began to make his many discoveries. That story always began with his testimony of faith. The story he told went like this:

> Years ago I went into my laboratory and said, "Mr. Creator, please tell me what the universe was made for." The great Creator answered, "You want to know too much for that little mind of yours. Ask for something more your size."
>
> Then I asked, "Dear Mr. Creator, tell me what man was made for." Again the great Creator replied, "Little man, you are still asking too much. Cut down the extent of your request and improve the intent."
>
> So then I asked, "Please, Mr. Creator, will you tell me why the peanut was made?" "That's better, but even that question is too infinite. What do you want to know about the peanut?"
>
> "Mr. Creator," I asked, "can I make milk out of the peanut?" "What kind of milk to you want?" He asked me. "Good Jersey milk or just plain boarding house milk?" "Good Jersey milk," I said. And then the great Creator taught me how to take the peanut apart and put it together again. And out of this process have come forth all these products.[1]

And then Dr. Carver would draw forth from his box samples of all kinds of products from face powder, shampoo, soaps, salads, wood stains, butter, to dandruff cure and instant coffee. He had discovered over 300 uses for the peanut! Each discovery had come after he narrowed his request down and made it very specific. That is how it is with all prayer.

CHAPTER 42

HOMEWORK: PRAYING UP A STORM

Prayer is family talk. Take your list and sit down with your family: your Father, your Brother, and your Teacher. Be prepared to spend a lot of time in silence and a lot of time listening. Present each prayer by itself. Ask if you've got it right. Ask if there is something they want you to do. The Bible emphasizes sowing and reaping. You don't get a harvest if you don't sow. Jesus said that it is the measure we use when we give, that is used to measure back to us. So you may ask if there is something you need to do as a way of sowing seed. For example, perhaps your greatest need is to get a job. Your father may suggest that you go out and bless people by giving your time, talents and strength doing odd jobs for those who cannot afford to pay you.

When I was young we sang "Stand up, stand up for Jesus, ye soldiers of the cross," and "Onward Christian soldiers." We thought those were only pep songs. But Paul tells us, in Ephesians chapter six, we are fighting a real war. We are told to be adequately prepared. We are to put on God's armor and become skilled in its use because we are attacking, not defending. To attack is to go after the enemy with all our weapons blazing. The Bible teaches that our blazing weapons are prayer and the name of Jesus. You have learned how to use your weapons. Go forth and use them.

ENDNOTES

Introduction

1. Twenty Years of Hus'ling by J.P. Johnston, (Thompson & Thomas, Chicago © 1906)
2. Who We Are Is How We Pray by Dr. Charles Keating, (Twenty-Third Publications, Mystic, CT, © 1987)

Chapter 4: Guess When God Throws a Party

1. Biblia Hebraica ed. by Rudolph Kittel, (Priveleg. Wurtt. Bibelanstalt Stuttgart 1951)

Chapter 8: At Last I See

1. The Transformation of the Inner Man by John and Paula Sandford, (Bridge Publishing, Inc., Plainfield, NJ, 1982).
2. To learn more about the Camps Farthest Out visit their web site at www.acfona.org
3. More of Tommy Tyson's stories and teachings are available on our website, www.cfoclassicslibrary.org.)
4. CFO Classics Library (references are taken directly from recordings made by Matt W Leach, and which are available from www.cfoclassicslibrary.org)
5. Prayer the Mightiest Force in the World by Frank Laubach (Fleming H. Revell Co; New York, 1946, used by permission)

Chapter 9: Learn to Trust

1. The Lord of the Rings trilogy by J.R.R. Tolkien, (Ballantine Books, New York, © 1965.)

Chapter 12: The Lifter Up of the Fallen

1. Summa Theologica, Q92, art.I, Reply Obj.I by Thomas Aquinas).

Chapter 18: Get a New Mind

[1] "The Divine Plan" by Glenn Clark (1939 free from www.unitedprayertower.org)

Chapter 19: Breaking the Unbreakable

[1] Something More: In Search of a Deeper Faith by Catherine Marshall (Avon Books, New York, ©1974).

[2] Free at Last by Larry Huch (Larry Huch Ministries, Portland, OR, ©2003)

[3] The Healing Light by Agnes Sanford (Macalester Park Publishing Company, Minneapolis, MN © 1947)

Chapter 20: They Broke Through

[1] The Adventures of Huckleberry Finn by Mark Twain (© 1885, Chapter 16).

[2] Love Can Open Prison Doors by Starr Dailey, (Willing Publishing Company, San Gabriel, CA, © 1934)

[3] Release by Starr Daily, (Harper & Brothers Publishers, New York © 1942)

Chapter 25: Walking Like Giants

[1] The Lord of the Rings trilogy by J.R.R. Tolkien, (Ballantine Books, New York, © 1965.)

Chapter 26: The Blessings of Dreaming Large

[1] A Man's Reach by Glenn Clark, (Harper & Brothers Publishers, New York © 1949)

Chapter 28: Homework: Experimenting with Prayer

[1] God's Healing Power by Edgar L Sanford, (Prentice – Hall, Inc., Englewood Cliffs, NJ, © 1959, p26)

Chapter 30: Ambassadors with Authority

[1] The Wonderful Name Of Jesus by E. W. Kenyon, (Lynnwood, Washington, Kenyon's Gospel Publishing Society, 1889)

Chapter 31: Living in the Power of His Name

[1] The Screwtape Letters by C.S. Lewis

[2] Steps to Prayer Power by Jo Kimmel (p38-41, Abingdon Press, Nashville, © 1972)

Chapter 32: Learning Love

[1] Prayer Evangelism by Ed Silvoso, (Regal Books, Ventura, VA © 2000 Used by permission).

Chapter 34: Love Redeems the Present

[1] CFO Classics Library (references are taken directly from recordings made by Matt W Leach, and which are available from www.cfoclassicslibrary.org)

Chapter 35: Love Redeems the Future

[1] "Discovery" by Toyohiko Kagawa (1922 Put in Public Domain by the copyright owners.)

Chapter 41: Different Kinds of Prayer

[1] The Man Who Talks With the Flowers by Glenn Clark, (Macalester Park Publishing Company, Austin MN, © 1939, p34 used by permission.)

Printed in the United States
By Bookmasters